Car-Free®
in Boston

The Guide to Public Transit in
Greater Boston & New England

9th Edition

Editors
Robert Gentile
Anne L. McKinnon
James Taylor

Photography
Kenneth Martin

Cover Design
James Parry

Consultants
Robert M. Davis • Sally Mayer • James Parry

Publisher
Association for Public Transportation, Inc.

Officers
Dennis M. Campbell, President
Barry D. Andelman, Vice-President
Ian C. Palmer, Treasurer
Carolyn Mieth, Clerk

For additional copies send $6.95 plus $1.25 postage and handling to:
APT, P. O. Box 1029, Boston, MA 02205. A bulk discount is available for orders
of 84 or more copies. Call (617) 482-0282 for more information.

Note: Every effort has been made to obtain accurate information prior to
publication. However, transit services and schedules do change. We urge
you to confirm schedules with the carrier before making your trip.

Contents

Using *Car-Free*

The four parts of this book are designed to answer your transit questions.
☛ Are you clueless about Boston-area transit? Or do you need to know the basics about getting around (or out of) town? See **Part I**.
☛ Do you need an idea for a trip? See **Part II**.
☛ Do you already know where you want to go, but need directions? See **Part III**. You should also check out **Part IV** for routes and schedules. If you need to call a train, bus, or ferry line for further information, see the telephone list on pages 168-169. Unless otherwise indicated, all phone numbers in this book are in the 617 area code.

Introduction .... *v*
APT membership information .... *vi*

Part I. Using Transit
    An introduction to Boston-area transit services
  1. **The T (MBTA System)** 3
    Rapid transit, buses, commuter rail, and commuter boats: information sources; hours of operation; holidays; fares; visitor and monthly passes; commendations and complaints
  2. **Not the T** 11
    Intercity, commuter, and local buses; railroads; ferries; regional transit authorities, tours and charters
  3. **Other Transportation Options** 13
    Ridesharing—carpools, vanpools, subscription buses; taxis and rental cars; bicycles
  4. **Services for Persons with Disabilities** 15
    Wheelchair-accessible services on the MBTA and on other trains, buses, and ferries; "The Ride"
  5. **Downtown Boston and Cambridge** 17
    Public transit serving Boston's business district, Back Bay, and Cambridge; rapid transit stations; MBTA bus routes; train, bus, and ferry terminals
  ☞Map of Boston terminals
  ☞Maps of downtown Boston, Back Bay, and selected other neighborhoods
  6. **Logan Airport** 30
    Access to the airport by subway, ferry, bus, limousine, and taxi; airport terminal map; airline telephone numbers

Part II. Places to See and Things to Do
*Ideas for an afternoon or a day trip in the Boston area and
eastern Massachusetts*
7. **Historical, Cultural, and Other Attractions** 35
*Greater Boston visitor information; sightseeing tours and
cruises; the Freedom Trail; the Black Heritage Trail; the
Women's Heritage Trail; and places to visit along the four rapid
transit lines*
8. **Parks and Recreation** 44

Part III. Destination Listings
How to get to hundreds of specific destinations
9. **Museums, Attractions, and Points of Interest** 57
10. **Theaters, Cinemas, and Auditoriums** 61
11. **Nightlife** 65
12. **Major Spectator Sports** 68
13. **Shopping Centers** 70
14. **Educational Institutions** 73
15. **Hospitals** 78
16. **Cities, Towns, and Neighborhoods** (with selected Park &
Ride facilities) 82
☞Related maps

Part IV. Routes and Schedules
A guide to virtually every Boston-area transit route
17. **MBTA Rapid Transit and Buses** 111
☞Maps of rapid transit lines with station addresses, fare
zones, and connecting routes
☞Map of crosstown bus routes
18. **MBTA Commuter Rail and Boats** 139
☞Commuter Rail map with station addresses.
19. **Other Trains, Ferries, Buses** 144
In greater Boston and eastern Massachusetts
20. **Regional Transit Authorities** 153
Local transit in other Massachusetts and Rhode Island cities
21. **Transit in New England and Beyond** 160
Train, bus, and ferry services from Boston; local transit services
☞New England map

Index 165
Transit telephone numbers 168
Car-Free Updates information 170
Rapid Transit Map ....*Inside Front Cover*
Regional Transit Map ....*Inside Back Cover*

Introduction

In this, the ninth edition of *Car-Free in Boston*, our goal remains the same as when we started in 1977: to provide a quality, comprehensive guide to Boston's public transportation services. Included is information on almost every train, bus, and ferry route (both publicly and privately owned) in eastern Massachusetts as well as selected services throughout New England. *Car-Free* also contains directions to hundreds of destinations to which you *can* get without a car.

Our job is made easier by the fact that Boston remains transit-friendly, having survived some ill-conceived highway schemes and criminal hanky-panky perpetrated during the last 25 years or so. (The ultimate effect on Boston of the current project, the depressing of the Central Artery highway —the "Big Dig"— may not be known for a decade. For sure, during construction driving in Boston will be even less pleasant than it is now, if that is possible. Stay tuned.)

Boston's primary transit operator, the Massachusetts Bay Transportation Authority (the MBTA or the "T"), has been making big strides as of late and is basically clean, reliable, safe, and even friendly. The result is that a significant proportion of Boston commuters, students, and visitors use it. The "T" must be doing something right.

Car-Free's nearly two decades of publication suggest we too must be doing something right. But there is always room for improvement. In this edition we have added:

- A new destination category, "Nightlife" (Chapter 11), including music, dance, billiards, and comedy clubs.
- More phone numbers.
- An improved Boston map section.
- Commuter rail station addresses.
- Free *Car-Free* updates. In a perfect world, service changes would not be allowed between editions of *Car-Free*. It is not a perfect world. Therefore, we are now offering our readers updated information (annually or better) at no charge until the next edition is published. A guarantee of freshness, if you will. Items to watch for in these updates include Amtrak service, new commuter rail service to the south shore, and crosstown bus service.

All you have to do to get on the Update mailing list is send your name and address on a postcard to the Association for Public Transportation (APT), P.O. Box 1029, Boston, MA 02205.

Or call our answering machine at (617) 482-0282 to leave your name address and zip code.

The Association for Public Transportation is a nonprofit organization that, in addition to publishing this book, works to improve Boston's public transit for the benefit of both the rider and the environment. We have been doing this for the last 21 years. We urge all our readers to become a part of the process:

- Let your elected officials know that public transportation is important to you.
- Become a member of APT. If you would like to become an active member, we welcome your participation. For more information on APT, contact us.

> Association for
> Public Transportation
> Boston, Massachusetts
> February 1995

_____ I'd like to join APT; enclosed is my tax-deductible donation of $_____.

$12.50 student/senior	$50.00 donor
$20.00 regular	$100.00 sponsor

APT members receive *mass. transit* and a copy of the next edition of *Car-Free* when it is published.

NAME

ADDRESS

CITY   STATE   ZIP CODE

PHONE (H)   (W)

Association for Public Transportation, PO Box 1029, Boston, MA 02205

Part I
Using Transit

Orange Line, Back Bay Station, Boston

1. The T (MBTA System)
2. Not the T
3. Other Transportation Options
4. Services for Persons with Disabilities
5. Downtown Boston and Cambridge
6. Logan Airport

HELPFUL TIPS FOR SUBWAY RIDERS

• The MBTA Information Booth is located at Park Street (on the Green Line outbound platform).

• **"Inbound"** is always toward downtown Boston— Park Street, State, Downtown Crossing, or Government Center. **"Outbound"** *means away from downtown.*

• **Green Line** trains (also called "streetcars" or "trolleys") have letters for different branches: B—Boston College; C—Cleveland Circle; D—Riverside; E—Heath St. A red line through the letter on a sign means that the train goes only part way on that branch (for example, a D-line car terminating at Reservoir). All trains stop at Park Street, Boylston, Arlington, and Copley. All trains except "E" also stop at Hynes Convention Center/ICA and Kenmore. Only "E" trains stop at Prudential and Symphony.

There is no free transfer between inbound and outbound at Copley; use Arlington instead.

• Bowdoin on the **Blue Line** closes at 6:30 pm Monday through Friday and is closed on Saturdays and Sundays.

• Most **Red Line** trains stop at all stations between Alewife and Andrew, including Harvard and Park Street. During rush hours, some trains may terminate at Park Street. The last transfer point between the two Red Line branches (Braintree and Ashmont) is at JFK/UMass.

• Finally, a rainy-day tip for the **Orange Line.** At Back Bay Station, you can go, via the Dartmouth Street underpass, through the Copley Place shopping area, across the Huntington Avenue bridge, then through the Prudential Center to Boylston Street.

Chapter 1
The T (MBTA System)

Many Bostonians, especially those who give directions to tourists, refer to their public transit system as "the T," after the Ⓣ₍ symbol that flags subway entrances. The official name of the transit agency is the Massachusetts Bay Transportation Authority (MBTA). In addition to its four rapid transit lines, the MBTA operates buses, commuter trains, and commuter boats in Boston and surrounding communities.

Rapid Transit (Subway)

The four transit lines—Red, Green, Orange, and Blue—that radiate out from downtown Boston are often called "the subway," even though every line comes above ground for much of its route.

There are over 75 transit stations, usually named for a nearby square, street, or landmark. In addition, Green Line trains stop at many street corners along the surface portions of their routes. (Some helpful hints for subway riders are listed on the facing page.)

A simplified, color-coded rapid transit map can be found in most subway stations, and one is printed on the back cover of this book. Detailed maps of each of the four lines, showing all MBTA stations, their street addresses, and bus connections, are on pages 113—123.

All four lines intersect in downtown Boston. You can transfer between lines, *at no extra charge*, at the following stations:

- **Park Street**—Red Line and Green Line (with underground walkway to the Orange Line at Downtown Crossing). You can transfer to the Blue Line by taking the Green Line to Government Center.
- **Downtown Crossing** (formerly "Washington")—Red Line and Orange Line (with underground walkway to the Green Line at Park Street).
- **Government Center**—Blue Line and Green Line.
- **State**—Blue Line and Orange Line.
- **Haymarket** and **North Station**—Green Line and Orange Line.

Fares

All fares in this book are those in effect at press time (February 1995). The MBTA's basic rapid transit fare is 85¢. At some outlying stations, however, a different fare is charged. Under the T's zone fare system, the fare you pay is determined by where you get on the train. Once you have paid, you can ride as far as you want (except to Quincy Adams or Braintree) without paying anything extra.

In some cases, then, a trip in one direction costs more than the return trip. For example, the fare from Riverside to Park Street on the

3

Green Line is $2.00, while from Park Street to Riverside is just 85¢. A **ten-ride ticket** for inbound rides on the Riverside line is available at all Green Line collector's booths (except Symphony and Prudential) at a 15 percent discount.

A different fare is charged at the following stations:

- **Green Line surface streetcars**—stops west of Kenmore ("B" and "C" trains) or west of Symphony ("E" trains): regular fare, 85¢, when boarding inbound. *No fare when boarding outbound at these stops.*
- **Green Line-D (Riverside)**—stops from Reservoir to Fenway, inclusive: $1.00 when boarding inbound. *No fare when boarding outbound.*
- **Green Line-D (Riverside)**—stops from Riverside to Chestnut Hill inclusive: $2.00 when boarding inbound; or $1.00 plus a Newton Local Coupon. (Coupons are issued when you get off an inbound train between Woodland and Chestnut Hill, inclusive; they are good for a discount on your next trip.) *No fare when boarding outbound.*
- **Red Line (Braintree Branch)**—Quincy Center, Quincy Adams, and Braintree: two tokens ($1.70) when boarding at these stations. At Quincy Adams and Braintree, an additional token is also charged when you leave the station. (The local fare between North Quincy and Braintree is 85¢; ask the token seller for instructions before you pay your fare.)
- **Red Line (Ashmont-Mattapan Line)**—Mattapan Line: The local fare between Mattapan and Cedar Grove is 60¢, on inbound trolleys only. *No fare on outbound trains.*

Turnstiles in subway stations accept only tokens and passes. Tokens are sold (and change for buses is available) at the collector's booth in most subway stations. Some stations also have token-vending machines.

Exact change, in coins and tokens only, is required on all streetcars. Dollar bills are not accepted. Exact change is also required at Science Park, Symphony and, sometimes, at Lechmere and Prudential. There are change machines at each of these stops. *For special fares, see page 8.*

Buses

Most of the MBTA's bus routes operate *feeder service*, linking subway stations to neighborhoods not directly served by rapid transit. Some *crosstown* routes connect stations on different subway lines without going into downtown. Only a few MBTA buses actually enter downtown Boston, and most of these are express buses from outlying areas. Maps showing downtown Boston bus stops are on page 23 and crosstown bus routes are on page 125. For cities, towns, and neighborhoods served by MBTA buses, see Chapter 16; for routes and schedules, see Chapter 17.

Buses stop only at designated stops, marked in most areas, but not all, by white or yellow signs with the "T" logo, a picture of a bus, and a "no parking" symbol. The MBTA has begun installing new signs, which include bus schedules, throughout its system.

Fares

The basic bus fare is 60¢. On a few very long routes, a zone fare—40¢ extra for travel in three zones—is charged. Express bus fares range from $1.50 to $2.25, depending on the length of the route. A **ten-ride discounted ticket** is available for all express buses.

As on streetcars, **exact change** is required on buses; no dollar bills are accepted. MBTA tokens are accepted but no change is returned.

In general, there is **no free transfer** between buses, or between buses and the subway. Unless you have a monthly pass, you must pay the full fare on each bus. There are three exceptions, however:

- A free transfer between **T-Bus 39** (Forest Hills-Back Bay Sta.), which substitutes for the Green Line-E (Arborway) streetcar, and the Green Line at Copley or the Orange Line at Back Bay Station.
- A free transfer between **T-Bus 1** (Harvard-Dudley), to or from Dudley Sq. only, and the Orange Line at Mass. Ave. station.
- A free transfer inbound between **T-Bus 49** (Dudley-Downtown) and New England Medical Ctr and Chinatown stations.

In all cases, riders should pay 85¢ on the bus and ask the driver for a subway transfer. Free transfer coupons to the buses are issued inside subway stations at Copley, Back Bay Station, Mass. Ave., and New England Medical Center. *For special fares, see page 8.*

Commuter Rail

MBTA Commuter Rail, shown in purple on MBTA maps and sometimes called the "Purple Line," extends from downtown Boston to as far as 60 miles away. Most routes have midday, night, and weekend service, making them more than just rush-hour "commuter rail." A map of all nine commuter rail lines is on page 143.

Commuter trains to suburbs north and northwest of Boston depart from North Station, on the Green and Orange lines.

Commuter trains to points south and west of the city leave from South Station, on the Red Line. All southside commuter trains, except the Fairmount Line, also stop at Back Bay Station, on the Orange Line.

Connections between rapid transit and commuter rail can also be made at Porter (Red Line), and at Malden Center, Ruggles, and Forest Hills (Orange Line).

For cities, towns, and neighborhoods served by commuter rail, see Chapter 16; for routes and schedules, see Chapter 18.

Fares

Commuter rail fares are zoned from a minimum of 85¢ to a maximum of $6.00. Zone fare prices are listed below under "Monthly Passes."

Commuter rail tickets are sold at North Station, South Station, and Back Bay Station, and at or near some suburban stations. You may also buy a ticket on the train. If a ticket office at your station is open at train time, there is a $2.00 extra charge for buying your ticket on the train during rush hours and a $1.00 extra charge during off-peak hours.

Twelve-ride commuter rail tickets, valid for 180 days, cost about the price of 10 one-way fares. *For special fares, see page 8.*

Commuter Boats

The Hingham commuter boat sails from Rowes Wharf, Monday through Friday; the one-way fare is $4.00. The Navy Yard Water Shuttle sails from Long Wharf to the Charlestown Navy Yard, daily; the fare is $1.00. *For special fares, see page 8.*

Information

Printed schedules are available for all MBTA rapid transit, bus, commuter rail, commuter boat, and privately operated MBTA "commuter coach" services.

Rapid transit and bus schedules are issued four times a year, in early September, late December, late March, and mid June. Schedules are sometimes available at subway stations and from bus drivers. Schedules for all routes are available at the information booth in Park Street station, at the MBTA Operations Center at 45 High St. in downtown Boston, and at the Library in the State Transportation Building at 10 Park Plaza (near Boylston station; see the Downtown Boston/Back Bay map). Schedules are also distributed to over 400 community locations, including public libraries, city and town halls, stores, banks, and colleges. To have a schedule mailed to you, call 722-3200 or 800-392-6100.

Commuter rail schedules are updated less frequently, usually in April and October. Copies are available at North Station, South Station, and Back Bay Station, at the State Transportation Library, and from commuter rail ticket agents.

For schedule information you may also call the MBTA's Travel Information Line at 722-3200 or 800-392-6100.

Hours of Operation

MBTA rapid transit operates 20 hours each day—from shortly after 5:00 am until past 1:00 am. On Sunday, service begins about 40 minutes later than other days. The last trains leave downtown Boston at 12:45 am. Times of the first and last trains are on page 110.

Bus schedules vary greatly. Some routes have full 20-hour, 7-day service. Others operate weekdays only, daytime only, or even rush hours only.

Most commuter rail trains operate seven days a week. Excep-

HOLIDAY SERVICE

MBTA service operates every day of the year. Bus and subway lines observe special holiday schedules, as follows:

- **Sunday schedule:** New Year's Day, Memorial Day, July
  4th, Labor Day, Columbus Day, Thanksgiving, and
  Christmas.
- **Saturday schedule:** Martin Luther King Day, Presidents
  Day, Patriots Day, and Veterans Day.
- On **Patriots Day,** due to the Boston Marathon, Copley
  station (Green Line), at the finish line, is closed and some
  bus routes are rerouted or rescheduled.

Commuter rail lines follow slightly different holiday schedules:

- **Sunday schedule:** New Year's Day, Memorial Day, Labor
  Day, Thanksgiving, and Christmas.
- **Saturday schedule:** Presidents Day, July 4th, Columbus
  Day, Veterans Day.
- **Regular weekday schedule:** Martin Luther King Day and
  Patriots Day.

---

tions: Ipswich, Needham, and Stoughton line trains operate six days
a week and the Fairmount line is Monday through Friday only.

On New Year's Eve (First Night), the last trip on all lines is
approximately one hour later than normal.

See Chapters 17 and 18 for more specific information on all MBTA
routes and hours of operation.

Monthly Passes

A monthly T pass is convenient and can also save you serious
money. Monthly subway and local bus passes cost the same as 14 to
16 round trips; other passes are an even greater bargain. A pass gives
you unlimited rides—at night, on weekends, anytime. *You can take a
friend along on Sunday at no extra charge.*

Several museums and tourist attractions offer discounts to T
passholders, as noted in Chapter 9; and special offers are featured on
the back of each month's pass. If you own a car, you can save up to
$75 a year on auto insurance, too; ask your agent for details.

Over 800 companies make passes available directly to their
employees, and many even pay part of the cost as an employee benefit.

MBTA monthly passes are sold at Downtown Crossing, Government Center, and Harvard stations, on the last four and first four
working days of each month (cash only at these outlets); at North
Station, South Station, and Back Bay Station passes are sold during

SPECIAL FARES

Senior citizens (over 65) with MBTA I.D. cards pay only 20¢ for all rapid transit lines and 15¢ for local buses. On zoned and express buses, and on commuter rail, senior citizens pay half the regular fare. A driver's license and other I.D. forms showing proof of age are accepted on commuter rail, but on buses and the subway you must have an MBTA senior citizen card.

Persons with disabilitieswho have an MBTA Transportation Access Pass (TAP) pay the same fares as senior citizens. TAPs from other regional transit authorities in Massachusetts are also accepted on the T. Blind persons ride the MBTA free at all times (they need a travel card from the Massachusetts Commission for the Blind).

Senior citizen cards and TAPs can be obtained at Downtown Crossing station on weekdays, 8:30 am-4:15 pm. Call 722-5438 (TDD 722-5854) for further information. Senior citizens' cards are 50¢; TAPs are $3.00 (valid for five years for persons with permanent disabilities; valid for one year for persons with a temporary disability). Call first to have an application mailed.

Children under five ride the MBTA system free when accompanied by an adult. Children age 5—11 pay half fare.

Students through high school pay half fare for travel to and from classes on buses and boarding at Quincy Center, Quincy Adams, and Braintree on the Red Line and 40¢ on rapid transit with an MBTA student badge. A monthly student pass is available through some schools for $11.00. Students' fares and passes are not valid after 6:00 p.m.or on days when school is not in session. **The MBTA also has special semester rates for participating colleges (722-5218).**

Commuter rail **family fares** allow a group of up to five people—one adult and four children or two adults and three children—to travel round-trip on off-peak trains for a special fare, usually the price of two adult round-trips. For the family fare, "children" are under age 18.

Note: The fares listed above were correct when this book went to press in February 1995.

the last five and first ten days of the month and can be paid for by personal check or charged on Mastercard or Visa.

T passes are also sold at some neighborhood banks, stores, and at some colleges; and they are available by mail if you send in your order by the 10th of the preceding month. There is a $1.00 service charge for mail orders. A prepaid "annual pass-by-mail," 12 passes for the price of 11, is also available. Call 722-5218 for more information on monthly T passes, including a list of neighborhood pass outlets or a pass-by-mail order form.

There are four basic passes, which cover the entire MBTA subway and local bus system; plus passes for express buses, commuter rail, and commuter boats:

60¢ Local Bus — $20.00/month
- Valid for 60¢ fare on all local buses and Crosstown buses CT1, CT2, and CT3; additional zones payable in cash.
- Valid for 85¢ and $1.00 surface fares on the Green Line.
- Valid, with $1.00 cash or Newton Local Coupon, for $2.00 fare on the Green Line-D (Riverside).
- Valid on the Red Line between Mattapan and Ashmont only.
- *Not valid* on any other subway line or on express buses 300-326 and 352-354.

85¢ Subway — $27.00/month
- Valid at all 85¢ rapid transit stations.
- Valid for 85¢ and $1.00 fares on the Green Line.
- Valid on the Red Line between Mattapan and Ashmont.
- *Not valid* at Green Line-D (Riverside) stops Chestnut Hill-Riverside, inclusive.
- *Not valid* on the Red Line at Quincy Center, Quincy Adams, or Braintree.
- Valid on T-Buses 1 (Harvard-Dudley, between Mass. Ave. station and Dudley *only*), 39 (Forest Hills-Back Bay Sta.), 49 (Dudley-Downtown), and Crosstown buses CT1, CT2, and CT3.
- *Not valid* on any other bus.
- Valid for commuter rail zones 1A (85¢) and 1B ($1.20).

$1.50 Combo — $46.00/month
- Valid at all rapid transit stations *except* Quincy Adams and Braintree.
- Valid at all Green Line stops.
- Valid for up to $1.50 fare on all buses; additional fare payable in cash.
- Valid for commuter rail zones 1A and 1B.

$1.70 Combo Plus — $48.00/month
- Valid at all rapid transit stations and Green Line stops.
- Valid for up to $1.70 fare on all buses; additional fare payable in cash.
- Valid for commuter rail zones 1A and 1B.

$2.00 Commuter Rail Zone 1 — $64.00/month
$2.25 Commuter Rail Zone 2 — $72.00/month
$2.50 Commuter Rail Zone 3 — $82.00/month
$3.00 Commuter Rail Zone 4 — $94.00/month
$3.25 Commuter Rail Zone 5 — $104.00/month

$3.50 Commuter Rail Zone 6 — $112.00/month
$3.75 Commuter Rail Zone 7 — $120.00/month
$4.00 Commuter Rail Zone 8 — $128.00/month
$4.75 Commuter Rail Zone 9 — $136.00/month
$6.00 Commuter Rail Zone 11 — $150.00/month
  • Valid at all rapid transit stations and Green Line stops.
  • Valid for up to the indicated fare on all buses; additional fare
    payable in cash.
  • Valid for up to the indicated fare zone on all commuter rail lines.

$4.00 Commuter Boat — $136.00/month
  • Valid on MBTA commuter boats between Boston and Hingham.
  • Also valid for the same services as the Combo Plus pass.

Note: These pass prices and descriptions were correct when this
book went to press in February 1995.

Boston Passport Visitor Pass

Although the Boston Passport is aimed at tourists, anyone can
buy and use it. A one-day Passport costs $5.00; a three-day Passport,
$9.00; a seven-day Passport, $18.00. Each Passport allows unlimited
use of all subway lines, including surface Green Line branches, plus
MBTA buses up to $1.70 fare (additional fare, if any, payable in cash),
and commuter rail zones 1A and 1B—the same as a Combo Plus
monthly pass. With the Passport you can also get discounts at some
tourist attractions and restaurants. It is a good way to test-ride the T.

Boston Passports are sold at North Station, South Station, and
Back Bay Station; at Airport, Government Center, Harvard, and
Riverside MBTA stations; at visitor information centers on Boston
Common, in Quincy Market, and at several hotels and newsstands.
They are also available by mail; call 722-5218 for mail orders.

Commendations, Complaints, and Suggestions

To comment about MBTA service, or to suggest improvements,
call MBTA Customer Relations at 722-5215. Or write: MBTA Customer Relations, 120 Boylston St., 3rd floor, Boston, MA 02116.

If you are commenting—good or bad—about an MBTA employee, try to get the employee's number or name. The exact time and
place, bus route number, and vehicle number will also help identify
the employee. If there is a problem with equipment, please provide
the vehicle number as well as the bus route number.

All MBTA services rely on financial assistance from federal, state,
and local governments. If you use transit, you should let your elected
officials know how important the T is to you. These officials may also
be able to help get better service in your community. If you have a
question or comment about the level or quality of service, or a
suggestion for improving service, you can contact your senator or
representative in the state legislature, or your city or town's repre-

sentative on the MBTA Advisory Board. Call 426-6054 for the name of your Advisory Board representative.

The Association for Public Transportation, the private, non-profit group that publishes this book, is also interested in your comments on transit service. Send them to APT, P.O. Box 1029, Boston, MA 02205.

Chapter 2
Not the T

A number of other carriers besides the MBTA operate public transit services in and near Boston.

Buses

Several intercity bus companies serve Boston. The two largest, Greyhound and Peter Pan, both have frequent daily buses to New York City and to Albany, as well as service to points within New England. Greyhound serves the entire United States and parts of Canada.

There are three intercity bus terminals in Boston-South Station, the Peter Pan terminal, across from South Station, and the Bonanza Bus Lines terminal, located in Back Bay Station. The Peter Pan terminal is used by other companies; The Greyhound terminal is located at South Station; see Chapter 5 for details.

Both Greyhound and Peter Pan also have terminals at Riverside in Newton, on the "D" branch of the Green Line.

Commuter buses connect downtown Boston with nearby towns and suburbs. Some routes operate only during rush hours, while others have midday, night, and weekend service. Most commuter buses leave from Park Plaza (formerly called "Park Square"), Copley Square, Haymarket, or South Station. For more details, see Chapters 5 and 19, or call the bus company.

Local bus service in some communities is operated by private companies, or by the local city or town government.

Boston-area bus services are listed in Chapter 16, "Cities, Towns, and Neighborhoods," and in Part IV, "Routes and Schedules."

Railroads

Amtrak, the United States' nationwide passenger rail system, has frequent daily trains to New York, NY, and Washington, DC, via Providence, RI. There are also daily trains to New York, NY, via Springfield, and to Chicago via Springfield and Albany.

Amtrak trains depart from South Station (on the Red Line); they also stop at Back Bay Station (Orange Line). Trains via Providence

stop at Route 128 Station (Rt. 128/I-95, exit 13), and trains via
Springfield make stops in Framingham and Worcester.

In summer, Amtrak also operates direct trains from New York to
Cape Cod. These trains do not go through Boston.

Note: some of the above routes may be cancelled.

Ferries

In addition to ferries operated by the T (see page 141), there are
other boats serving Boston Harbor. For example, the Airport Water
Shuttle links downtown Boston with Logan Airport, and there is
commuter boat service to Hull.

The Airport Water Shuttle links downtown Boston with Logan
Airport and connects with boats from Hingham. (See Chapter 6.)

In summer, there are boats to Boston's harbor islands and to
Gloucester, Nantasket, and Provincetown, plus a variety of harbor
cruises.

Sightseeing cruises and service to the Boston Harbor Islands are
described in Chapter 8. For route-by-route listings, see Chapter 19.

Regional Transit Authorities

In many Massachusetts cities and towns, Regional Transit Authorities operate local buses. A complete list of these authorities is in
Chapter 20.

Tours and Charters

A wide variety of sightseeing tours are available in the Boston
area, from one-hour "trolley" tours of downtown to weekend or
week-long tours of New England. For information, see Chapter 7. If
your group is planning an outing, you can obtain group rates on
many carriers, including MBTA Commuter Rail. If you have enough
people, you can charter a bus or a boat, or even a whole train.

Chapter 3

Other Transportation Options

Ridesharing—Carpools, Vanpools, Subscription Buses

CARAVAN for Commuters, Inc., is a private, non-profit, state-supported organization that helps commuters in Massachusetts find alternatives to driving alone. Their Commuter Information Line, 227-7665 (CAR-POOL) or 800-248-5009, provides free information on train, bus, and ferry routes, carpools, vanpools, and park-and-ride lots.

CARAVAN can also help you join or organize a vanpool. Everyone pays a monthly fee except for the volunteer driver. Vanpools are designed for people who work in locations where public transit is limited. Some vanpools accept part-time riders.

Many employers offer special buses or vans to their workers, leaving from subway or commuter rail stations. Some apartment and condominium developments also offer special buses to transit stations or to downtown Boston. If your employer or management office does not already offer this service, ask them to call CARAVAN for a free consultation.

Taxicabs and Rental Cars

Occasionally you *will* need a car, so rent one, by the mile (taxi) or by the day (rental car). It's cheaper and easier than owning (and parking) one full time.

See the Yellow Pages under "Taxicabs" for cab companies; see "Automobile Rental & Leasing" for a list of rental companies.

Bicycles

Many Bostonians ride bikes to work or school, and more and more employers are providing facilities for cyclists. New, more secure bicycle racks have been installed at many T stations. With a permit, which costs $5.00 for four years, you can take your bike on the T (see box).

Bus and boat companies and Amtrak allow you to take your bike on board or ship it as luggage. Many ferries and intercity buses will accept a bike (on a space-available basis) "as is," ready to ride when you get off. They usually require that you take the same boat or bus as your bike. Many bus companies charge from $3.00 to $15.00; some are free. On Amtrak and Greyhound, you must pack the bike in a box, available from Amtrak or bike shops, and since few trains have baggage cars you should ship the bike a day in advance so it will be there when you arrive. Consult the carrier for details.

Bicycles can also be rented in many towns. See Chapter 8 in this book or look under "Bicycles—Renting" in the Boston Yellow Pages.

There are several commuter bikepaths in the Boston area that either bring you downtown or lead to a rapid transit station where you can board the train. They are:

- **Paul Dudley White Bikepath** runs along the Charles River from Watertown Sq. to the Museum of Science.
- **The Southwest Corridor linear park** includes a bikepath from Forest Hills to Copley Place.
- **Bikepaths at Alewife station** (Red Line) link Belmont and Somerville.
- **Jamaicaway Bikepath** goes from Jamaica Pond to Brookline Village
- **Muddy River Bikepath** runs along the Muddy River bordering the Longwood Medical Area and on to Fenway station.
- **Minuteman Commuter Bikeway**, an 11-mile route from Arlington to Lexington and Bedford, terminates very close to Alewife.

The following resources may be of help to cyclists:
- **Bicycle Coalition of Massachusetts**, 214A Broadway, Cambridge 02139; phone 491-RIDE. BCOM publishes pamphlets, available at many bike shops and by mail, on a variety of topics related to biking.
- **Charles River Wheelmen**, 19 Chase Ave., W. Newton 02165; phone 325-BIKE. The CRW sponsors group rides of varying lengths and difficulties, every weekend of the year.
- **Boston's Bikemap**—available at bookstores, bike shops.
- **Explorer Map and Guide**—available at bookstores, bike shops.
- **Cape Ann and North Shore, Cape Cod and the Islands Bicycle Map**—Bike routes, parks, and beaches on the North Shore and Cape Cod; available at bookstores and bike shops.

BIKES ON THE Ⓣ PROGRAM

- **Red, Orange, Blue lines:**
    Weeknights after 8:00 pm; Saturdays before 8:30 am and after 8:00 pm; Sundays all day.
- **Green Line, T buses:**
    Bikes not allowed.
- **Commuter Rail:** Non-rush hours: 9:30 am to 3:00 pm. Rush hours (reverse commute only): outbound from start of service until 3:00 pm and inbound from 9:30 am to 6:30 pm.

The program operates year-round except for the weeks between Thanksgiving and Christmas, and bikes are not allowed on days or nights of Boston Garden events and games at Fenway Park and at Aquarium, Park Street, Downtown Crossing, and Government Ctr.
    All cyclists must have a permit ($5.00 for four years) from the Senior and Access Pass Office at Downtown Crossing, open 8:30 am to 4:15 pm, closed noon to 1:00 pm.
    Call 722-5438 for information.

Chapter 4
Services for Persons with Disabilities

The Americans with Disabilities Act (ADA), which became effective in 1992, requires all public carriers to provide services for persons with disabilities. It is best to call the individual train, bus, or ferry line for the latest information on these services (see phone list on pages 168-169).

An increasing number of MBTA services are accessible to persons who use mobility aids, including wheelchairs. Many more accessible stations are under construction or planned for construction.

Buses with wheelchair lifts and kneelers are now available on all MBTA routes. Some routes are fully accessible all of the time; on others, you must schedule your trip a day in advance. For more information or to schedule a trip, call 1-800-LIFT-BUS (1-800-543-8287) on the day before you wish to travel.

THE RIDE is the MBTA's door-to-door lift-equipped van service. It now operates, by advance reservation, in 41 cities and towns. A total of 62 communities will be served by May 1996.

All Regional Transit Authorities (RTAs) in Massachusetts operate accessible services, including lift-equipped vans; some RTAs also have lift buses on their regular routes. If you are eligible for local accessible services, you are also eligible to receive such services from the MBTA and any other RTA; your MBTA or RTA Transportation Access Pass allows you reduced fares across the state (see page 8).

Some WAVE (wheelchair accessible vehicle) taxis are now available in Boston.

All Amtrak trains departing Boston are wheelchair accessible at South Station and Back Bay Station. Amtrak stations in most large cities are accessible. Advance reservation is required. Call 482-3660 (TDD 800-523-6590).

At Logan Airport, the Airport Handicapped Van (561-1770; 561-1990, off-peak) provides transportation between terminals.

For more information or contact:
- **Information Center for Individuals with Disabilities,** 27-43 Wormwood St., 1st floor, Boston, MA 02210. Call 727-5540 or 800-462-5015 (Voice or TDD).
- **Massachusetts Coalition for Citizens with Disabilities,** 20 Park Plaza, Suite 603, Boston, MA 02116. Call 482-1336 or 1-800-TRY-MCCD (Voice or TDD).

MBTA Access, a free booklet available from the MBTA, describes all of the T's services and programs for persons with disabilities. For a copy, or for more information on any of these services, including THE RIDE, call the MBTA Office for Transportation Access at 722-5123 (TDD 722-5415). For an update on MBTA elevator service, call 451-0027 (TDD 722-5415).

Boston Terminals

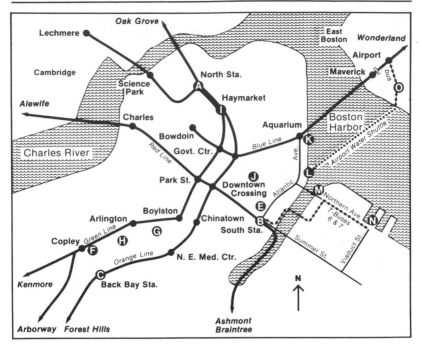

Ⓐ North Station
126 Causeway St.
T-Commuter Rail

Ⓑ South Station
Summer St. & Atlantic Ave.
T-Commuter Rail
Amtrak
See Downtown Boston Map for commuter bus stops:
Brush Hill
Carey's
Greyhound
Interstate
Plymouth & Brockton
Trombly
Vermont Transit
Yankee Line

Ⓒ Back Bay Station
145 Dartmouth St.
T-Commuter Rail
Amtrak
Bonanza

Ⓔ Peter Pan Terminal
555 Atlantic Ave.
American Eagle
Bloom Bus
C & J Trailways
Concord Trailways
Peter Pan
Plymouth & Brockton

Ⓕ Copley Square
See Back Bay map for commuter bus stops:
Cavalier Coach
Guilbankian's
Peter Pan *(some trips)*
Yankee Line
T-Buses to Newton,
Watertown & Burlington

Ⓖ Park Plaza
See Back Bay map for commuter bus stops:
Cavalier Coach
Gulbankian's
Interstate
Plymouth & Brockton
Trombly

Ⓗ St. James Ave.
See Back Bay Map for commuter bius stops:
Peter Pan
The Coach Co.

Ⓘ Haymarket
See Downtown Boston map for commuter bus stops:
Cavalier Coach
The Coach Company
T-buses to Lynn, Salem,
Marblehead, Medford, Woburn, &
Burlington

Ⓙ Federal St.
@ Franklin St.
See Downtown Boston map
T-buses to Newton, Watertown
& Waltham

Ⓚ Long Wharf
T-Commuter Boat
to Charlestown
Bay State Cruise Co.
Boston Harbor Cruises

Ⓛ Rowes Wharf
T-Commuter Boat to Hingham
Airport Water Shuttle

Ⓜ Pier One
A.C. Cruise Line

Ⓝ Commonwealth Pier
Bay State Cruise Co.
to Provincetown

Ⓞ Logan Airport

16

Chapter 5

Downtown Boston and Cambridge

While driving anywhere in Boston can be difficult, taking a car downtown is almost guaranteed to be a bad idea. Streets are crowded and poorly marked, and parking—if you can find it—is expensive. Public transit is a better way to go downtown. Walking and biking are good, too.

In the heart of the city is "Downtown Crossing," a pedestrian zone where private cars are banned. In this shopping area are Jordan Marsh and Filene's department stores, shopping malls, and many smaller stores. Another downtown shopping area, also closed to cars, is Faneuil Hall Marketplace (or "Quincy Market"). Nearby are Boston's financial district and Government Center.

Back Bay is the area west of downtown, from the Public Garden to Massachusetts Ave. It includes the Newbury Street, Copley Place and Prudential Center shopping areas and offices of several insurance companies and other firms.

Cambridge, across the Charles River, is easily accessible by public transportation. Many Boston workers live in this area, famous for its colleges, bookstores, and cosmopolitan ambience (reflected by the international publications available at Out of Town News, along side the Harvard T entrance).

Maps of downtown Boston, the Back Bay, and Cambridge are on pages 20-23, 24, and 26.

Downtown Boston

All four subway lines serve Downtown Boston. The stops are close together—in some places only a few blocks apart. For more detailed information on T services mentioned here, see Chapters 17 and 18. For other services, Chapter 19. The following subway stations serve downtown:

- **Park Street**, Park and Tremont Sts. *Red and Green lines.* The hub of the MBTA system; T information booth, Boston Common, State House, Beacon Hill; near Downtown Crossing shopping area. *T-Buses: 34, 55*

- **Downtown Crossing** (formerly "Washington"), Washington and Summer Sts. *Red and Orange lines.* Downtown Crossing shopping area (Filene's, Jordan Marsh, etc.), financial district. *T-Buses: 7, 11, 49, 53, 54, 92, 93, commuter express buses.*

- **Charles/MGH**, Charles and Cambridge Sts. *Red Line.* Borders Beacon Hill, Massachusetts General Hospital, Holiday Inn, the Massachusetts Department of Employment and Training in the Charles F. Hurley Building, and Suffolk University.

- **South Station**, Atlantic Ave. and Summer St. *Red Line*. Financial district, Children's Museum, Fort Point Channel area, U. S. Post Office, "Leather District," Amtrak, commuter rail, Greyhound Terminal, intercity buses, World Trade Center shuttle bus, Peter Pan Terminal, commuter buses, Rowes Wharf ferries. *T-Bus 7.*

- **Government Center**, Court and Tremont Sts. *Blue and Green lines*. Boston City Hall, state and federal offices, Faneuil Hall, Quincy Market.

- **State**, Washington and State Sts. *Blue and Orange lines*. Financial district, Faneuil Hall, Quincy Market; near Government Center, Old State House. *T-Buses: 92 and 93 (one block E at State and Congress Sts.).*

- **Aquarium**, Atlantic Ave. and State St. *Blue Line*. Waterfront, ferry docks, New England Aquarium, Quincy Market, North End. *T-Bus 6 (rush hours only).*

- **Bowdoin**, Cambridge and New Chardon Sts. *Blue Line*. State offices, Beacon Hill.   Closes at 6:30 pm Mon.-Fri.   Closed Saturday and Sunday.

- **Haymarket**, Congress and New Sudbury Sts. *Green and Orange lines*. North End, near Government Center, weekend open-area markets. *T-Buses: 92, 93 and 111; MBTA commuter buses to the North Shore.*

- **Boylston**, Boylston and Tremont Sts. *Green Line*. Theatre district, Park Plaza, commuter buses, Chinatown. *T-Buses: 9, 10, 55 and 302.*

- **Chinatown** (formerly "Essex"), Washington and Boylston Sts. *Orange Line*. Chinatown, Combat Zone, theatre district. *T-Buses: 11 and 49.*

- **New England Medical Center**, Washington St. south of Stuart St. *Orange Line*. New England Medical Center, theatre district, near Chinatown. *T-Buses: 3, 11, 43 and 49.*

Back Bay
Back Bay is served by the Green Line and the Orange Line:

- **Arlington,** Boylston and Arlington Sts. *Green Line*. Public Garden, Park Plaza, insurance district, Newbury St. shopping, commuter buses. *T-Buses: 9 and 55.*

- **Copley,** Boylston and Dartmouth Sts. *Green Line*. Insurance district, several hotels, Boston Public Library, Copley Place, Newbury Street, Prudential Center; two-block walk to Back Bay Station (Amtrak and commuter rail). *T-Buses: 9, 10, 39, 55, and commuter express buses.*

continued on page 22

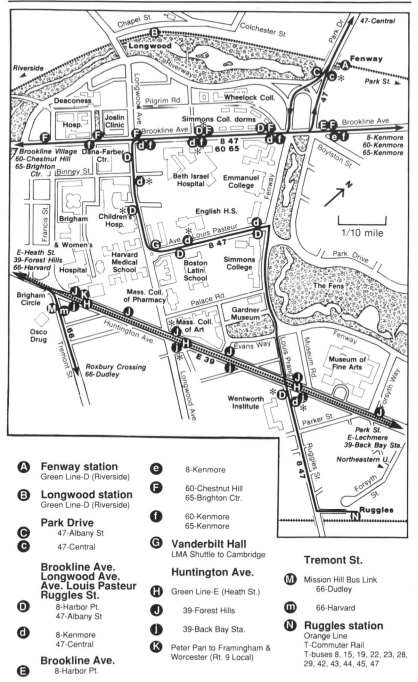

A Fenway station
Green Line-D (Riverside)

B Longwood station
Green Line-D (Riverside)

Park Drive
C 47-Albany St
c 47-Central

Brookline Ave.
Longwood Ave.
Ave. Louis Pasteur
Ruggles St.
D 8-Harbor Pt.
47-Albany St
d 8-Kenmore
47-Central

Brookline Ave.
E 8-Harbor Pt.

e 8-Kenmore

F 60-Chestnut Hill
65-Brighton Ctr.

f 60-Kenmore
65-Kenmore

G Vanderbilt Hall
LMA Shuttle to Cambridge

Huntington Ave.

H Green Line-E (Heath St.)

J 39-Forest Hills

j 39-Back Bay Sta.

K Peter Pan to Framingham &
Worcester (Rt. 9 Local)

Tremont St.

M Mission Hill Bus Link
66-Dudley

m 66-Harvard

N Ruggles station
Orange Line
T-Commuter Rail
T-buses 8, 15, 19, 22, 23, 28,
29, 42, 43, 44, 45, 47

✳**Crosstown express bus stops:**
CT2 (Kendall-Ruggles): all marked stops except Ave. Louis Pasteur, Fenway (Park Dr.)
CT3 (Beth Israel Hosp.-Andrew): all marked stops except Mass. College of Art

Back Bay Boston

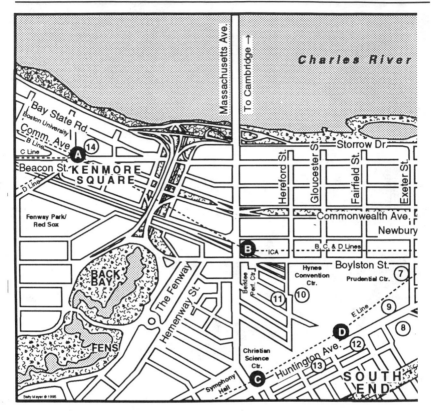

Key to Back Bay Map

Ⓐ Kenmore station
Green Line-B,C,D
T-Bus 8 - Harbor Pt./Umass
T-Bus 57 - Watertown via Brighton
T-Bus 60 - Chestnut Hill Mall
T-Bus 65 - Brighton Ctr. via Brookline Village

Ⓑ Hynes Convention Ctr./I.C.A. station
Green Line B,C,D
T-Bus 1 - Harvard/Dudley
T-Bus CT1 - Central/B.U. Med. Ctr.
T-Bus 55 - Queensberry/Park St.
(on Boylston St.)

Ⓒ Symphony station
Green Line - E
T-Bus 1 - Harvard/Dudley
T-Bus CT1 - Central/B.U. Med. Ctr.

Ⓓ Prudential station
Green Line - E

Ⓔ Copley Square
Boylston St.
Green Line (Copley) Inbound
T-Buses 9 - City Point/Copley via Broadway
T-Bus 10 - City Point/ Copley via Back Bay
T-Bus 55 - Queensberry/Park St. (on Boylston St.)
T-Bus 302 - Watertown/Copley (Rush/Sat. Expr.)

Ⓕ Boylston & Dartmouth Sts.
Green Line (Copley) outbound

Ⓖ St. James Ave.
T-Bus 39 - Forest Hills/Copley
T-Bus 300 - Riverside/Downtown (Rush/
Ltd. Eve Expr.)
T-Bus 304 - Watertown/Downtown (Rush/
Day/Sat. Expr)
T-Bus 352 - Burlington/Boston (Ltd. 1 Trip
Rush Expr.)
Cavalier Coach
Gulbankian's, Copley Sq. Stop
Peter Pan, Copley Sq. Stop
Trombly (PM rush hour)
Yankee Line

Ⓗ Back Bay Station
Orange Line
T-Commuter Rail
Amtrak
Bonanza

Ⓘ Dartmouth St. at Southwest Corridor Park
T-Bus 10 - City Point/Copley via Broadway

Ⓙ Clarendon St. busway
T-Bus 39 - Forest Hills/Copley via Back
Bay

Key to Back Bay Map

K **Arlington Station**
Green Line

L **Arlington Street**
T-Bus 9 - City Point/Copley via Broadway

M **St. James Ave.**
Peter Pan, Arlington St. Stop

N **Park Plaza**
At statue
T-Bus 352 - Burlington/Boston (Ltd.1 Trip Rush Expr.)
Gulbankian's, Park Plaza Stop

O **Transportation Building**
T-Bus 43 - Ruggles/Downtown via Tremont St.
T-Bus 55 - Queensberry/Park St. (on Boylston St.)
Trombly

P **Stuart St. @ U.Mass.**
Interstate

Q **Plymouth & Brockton Buses**

R **Charles/MGH Station**
Red Line (via Park St.)
Mass. General, Mass. Eye & Ear, & Shriners Hospitals

Back Bay Area Hotels

1. Four Seasons Hotel
2. 57 Hotel
3. Boston Park Plaza Hotel & Towers
4. Ritz-Carlton Hotel
5. Copley Plaza Hotel
6. Westin Hotel
7. Lenox Hotel
8. Copley Marriott Hotel
9. Copley Square Hotel
10. Sheraton Hotel & Towers
11. Boston Back Bay Hilton Hotel
12. Colonnade Hotel
13. Midtown Hotel
14. Howard Johnson Motor Lodge

Key To MBTA Branches

- - - - - Green Line
— — — Orange Line
— — Red Line

Map by Sally Mayer

21

- **Hynes Convention Center/ICA** (formerly "Auditorium"), Massachusetts Ave. between Newbury and Boylston Sts. *Green Line-B, C, and D.* Hynes Convention Center, Institute of Contemporary Art, Tower Records; also near Christian Science Center, Prudential Center, Newbury Street shopping, Berklee Performance Center. *T-Buses: 1 and 55 and CT1.*

- **Prudential**, Huntington Ave. and W. Newton St. *Green Line-E.* Prudential Center, Christian Science Center, Copley Place, South End. *T-Bus 39.*

- **Symphony**, Huntington and Massachusetts Aves. *Green Line-E.* Symphony Hall, YMCA, Huntington Theatre, Jordan Hall, New England Conservatory, Horticultural Hall. *T-Buses 1 and CT1.*

- **Back Bay Station**, Dartmouth St. south of Stuart St. *Orange Line.* Copley Place, Copley Square, John Hancock Building, Prudential Center, insurance district, Amtrak, commuter rail, Bonanza terminal, South End. *T-Buses: 10 and 39.*

continued on page 27

Key to Downtown Map

(A) **Haymarket**
Busway
*Inner lane:*T-Buses 352, 353, 354, 426, 436, 439, 441, 442, 450, 455, 458
Outer lane: T-Buses 6, 92, 93, 111

(B) **Congress St. (under garage)**
T-Buses 325, 326

(C) **New Sudbury St.**
The Coach Co.

(D) Cavalier Coach

(E) **State House**
Beacon St.
T-Buses 43, 55
Peter Pan

(H) **Tremont St.**
T-Buses 43, 55

(I) **Congress St.**
North St.
T-Buses 325, 326

(J) **Franklin St.**
Washington St.
Post Office Sq.
Congress St.
T-Buses 92, 93

(K) **Franklin St.**
Otis St.
Summer St.
T-Bus 7

(L) **Federal St./Otis St.**
T-Buses 53, 54, 56, 58, 300, 301, 304, 304A, 305

(M) **Washington St.**
Bedford St.
T-Buses 11, 49

(N) **Surface Artery**
T-Buses 11, 49, 53, 54, 56, 58, 300, 301, 304, 304A, 305

(O) Cavalier Coach

(P) **State St.**
Court St.
Cambridge St.
Congress St.
Carey's

(Q) **South Station**
Amtrak
T-Commuter Rail
Greyhound

(S) Brush Hill
Plymouth & Brockton

(T) Carey's

(U) **Essex St.**
Trombly
Yankee Line

(V) **Lincoln St.**
Interstate

(W) **Summer St.**
World Trade Center shuttle

(X) **Peter Pan Terminal**
See "Boston Terminals" map

(?) **Visitor Information**
Freedom Trail

Downtown Boston

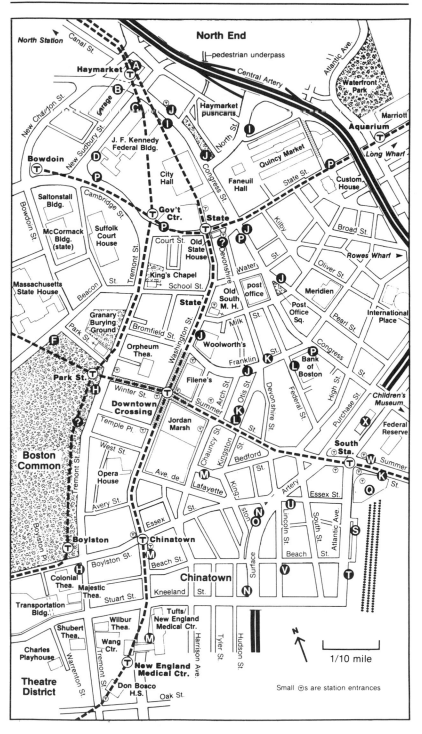

Brookline Village

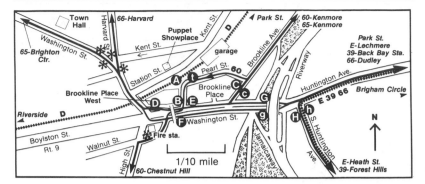

ⓐ Brookline Village station
Green Line-D (Riverside)

ⓑ Pearl St.
60-Chestnut Hill

Brookline Ave.

ⓒ 65-Brighton Ave.

ⓒ 60-Kenmore
65-Kenmore

Washington St.

ⓓ 65-Brighton Ctr.
66-Harvard

ⓔ Peter Pan to Framingham &
Worcester (Rt. 9 local)

ⓕ 60-Kenmore
65-Kenmore
66-Dudley

ⓖ 66-Harvard

ⓖ 66-Dudley

S. Huntington Ave.

ⓗ Green Line-E to Heath St.
39-Forest Hills

ⓗ Green Line-E to Lechmere
39-Forest Hills

✳ Other bus stops

⒪ Taxi Stand

Central Square Cambridge

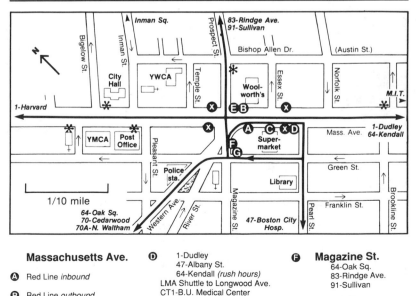

Massachusetts Ave.

ⓐ Red Line *inbound*

ⓑ Red Line *outbound*

ⓒ 70-Cedarwood (Waltham)
70A-N. Waltham

ⓓ 1-Dudley
47-Albany St.
64-Kendall *(rush hours)*
LMA Shuttle to Longwood Ave.
CT1-B.U. Medical Center

ⓔ 1-Harvard

ⓕ Magazine St.
64-Oak Sq.
83-Rindge Ave.
91-Sullivan

ⓖ Green St.
47-Albany St.

✳ Other subway exits

❌ Other bus stops

Boston **Cleveland Circle**

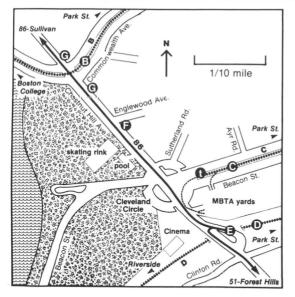

Ⓑ Commonwealth Ave.
Green Line-B (Boston College)

Ⓒ Cleveland Circle
Green Line-C
(Cleveland Circle)

Ⓓ Reservoir station
Green Line-D (Riverside)

Ⓔ Reservoir busway
51-Forest Hills
86-Sullivan
Newbury College Shuttle

Chestnut Hill Ave.

Ⓕ　86-Sullivan
　　Boston College Buses

Ⓖ　86-Sullivan

❶ Taxi Stand

Somerville **Davis Square**

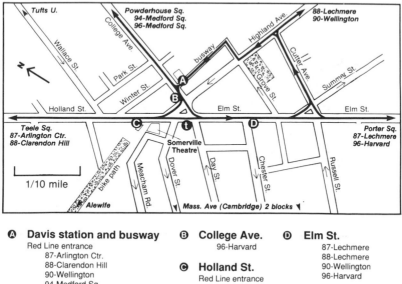

Ⓐ Davis station and busway
Red Line entrance
87-Arlington Ctr.
88-Clarendon Hill
90-Wellington
94-Medford Sq.
96-Medford Sq.

Ⓑ College Ave.
96-Harvard

Ⓒ Holland St.
Red Line entrance
87-Lechmere
88-Lechmere

Ⓓ Elm St.
87-Lechmere
88-Lechmere
90-Wellington
96-Harvard

❶ Taxi Stand

Harvard Square Cambridge

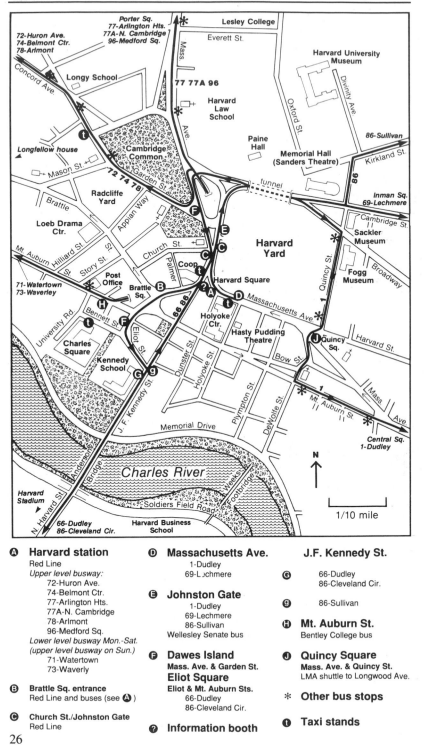

Ⓐ Harvard station
Red Line
Upper level busway:
72-Huron Ave.
74-Belmont Ctr.
77-Arlington Hts.
77A-N. Cambridge
78-Arlmont
96-Medford Sq.
Lower level busway Mon.-Sat.
(upper level busway on Sun.)
71-Watertown
73-Waverly

Ⓑ Brattle Sq. entrance
Red Line and buses (see Ⓐ)

Ⓒ Church St./Johnston Gate
Red Line

Ⓓ Massachusetts Ave.
1-Dudley
69-Lechmere

Ⓔ Johnston Gate
1-Dudley
69-Lechmere
86-Sullivan
Wellesley Senate bus

Ⓕ Dawes Island
Mass. Ave. & Garden St.
Eliot Square
Eliot & Mt. Auburn Sts.
66-Dudley
86-Cleveland Cir.

❓ Information booth

J.F. Kennedy St.

Ⓖ 66-Dudley
86-Cleveland Cir.

ⓖ 86-Sullivan

Ⓗ Mt. Auburn St.
Bentley College bus

Ⓙ Quincy Square
Mass. Ave. & Quincy St.
LMA shuttle to Longwood Ave.

✳ Other bus stops

ⓣ Taxi stands

26

Cambridge

Cambridge is served by the Green Line and the Red Line.

- **Lechmere**, Cambridge St. and O'Brien Highway. *Green Line.* CambridgeSide Galleria shopping (free shuttle bus), Lechmere Sales, Riverfront Park. *T-Buses: 69, 80, 87, 88.*

- **Kendall**, Main St. at Carleton St. and 3 Cambridge Center. *Red Line.* MIT Press bookstore, MIT Coop, CambridgeSide Galleria (free shuttle bus), John A. Volpe National Transportation Systems Center. *T-Buses: 64 (rush hours only) and 85.*

- **Central**, Massachusetts Ave. at Prospect St. *Red Line.* Cambridge City Hall, U. S. Post Office. Ethnic restaurants, discount clothing, furniture, and record shops highlight this area. *T-Buses: 1, 47, 64, 70, 70A, 83, 91, and CT1.*

- **Harvard**, Massachusetts Ave. at Harvard Square. *Red Line.* Harvard University, Radcliffe College, Lesley College; book and record stores, street music; the Loeb Drama Center and the American Repertory Theatre, the Hasty Pudding Theatre; and the Harvard Coop. *T-Buses: 1, 66, 69, 71, 72, 73, 74, 77, 77A, 78, 86, and 96.*

- **Porter**, Massachusetts Ave. at Somerville Ave. *Red Line.* Porter Square Shopping Center, Fitchburg line commuter rail. *T-Buses: 77, 77A, 83, and 96.*

- **Davis**, College Ave. and Holland St., Somerville. *Red Line.* Tufts University, Somerville Theatre, Boston Baked Theatre, and the Seven Hills Linear Park on the bikepath to Cambridge. *T-Buses: 87, 88, 90, 94, and 96.*

- **Alewife**, Alewife Brook Pkwy. at Rindge Ave. and Rt. 2. *Red Line.* The Fresh Pond Shopping Center is a 1/4 mile walk. Bikepaths to Somerville and the Minuteman Bikeway begin here. *T-Buses: 62, 67, 76, 79, 83, 84 and 350.*

The Back Bay, Downtown Boston and Cambridge maps on pages 21-23, 24 and 26 show the exact locations of most bus stops. See Chapters 17-18 for detailed service information.

Railroad Stations

- **North Station**, 126 Causeway St., Boston, under Boston Garden/FleetCenter sports arena. *Green and Orange lines.* Serves northside MBTA Commuter Rail.

- **South Station**, Atlantic Ave. and Summer St., Boston. *Red Line.* Serves Amtrak and southside MBTA Commuter Rail. This station has been extensively renovated and now features a comfortable waiting room and several eateries.

- **Back Bay Station,** 145 Dartmouth St., two blocks south of Copley Square. *Orange Line.* Serves Amtrak and south side MBTA Commuter Rail (except Fairmount Line). Bonanza bus terminal.
- **Porter Square Station,** 1900 Massachusetts Ave., Cambridge. *Red Line .* Serves Fitchburg Line Commuter Rail.

Bus Terminals

- **Peter Pan Terminal,** 555 Atlantic Ave. *Red Line to South Station.* Serves American Eagle, Bloom Bus, C & J Trailways, Concord Trailways, Peter Pan, Plymouth & Brockton. (This was formerly the Trailways terminal.)
- **Bonanza Bus Terminal.** See **Back Bay Station** above.
- **South Station,** 200 Summer St. and 600 Atlantic Ave. *Red Line to South Station.* Serves Greyhound, Plymouth & Brockton, Vermont Transit, Brush Hill, and Carey's.

Commuter Bus Stops

Listed below are some of the major commuter bus stops in downtown Boston and the Back Bay. Different companies may stop at slightly different locations; and some buses make other stops besides those listed here. See the maps in this book or call the bus company for information.

- **Otis and Summer Sts.** *Red or Orange lines to Downtown Crossing.* Serves MBTA commuter express buses 300-305 (see also T-Buses 53, 54, 56, 58-rush hour).
- **Park Plaza.** (formerly called "Park Square"). *Green Line to Boylston or Arlington.* Serves Gulbankian's, Hudson, Interstate, Plymouth & Brockton, Trombly.
- **St. James Ave.** *Green Line to Arlington.* Serves The Coach Co., Peter Pan.
- **Copley Square.** *Green Line to Copley or Orange Line to Back Bay Station.* Serves Gulbankian's, Peter Pan, Trombly (rush hour only), Yankee Line.
- **South Station.** *Red Line.* Serves Brush Hill, Carey's, Plymouth & Brockton. Nearby stops include Essex St.: Trombly, Yankee Line; Lincoln St.: Interstate.
- **Haymarket.** *Green and Orange lines.* Serves The Coach Co. MBTA buses to North Shore points., Atlantic Ave. at State St. Blue Line to Aquarium. Serves Bay State Cruise Co., Boston Harbor Cruises, MBTA Commuter Boat to Charlestown.

Logan Airport Water Shuttle at Rowes Wharf

Ferry Docks

- **Long Wharf,** Atlantic Ave. at State St. *Blue Line to Aquarium.* Serves Bay State Cruise Co., Boston Harbor Cruise, MBTA Commuter Boat to Charlestown, shuttle boat to Commonwealth Pier.

- **Rowes Wharf,** 350 Atlantic Ave. behind the Boston Harbor Hotel. *Blue Line to Aquarium, follow Atlantic Ave. two blocks south. Or: Red Line to South Station, follow Atlantic Ave. three blocks north.* Serves Airport Water Shuttle, MBTA Commuter Boat to Hingham.

- **290 Northern Ave.,** *Red Line to South Station; then T-Bus 7.* Serves AC Cruise Line.

- **Commonwealth Pier,** 164 Northern Ave. at Viaduct St. *Red Line to South Station; then T-Bus 6 (Marine Industrial Park) or 7 (City Point), or walk 3/4 mile east on Summer St. (away from downtown), and turn left on Viaduct St. Or: shuttle boat from Long Wharf.* Serves Bay State Cruise Co. to Provincetown.

Chapter 6
Logan Airport

Logan International Airport, in East Boston, is served by the MBTA Blue Line and the Airport Water Shuttle from downtown Boston, as well as buses, limousines, and taxis.

Although the airport is just two miles from downtown, it can seem like an eternity away when you're stuck in traffic. Traffic tie-ups are now common, not just at rush hours, but also at other times such as Sunday afternoons and major holidays.

For up-to-date information on ground transportation to Logan Airport, call 800-23-LOGAN.

Rapid Transit

The Blue Line goes to **Airport** station; from there, free Massport shuttle buses leave for all airline terminals every 8–12 minutes, 365 days a year, 5:30 am to 1:00 am. There are three shuttle bus routes:

- Airport bus 22 stops at Airport station, Terminals A and B, and the airport tower.
- Airport bus 33 stops at Airport station and Terminals C, D, and E.
- Airport bus 11 stops at all terminals (A, B, C, D, and E) and the airport tower; it does *not* go to Airport station.
- Late at night and early in the morning, these three routes are sometimes combined into a single route stopping at all terminals *and* Airport station.
- Massport employee shuttle bus stops at Airport station, *all* terminals, and can be used by persons with bicycles to arrive and depart via the Maverick Gate area.

Ferries

The Airport Water Shuttle links Logan Airport with **Rowes Wharf** in downtown Boston. Free shuttle buses operate between the airport ferry dock and all airline terminals.

The Airport Water Shuttle operates every 15 minutes on weekdays (6:00 am-8:00 pm); every half hour on Friday evenings (8:00 pm-11:00 pm), Saturdays (10:00 am-11:00 pm), and Sundays and holidays (12:00 noon-8:00 pm). The trip from dock to dock takes about seven minutes. There is no service on New Year's Day, July 4, Thanksgivng, Christmas. The adult fare is $8.00, $4.00 for seniors, and children under 12 ride free. The Water Shuttle transports bicycles at no extra charge.

At Rowes Wharf, the Water Shuttle connects with MBTA commuter boats from Hingham.

Logan Airport Terminal Guide

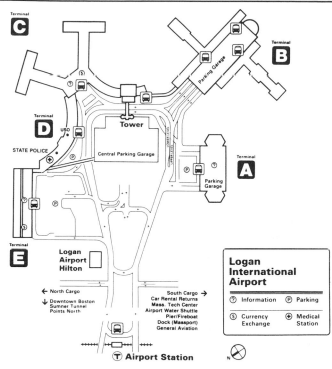

Logan International Airport

⑦ Information   ⑨ Parking

Ⓢ Currency Exchange   ⊕ Medical Station

Ⓣ **Airport Station**

Terminal A
Cape Air	800-352-0714
Colgan Air	800-272-5488
Continental	800-525-0280
Spirit Airlines	800-772-7177
USAir Shuttle	800-428-4322

Terminal B
America West	800-235-9292
American	800-433-7300
American Eagle	800-433-7300
Cape Air	800-352-0714
Delta Shuttle	800-221-1212
Midwest Express	800-452-2022
Qantas	800-227-4500
USAir/USAir Express	800-428-4322
Virgin Atlantic	800-862-8621

Terminal C
American Trans Air	800-543-3710
Business Express	800-345-3400
Delta	800-221-1212
Sabena*	800-955-2000
TWA*/TW Express	800-221-2000
United/United Express	800-241-6522

Terminal D
Charters
Alitalia*	800-223-5730

Terminal E
Aer Lingus	800-223-6537
Air Alliance	800-776-3000
Air Atlantic/Canadian Air	800-426-7000
Air Canada	800-776-3000
Air Nova	800-776-3000
British Airways	800-247-9297
El Al Israel Airlines	800-223-6700
Lufthansa	800-645-3880
Northwest/NW Airlink	800-225-2525
Olympic	800-223-1226
Swissair	800-221-4750
TAP Air Portugal	800-221-7370

*International arrivals on Alitalia, American, American Trans Air, Sabena, TWA and Virgin use Terminal E. All other flights use the terminal indicated above.

Buses and Limousines

Several bus and scheduled limousine companies go to Logan Airport. Service is available from most Boston hotels, plus the South Station and Peter Pan terminals, and from many outlying suburbs and distant cities. For complete listings of buses and limousines, look in Chapter 16, "Cities and Towns'; or check listings for the following carriers in Chapter 19:

Bonanza	Logan Express
C & J Trailways	M & L Transportation
City Transportation	Mass Limousine
Concord Trailways	Peter Pan
Flight Line	Plymouth & Brockton
Green Harbor Transportation	Vermont Transit

Overnight parking is permitted at Logan Express lots in Braintree, Framingham, and Woburn with seven consecutive parking days discounted to the six-day rate.

Taxis

Taxi fares between downtown and Logan average about $12.00, depending on traffic, plus tolls. Passengers boarding at the airport must also pay a 50¢ surcharge. Taxis are available at all terminals at all times.

Flat-rate fares are in effect to points beyond a 12-mile radius from downtown Boston. You should confirm the fare in advance with the driver or the Logan taxi dispatcher.

Airport Telephone Numbers

Public Information Office	561-1800
State Police	567-2233
Medical Station	569-8652
Fire Emergency/First Aid	567-2020
Airport Handicap Van	561-1769
Foreign Language Translators	561-1803

Part II

Places to See, Things to Do

Downtown Providence, as seen from South Water St.

7. Historical, Cultural, and Other Attractions
8. Parks and Recreation

VISITOR INFORMATION

Following are the city's major tourist information centers. The centers marked with "*" sell Boston Passport MBTA visitor passes. Guidebooks to the Freedom Trail and other Boston neighborhoods are available at visitor information centers and at local bookstores.

- **Boston Visitor Information Line** —call 536-4100 weekdays.

- **Boston Common Information Booth***—Tremont St. near Park Street station. Red Line or Green Line to Park Street.

- **Boston National Historical Park Visitor Center** (242-5642)—15 State St., corner of Devonshire St., across from the Old State House. Freedom Trail information and tours; public restrooms; wheelchair accessible. Orange Line or Blue Line to State; Green Line to Government Center.

- **Bostix***—adjacent to Faneuil Hall, off Congress St., and in Copley Square directly across from the Dartmouth Street entrance to the Boston Public Library. Information on cultural events and organizations; ticket sales, including some half-price, same-day tickets. (Closed Mondays.) Orange Line or Blue Line to State; Green Line to Government Center.

- **Faneuil Hall Marketplace Information Center***—South Market St., adjacent to Quincy Market. Orange Line or Blue Line to State; Green Line to Government Center.

- **Cambridge Discovery Information Booth** (497-1630)—Harvard Square. Cambridge information and tours. Red Line to Harvard.

- **The Travelers Aid Society** (542-7286)—offices at 17 East St., Boston (near South Station); booths at South Station and Logan Airport, Terminals A and E.

Chapter 7
Historical, Cultural, and Other Attractions

"Trip time" indicates approximate time from downtown Boston. Estimates include expected waiting times when transfers are required (some pre-trip planning is assumed!) Additional time will be required to get to specific destinations within a city or town from the station (e.g., Old North Bridge in Concord). Destinations without an indicated trip time (e.g., Charlestown) take 30 minutes or less from downtown Boston.

Destinations in **bold type** have detailed listings in Chapter 9. Names of MBTA rapid transit stations are capitalized (e.g., STATE).

Sightseeing Tours and Cruises

Guided walking tours allow you to visit many Boston neighborhoods—including Beacon Hill and the North End—where narrow streets prevent buses from entering. Many different groups offer tours in warm weather months, catering to diverse interests including architectural sites, historical areas (one such tour is led by "Benjamin Franklin"), and murder and mystery locations (Boston, after all, is the birthplace of Edgar Allan Poe). There's even an annual midnight-to-dawn bicycle tour of architectural and historic sites. Check newspaper calendar listings under "Walking Tours."

Several firms offer bus and "trolley" tours of the city. On so-called *trolley tours,* you can usually get off at any stop and then board a later trolley to complete the tour. *Motorcoach (bus) tours* do not allow reboarding. The following tours all include Boston and Charlestown; motorcoach tours also include Cambridge.

- **Boston Duck Tours** (723-DUCK)—amphibious tour of Boston, Charlestown and the Charles River.
- **Boston Trolley Tours** (427-TOUR)—Boston/Charlestown tour (The "Blue Trolley").
- **Brush Hill/Gray Line Tours** (236-2148)—"Beantown Trolley" and motorcoach tours.
- **Old Town Trolley** (269-7010)—Boston/Charlestown tour and Cambridge tour.

These companies offer sightseeing cruises of Boston Harbor:

- **Bay State Cruise Co.** (723-7800)—from Long Wharf (*Blue Line* to AQUARIUM): sightseeing; Nantasket Beach; lunch and dinner cruises; whalewatch cruises. Also, from Commonwealth Pier: Provincetown (Cape Cod) day trip.

- **Boston Harbor Cruises** (227-4321)—from Long Wharf (*Blue Line* to AQUARIUM): sightseeing; lunch cruises.
- **New England Aquarium** (973-5277)—from Central Wharf (*Blue Line* to AQUARIUM): whalewatch cruises.
- **Odyssey Cruises** (654-9700)—from Rowes Wharf (*Blue Line* to AQUARIUM, or *Red Line* to SOUTH STATION): dinner cruises.
- **Spirit of Boston** (457-1450)—from Rowes Wharf (*Blue Line* to AQUARIUM, or *Red Line* to SOUTH STATION): lunch and dinner cruises.
- **A. C. Cruise Line** (1-800-422-8419 or 261-6633)—290 Northern Ave., (*Red Line* to SOUTH STATION, or *Blue Line* to AQUARIUM): Gloucester day trip; whalewatch cruises.

Check newspapers for other cruises such as music cruises and see Chapter 19 for ferries to the Boston Harbor Islands State Park.

One-day sightseeing tours to many of the out-of-town places listed in this section—including Lexington and Concord, Salem, Plymouth, and Newport—are offered by Brush Hill/Gray Line (236-2148).

Boston: The Back Bay

This neighborhood of 19th-century townhouses, churches, and shopping areas is served by the *Green Line*, with stops at ARLINGTON, COPLEY, PRUDENTIAL, SYMPHONY, and HYNES CONVENTION CTR./ICA; and by the *Orange Line* at BACK BAY STATION. (See map, page 21.)

Among the Back Bay's museums and attractions are the Public Garden with its famed Swan Boats, the **Gibson House Museum**, **Trinity Church**, the **Boston Public Library**, the **Institute of Contemporary Art (ICA)**, and the **Christian Science Center** and **Mapparium**. Boston's two tallest buildings, the **John Hancock** and **Prudential** towers, both have public observation decks.

Two fictional creations have attracted visitors to the area. The duckling statues in the Public Garden are based on the Mallard family of ducks in Robert McCloskey's children's classic *Make Way for Ducklings*. The nearby Bull & Finch pub ("Cheers"), at 84 Beacon St., is a tourist magnet.

Boston: Beacon Hill

Beacon Hill remains a quiet enclave in the middle of the busy city. Since its one-way streets have been purposely designed to frustrate drivers, it is an excellent place for walking. Atop the hill is the **Massachusetts State House**, and below are some of the city's finest houses. Take the *Red Line* or *Green Line* to PARK STREET Louisburg Square, with its patrician homes, is the centerpiece of Beacon Hill.

The Black Heritage Trail winds its way across Beacon Hill; the **Boston African-American National Historic Site** (also known as the "African Meeting House") and the **Museum of Afro American History** are on the hill's north slope. For information about the trail, call 742-5415; or pick up a free brochure at one of the city's visitor centers. At the foot of Beacon Hill, Charles Street, with its many restaurants and antique shops, is a popular shopping area. Take the *Red Line* to CHARLES/MGH.

Boston: Charlestown

The **Bunker Hill Monument** towers over Charlestown's 18th- and 19th-century houses. On the waterfront below is the **Charlestown Navy Yard**, home of the U.S.S. *Constitution*, nicknamed "Old Ironsides." You can take a *T-Commuter Boat* from Long Wharf to the Navy Yard (free connecting shuttle bus within the Navy Yard); or take *T-Bus 92 or 93*, which you can board either at HAYMARKET *(Green* or *Orange lines)* or in front of Woolworth's on Washington Street in Boston (*Red Line* to DOWNTOWN CROSSING).

Boston: Chinatown

To get to Boston's Chinatown, take the *Orange Line* to CHINATOWN station. Or take the *Green Line* to BOYLSTON and walk one block east on Boylston Street to CHINATOWN station. From there, walk one block south on Washington Street, and turn left on Beach Street into the heart of Chinatown's retail district. This route will take you through what remains of Boston's adult-entertainment area, the Combat Zone. (See map, page 23.)

An alternative route is the *Red Line* to SOUTH STATION, then walk south along the "Surface Artery" to Beach Street, where you will see a large ceremonial Chinese gate at the entrance to Chinatown.

Beacon Hill, Boston

Boston: Downtown Crossing

The streets of Boston's downtown shopping area are now a pedestrian mall lined with pushcart vendors. Take the *Red Line* or *Orange Line* to DOWNTOWN CROSSING. You can walk from the subway station directly into Filene's or Jordan Marsh department stores without going outside. Or see Chapter 5 for a list of T-Buses serving downtown. (See map, page 23.)

Boston: Faneuil Hall and Quincy Market

These 19th-century markets, reincarnated as a modern shopping center, have become one of the nation's most popular tourist attractions. Take the *Orange Line* or *Blue Line* to STATE; or the *Green Line* to GOVERNMENT CENTER and walk across City Hall Plaza; or take *Orange Line* to HAYMARKET (use "City Hall" exit).

Boston: The Freedom Trail

The Freedom Trail is a self-guided walking tour of sites associated with this nation's early history. It goes from Boston Common, past **Faneuil Hall** and through the North End to Charlestown. Along the way are the **Old South Meeting House**, the **Old State House**, the **Paul Revere House** and the **Old North Church**, "Old Ironsides" **(U.S.S.** *Constitution*) and the **Bunker Hill Monument**. Several of these sites are now part of the Boston National Historical Park.

To start the trail, take the *Red* or *Green Line* to PARK STREET. The trail, which is marked by a red line on the sidewalk, begins at the Visitor Information Booth about 100 feet south of the station on Tremont Street Maps of the trail can be bought at this booth. The National Park Visitor Center at 15 State St. (242-5642), across from the Old State House, offers free maps, a free slide show, and (from April to November) free ranger-guided tours.

The Freedom Trail has provided inspiration for two other trails: The Black Heritage Trail (discussed above under "Beacon Hill") and the Women's Heritage Trail. Featuring walks in downtown, the North End, Chinatown, and Beacon Hill, the Women's Heritage Trail, visits sites associated with Amelia Earhart, Rose Kennedy, Phillis Wheatley, Mary Baker Eddy, Louisa May Alcott, and Julia Ward Howe, among others.

Boston: The North End

The North End, Boston's oldest neighborhood, is the heart of the city's Italian-American community. It is known for its festivals on summer weekends, and its restaurants and bakeries, as well as for the **Paul Revere House** and the **Old North Church**. Take the *Green Line* or *Orange Line* to HAYMARKET and walk through the pedestrian underpass beneath the Central Artery Expressway.

Boston: The Waterfront

Take the *Blue Line* to AQUARIUM, and you will be in the center of Boston's historic waterfront. At Long Wharf and Rowes Wharf, you can board cruise boats to explore the harbor; nearby are Waterfront Park and the **New England Aquarium**. If you're downtown, you can walk out State Street to the waterfront; the "Walk to the Sea" self-guided tour pamphlet is available at the National Park Visitor Center at 15 State St.

On the Fort Point Channel, near SOUTH STATION *(Red Line)* is the "Museum Wharf" complex· the **Children's Museum**, the **Computer Museum**, and the replica **Boston Tea Party Ship**.

Cambridge

Harvard Square in Cambridge is known for its many bookstores, restaurants, and shops, as well as the nation's oldest college. From Boston, take the *Red Line* to HARVARD. Cambridge Discovery's information booth (497-1630) is next to the subway entrance. Harvard University's information office is in Holyoke Center, a modern building behind an outdoor cafe, a block from the subway station. The university has several museums, including the **Busch-Reisinger**, **Fogg**, and **Sackler** art museums, the **Semitic Museum**, and the **Harvard University Museums of Natural History** complex with the Glass Flowers. (See map, page 26.)

On Brattle Street is the **Longfellow National Historic Site,** George Washington's headquarters during the American Revolution.

On Massachusetts Ave., facing the Back Bay across the river, is the Massachusetts Institute of Technology (M.I.T.), which also has a **museum**. Take T-Bus 1 (Harvard-Dudley) or the *Red Line* to KENDALL to the campus.

Both colleges offer tours of their campuses, and in summer, tours of historic Cambridge and Brattle Street start at the Cambridge Discovery booth.

Concord *(trip time: 45 min.)*

Concord was the site of the American Revolution's second battle, the "shot heard 'round the world'"; and later, home to the country's 19th-century literary flowering. Take a *Fitchburg Line commuter train* from NORTH STATION or PORTER *(Red Line)*. From the Concord train station turn right on Thoreau Street, then left on Sudbury Street (Friendly's at the corner) to the town center. The Old North Bridge is a 20-minute walk from the train station, as is the Concord Museum. The homes of Ralph Waldo Emerson and Louisa May Alcott may also be visited; directions to Thoreau's Walden Pond are on page 49. For information call the Chamber of Commerce at 508-369-3120 or the National Park Service at 484-6156.

Fall River *(trip time: 1 hour)*

Once the home of a thriving textile industry, Fall River today features two important maritime museums and an excellent local historical museum. *Bonanza* buses leave from Boston's BACK BAY STATION; local buses are operated by SRTA Mon.-Sat. Visitor

information is available at 72 Bank St. (508-679-0922) or at the
Heritage State Park (508-675-5759).

Battleship Cove, Water Street

Marine Museum, 70 Water St.

Fall River Heritage State Park, 100 Davol St.

• SRTA Bus 7 (Bay St.) to Columbia and Eagle streets, walk north
  on Eagle Street

• Or walk north from the bus terminal on Main Street, across I-
  195; turn left on Central Street parallel to the highway (3/4
  mile)

Fall River Historical Society, 451 Rock St.

• From the bus terminal walk 7 blocks north on Main Street, then
  right on Walnut Street 2 blocks to Rock Street

Gloucester and Rockport *(trip time: 1 hour, 15 min.)*

These two towns form Cape Ann, on Massachusetts' scenic North
Shore. They are served by *Rockport Line commuter trains* from Boston's
NORTH STATION; *CATA* local buses operate Mon.-Sat.

The ancient fishing village of Gloucester has grown into a city,
but it still retains much of its 18th- and 19th-century ambience. From
the commuter rail station, walk 1/2 mile south on Washington Street
to the center of town, or take CATA's Business Express bus. (See
map, page 90.)

The Gloucester Maritime Trail comprises four self-guided walking tours of Gloucester aided by signs, painted lines and a free map
and guide booklet.

To get to the Rocky Neck artist's colony, take *CATA's Red Line
(Thatcher Road) bus*, or *A. C. Cruise Line* direct from 290 Northern Ave. in
Boston.

Virtually everything in Rockport, including the Bearskin Neck
artist's colony, is a short walk from the train station. The town is full
of crafts shops, galleries, restaurants, and inns. (See map, page 92.)
CATA's Blue Line (Lanesville) and *Red Line (Thatcher Road) buses*—both
of which operate between Gloucester and Rockport—offer spectacu-
lar ocean views and are good alternatives to more expensive tours.

For information, call the Cape Ann Chamber of Commerce at 508-
283-1601.

Lexington *(trip time: 1 hour)*

Lexington's Battle Green is where the first shots of the American
Revolution were fired. Take the *Red Line* to ALEWIFE, then T-Bus 62
(Bedford) or 76 (Hanscom Field) to Lexington Center, Mon.-Sat. The
Battle Green, Munroe Tavern, Hancock House, and Old Belfry are all
within a short walk of the town center. The Buckman Tavern and the
Museum of Our National Heritage are located a few bus stops before
Lexington Center. For information call the Chamber of Commerce at
862-1450.

Lowell *(trip time: 45 min.)*

Lowell was the first planned city of the American industrial revolution. Today many of its early 19th-century mills are being restored, and the National Park Service leads popular Mill and Canal tours of the city.

Lowell Line commuter trains depart from NORTH STATION. Local buses are operated by LRTA, Mon.-Sat.; and an all-new, old-fashioned electric trolley links many of the historic sites.

The Boott Cotton Mills Museum, the first major National Park Service museum on industrial history, recently opened in Lowell National Historical Park, featuring a re-created 1920s weave room with 88 operating power looms. Visitors experience the clatter, heat, and smell of the factories.

Beat writer Jack Kerouac was born in Lowell, and each October there is a three-day celebration in his honor, with poetry readings and other events.

The National Park Visitor Center is at 246 Market St. From the Lowell train station, take LRTA's downtown shuttle bus; or walk 5 blocks north on Thorndike Street, then right 4 blocks on Dutton Street to Market Street. Sidewalks are on the *west* (left) side of both Thorndike and Dutton streets; and go over the underpass at Appleton Street (See map, page 92.) For information and tour reservations (required!), call 508-970-5000.

Marblehead *(trip time: 1 hour)*

This seaside town, with its twisting, narrow streets, is much as it was 200 years ago. Today it is also one of the world's sailing capitals. There are shops and restaurants, and two historic house museums. Take T-Bus 441 or 442 from HAYMARKET. For visitor information, call 1-617-631-2868.

New Bedford *(trip time: 1 hour, 30 min.)*

A hundred years ago, New Bedford prospered as a great whaling port. The Seamen's Bethel described in *Moby Dick* still stands, and across the street is a fine Whaling Museum. A Glass Museum is also in the restored historic waterfront just a few blocks from the bus terminal. Visitor information is at 47 N. Second St., or call 508-991-6200. (See map, page 92.)

American Eagle buses to New Bedford leave from the Peter Pan terminal in Boston, and SRTA operates local buses.

Newport, RI *(trip time: 1 hour, 30 min.)*

A century ago, Newport was a summer resort for wealthy families. Seven of their extravagant mansions are now open for tours. The city also has the Tennis Hall of Fame, and many surviving colonial-era buildings, including America's first synagogue. Sightseeing tours by "trolley," train, and boat are available, and bikes can be rented. Tours depart from the Gateway Visitor Center, which is also the stop for *Bonanza* buses from BACK BAY STATION. and local RIPTA buses. The mansions are on Bellevue Avenue, on RIPTA's Red and Yellow routes. For visitor information call 800-326-6030.

Old Sturbridge Village *(trip time: 1 hour, 45 min.)*

Located 50 miles west of Boston, Old Sturbridge Village is a re-creation of an early 19th-century New England rural town. Visitors learn about life in the United States when it was a young nation. Peter Pan has daily buses to this museum from Boston. For information, call 508-347-3362.

Plymouth *(trip time: 1 hour, 30 min.)*

Here the Pilgrims established the first English colony in New England. You can see Plymouth Rock and board a full-scale replica of the *Mayflower*. Take *Plymouth & Brockton* from either Park Plaza or SOUTH STATION. Service is limited, so call Plymouth & Brockton for details.

Plimoth Plantation, a stockaded living-history re-creation of Plymouth in 1627, is three miles south of the town center. The Plymouth Rock Trolley Co. (508-747-3419) runs shuttles between the center of Plymouth, Plimoth Plantation, and other visitor attractions.

For information call the Chamber of Commerce at 508-830-1620. Most sites are open from April to November.

Providence, RI *(trip time: 1 hour, 15 min.)*

Rhode Island's capital is served by *Bonanza* buses, *Amtrak* trains, and *MBTA Commuter Rail* from Boston. Among its many attractions is Brown University, 1/2 mile east of the Kennedy Plaza bus stop and the new train station. Nearby is Benefit Street's "mile of history," featuring over 100 preserved houses, and the Rhode Island School of Design with its renowned art museum. Local buses are operated by RIPTA; for visitor information call 401-274-1636. (See map, page 106.)

> **Museum of Rhode Island History**, Aldrich House, 110 Benevolent St.
> •RIPTA Bus 38 (Rumford/Tunnel), 40 (Butler/Tunnel), or 41 (Elmgrove/Tunnel) to Waterman and Cooke streets; walk one block south.
> **Roger Williams Park, Museum of Natural History, and Zoo**, Elmwood Avenue.
> •RIPTA Bus 20 (Elmwood).
> **Slater Mill Historic Site**, Roosevelt Avenue at Main Street, Pawtucket.
> •RIPTA Bus 98-99 (Providence-Pawtucket) to Roosevelt Avenue and Main Street.

Quincy

Quincy, the "Presidents' City," was the hometown of Presidents John Adams and John Quincy Adams. Their mansion, now the

Adams National Historic Site, is open from April to November. It and several other historic sites may be visited by taking the *Red Line (Braintree)* to QUINCY CENTER. For information call the Quincy Historical Society at 773-1144.

For information on tours of Quincy's historic granite industry, including America's first commercial railroad, call 436-8399. The quarries are off Ricciuti Drive; take T-Bus 215 (Quincy Center-Ashmont) to Willard and Copeland streets and follow Willard Street under the highway.

Note: Quincy **Market** is in downtown Boston, not in Quincy **Center**, which is 10 miles south of downtown.

Rockport. See Gloucester and Rockport.

Salem *(trip time: 35 min.)*

Salem, site of the witch trials of the 1690s and a prosperous port in the early 1800s, is served by *Rockport/Ipswich Line commuter trains* from NORTH STATION and by T-Buses 450 and 455 from HAYMARKET.

Among the city's many attractions are the Peabody Museum of Salem, the Essex Institute, the House of Seven Gables, the old Custom House (now part of the Salem Maritime National Historic Site), and the Salem Witch Museum multi-media show. All are within a 15-minute walk of the train station. From spring through fall, the Salem Trolley (508-744-5469) links these sites and others such as Salem Willows. For more information call the Chamber of Commerce at 508-744-0004 or the National Park Service at 508-741-3648. (See map, page 102.)

Worcester *(trip time: 1 hour)*

New England's second-largest city is known for its colleges and universities. Its excellent Art Museum, the scholarly collections of the American Antiquarian Society, and the Salisbury Mansion (restored to its 1830s splendor) are near Lincoln Square, one-half mile north of downtown Worcester. The city's historical museum is at 30 Elm St., one block from City Hall.

Worcester is served by *Peter Pan, Greyhound,* and *Amtrak* from Boston; local buses are operated by WRTA. For information call the Visitors Bureau at 508-753-2920. (See map, page 106.)

New England Science Center, 222 Harrington Way.
 •WRTA Bus 12 (Plantation/Lake View) to Plantation and Franklin streets or WRTA Bus 18 (Hamilton/Edgemere).

Higgins Armory Museum (medieval arms and suits of armor), 100 Barber Ave.
 •WRTA Bus 30N (Summit/W. Boylston or Summit/Holden) to Barber Avenue.

Chapter 8
Parks and Recreation

Many of Greater Boston's parks, beaches, and other recreation areas are accessible by public transit.

Parks marked "BP&R" are operated by Boston Parks and Recreation; call 635-4505 for information on special programs in these and other city parks.

Boston's Emerald Necklace is a seven-mile string of parks, most of which were designed by Frederick Law Olmsted. With a few short interruptions, you can hike in parkland from Boston Common to Franklin Park in Dorchester. All of the BP&R parks listed here are part of the necklace. For information on Boston Park Rangers tours, call 635-7383.

Parks marked "MDC" are operated by the Metropolitan District Commission. A guide to all MDC facilities is available by writing to the MDC at 20 Somerset St., Boston MA 02108 or by calling 727-5250. For specific information about MDC facilities, call 727-5250 or check the blue pages of the Boston-area phone book under "Commonwealth of Massachusetts, Government Offices."

"Trip time" indicates approximate time from downtown Boston. Estimates include expected waiting times when transfers are required (some pre-trip planning is assumed!) Additional time will be required to get to specific destinations within a city or town from the station (e.g., Crane's Beach in Ipswich).

Destinations without an indicated trip time (e.g., Quincy) take 30 minutes or less from downtown Boston.

Names of MBTA rapid transit stations are capitalized.

Boston: Downtown and the Back Bay

Boston Common is the oldest public park in America. *Red Line* to PARK STREET or *Green Line* to PARK STREET or BOYLSTON. (BP&R)

Public Garden—Stroll around the lagoon, feed the ducks, or take a ride on the Swan Boats (Apr.-Sept.). You can rent ice skates in winter. *Green Line* to ARLINGTON. (BP&R)

Charles River Esplanade—A popular spot for jogging, bike riding on the Paul Dudley White Bikepath, roller skating, and sunning. Take the *Red Line* to CHARLES/MGH and cross the overpass to the river; or take the *Green Line* to ARLINGTON, COPLEY, HYNES CONVENTION CTR./ICA, or KENMORE and walk two to four blocks north to the river. There is a public swimming pool near the Science Museum (*Green Line* to SCIENCE PARK, or *Red Line* to CHARLES/MGH.) You can hike or bike on both sides of the river for six miles, from the Science Museum to Watertown Sq. (MDC)

RECREATION INDEX

Beaches— *See Boston entries for Dorchester, East Boston, Boston Harbor and South Boston; Cape Cod; Gloucester; Lynn; Manchester, Marblehead; Nantasket; Quincy; Revere; Rockport; Winthrop.*

Beaches (fresh water)— *See Concord (Walden Pond); Milton (Houghton's Pond); Winchester (Mystic Lakes).*

Bicycle Rentals— Boston: Back Bay Bicycles (Green Line to HYNES CONVENTION CTR./ICA); Earth Bikes (Green Line to COPLEY or Orange Line to BACK BAY STA.); and Community Bicycle Supply (T-Bus 43 from PARK STREET to Berkeley St.). *See also Cape Cod; Gloucester; Ipswich; Lincoln; Manchester-by-the-Sea; Marblehead; Martha's Vineyard; Nantucket. (See page 14 for bike path listings.)*

Camping— *See Boston Harbor and Hingham.*

Canoeing— *See Concord, Newton (Charles River), and Brookline/Brighton (Christian Herter Park).*

Golf— *See Boston: Dorchester (Franklin Park); Cambridge (Fresh Pond); Lynn (Gannon); Milton (Ponkapoag).* Other courses not listed: Putterham Meadows in Brookline (T-Bus 51 from RESERVOIR or FOREST HILLS); George Wright Golf Course in Hyde Park (Boston, T-Bus 50 from FOREST HILLS); Newton Commonwealth Golf Course (Green Line-B to BOSTON COLLEGE).

Horseback Riding— *See Milton.*

Ice Skating— *See Boston: Downtown and the Back Bay (Public Garden); Brookline (Chestnut Hill) ; Waltham (Beaver Brook); or call the MDC for other rinks at 727-9547.*

Rowboats— *See Boston: Jamaica Pond and Brookline/Brighton (Christian Herter Park).*

Sailing— *See Boston: Downtown and the Back Bay; Boston: Jamaica Pond; Somerville.*

Skiing, cross-country— *See Lincoln; Lynn Woods; Weston. (Rentals available at all three. Many other parks have trails.)*

Skiing, downhill— *See Milton (Blue Hills, west).*

Swimming Pools— *See Boston: Downtown and the Back Bay (Charles River Esplanade), Brookline (Chestnut Hill), or call the MDC at 727-9547.*

Community Boating, Inc.—Learn to sail and enjoy inexpensive sailing on the Charles (523-1038). *Red Line* to CHARLES/MGH.

Back Bay Fens—Tree-lined lagoons make this one of Boston's most beautiful parks. Be sure to visit the Rose Garden on Park Drive, near Jersey St. Take the *Green Line-E (Heath St.)* or *T-Bus 39* (Forest Hills-Back Bay Sta.) to MUSEUM OF FINE ARTS and cross behind the Museum of Fine Arts. Or: *Green Line-(B, C, or D)* to HYNES CONVENTION CTR./ICA and walk two blocks west on Boylston St. to the Fenway. (BP&R)

Southwest Corridor Park–see listing under "Boston: Jamaica Plain."

Boston: Dorchester

Franklin Park—This is Boston's largest park and one of landscape architect Frederick Law Olmsted's masterpieces. Take the *Orange Line* to GREEN and walk four blocks east (to the right) into the park. To reach the park's eastern side, near the zoo and the golf course, take the *Orange Line* to RUGGLES, then *T-Bus 22 (Ashmont via Jackson Sq.)*, 28 (Mattapan), or 45 (Franklin Park). Or: *T-Bus 16* from either JFK/UMASS *(Red Line)* or FOREST HILLS *(Orange Line)*.

Malibu and Savin Hill Beaches—*Red Line (Ashmont)* to SAVIN HILL. Walk east on Savin Hill Ave. to Playstead St. and turn right. (MDC)

Boston: East Boston

Constitution Beach —*Blue Line* to ORIENT HEIGHTS. Walk one block east on Saratoga Street to Barnes Avenue and turn right past the library. (MDC)

Boston Harbor

There are eight islands in the **Boston Harbor Islands State Park:**

Georges Island is the park's gateway. It is the departure point for free water taxis to four of the other islands, and the site of historic Fort Warren. The *Bay State Cruise Co.* sails to Georges Island, from Long Wharf in Boston, mid-May through mid-October.

In summer, daily ferries to Georges Island also depart from Hingham *Bay State Cruise Co.).*

Bumpkin, Gallops, Grape, and **Lovells islands** are reached by free water taxi from Georges Island. You can camp on Bumpkin, Grape, and Lovells. Permits are required; for Bumpkin and Grape, call 740-1605; Lovells, 727-5290. Peddocks Island's pier is being rebuilt; the island will reopen in late 1996.

Non-profit groups and persons 62 or older can get free ferry tickets to the islands on weekdays; call 740-1605 for an application form or for more information about the Harbor Islands State Park.

The Friends of the Boston Harbor Islands (740-4290) organize special cruises to the islands, including trips to Boston Light on Little Brewster.

Boston: Jamaica Plain

Arnold Arboretum —T-Bus 39 to The Monument, then walk west on Centre Street to the Arboretum's main gate. Or: *Orange Line* to FOREST HILLS and walk north into the Arboretum. (BP&R)

Jamaica Pond —T-Bus 39 to Pond Street; walk one block west on Pond Street. You can rent a rowboat or sailboat, and the pond is stocked with fish. No swimming. (BP&R)

Olmsted Park —This quiet park is part of the Emerald Necklace. *T-Bus 39* to Bynner St.; walk one block west on Bynner St. You can walk north in the park to BROOKLINE VILLAGE *(Green Line-D)* or south to Jamaica Pond. (BP&R)

Southwest Corridor Park —A 52-acre park has been built along the route of the MBTA Orange Line, including a three-mile bike path from Forest Hills to Copley Place. Take the *Orange Line* to any station from BACK BAY STATION to FOREST HILLS. (MDC)

Franklin Park —See listing under "Boston: Dorchester."

Boston: South Boston

Castle Island —Linked to the mainland, Castle Island is a good fishing spot, and there is a small, sheltered beach. Historic Fort Independence is also located here. *Red Line* to BROADWAY, then *T-Bus 9 (City Point)* or *11 (Bayview)* to the end of the line. From the bus stop at 1st and P streets, walk 1/2 mile east along Pleasure Bay. Less frequent buses to City Point leave from SOUTH STATION *(T-Bus 7)* and COPLEY *(T-Buses 9 and 10)*. (MDC)

Carson Beach—*Red Line (Ashmont)* to JFK/UMASS then walk north along Day Blvd. to the beach. (MDC)

M Street Beach —*Red Line* to BROADWAY, then *T-Bus 11 (Bayview)*. Get off anywhere along E. 8th Street and walk two blocks south to the beach. (MDC)

Boston: West Roxbury

Stony Brook Reservation—This 600-acre wooded park has miles of hiking and skiing trails and scenic views from hilltops. *Orange Line* or *T-Bus 39* to FOREST HILLS; then *T-Bus 34 (Dedham Line), 34E (East Walpole)*, or *40 (Georgetowne)*. Get off at Washington and LaGrange streets. (MDC)

Brookline and Brighton

Riverway —Half in Boston and half in Brookline, this park is a pleasant oasis in the middle of the city. *Green Line-D (Riverside)* to FENWAY or LONGWOOD. (BP&R)

Chestnut Hill Reservoir —The 1.7-mile track around the reservoir is popular with joggers; there is also a picnic area, a public swimming pool, and a public ice skating rink. *Green Line-B* to CHESTNUT HILL AVE., *Green Line-C* to CLEVELAND CIRCLE, or *Green Line-D (Riverside)* to RESERVOIR; walk out Beacon Street past the Ground Round restaurant. (MDC)

Christian Herter Park —This park on the Charles River has a playground, wading pool, and picnic tables. Rent a canoe or kayak! Take *T-Bus 70 (Cedarwood-Central), 70A (N. Waltham-Central),* or *86 (Sullivan-Cleveland Circle)* to Everett Street; walk one block north to the river. (MDC)

Cambridge

Charles River Basin—*Red Line* to HARVARD, then walk along J. F. Kennedy Street to the river. On Sundays from April to November, Memorial Drive becomes "Riverbend Park," and cars are banned between Western Avenue and the Eliot Bridge. (MDC)

Fresh Pond—*Red Line* to HARVARD, then *T-Bus 72 (Huron Ave.)* to Fresh Pond Parkway. The footpath around the pond is popular for runners. No swimming. (MDC)

Mount Auburn Cemetery—The cemetery is also a botanical garden and a birdwatcher's paradise. *Red Line* to HARVARD, then *T-Bus 71 (Watertown), 72 (Huron Ave.),* or *73 (Waverley).*

Cape Cod *(trip time: 90 min. to 3 hours)*

Plymouth & Brockton (P&B) buses to Hyannis depart from Park Plaza and the Peter Pan terminal in Boston. *Bonanza* buses to Falmouth and Woods Hole leave from BACK BAY STATION. (See maps, pages 88 and 90.) And the *Bay State Cruise Co.* has a daily summer ferry to Provincetown, at the tip of the Cape, from Boston's Commonwealth Pier.

Riding through Lexington on the Minuteman Bikeway (see page 14)

Bonanza also has daily buses to the Cape from New York, NY, and Providence, RI; and Amtrak runs trains from New York to Hyannis in summer.

The Cape Cod Regional Transit Authority operates year-round buses, Mon.-Sat., along the Cape's southern shore between Hyannis and Woods Hole. Bicycles can be rented in Hyannis, Falmouth, and Provincetown. The Cape Cod Scenic Railroad (508-771-3788) operates sightseeing trains from Hyannis, June–October, four days a week.

Kalmus Beach—From the Hyannis bus station, a 30-minute walk south on Ocean Ave.

Provincetown—The *Bay State Cruise Co.* offers a three-hour ferry trip from Boston. Or take a *P&B* bus to "P-town" via Hyannis (change buses in Hyannis). In summer, Lower Cape Bus runs local buses in Provincetown.

Orleans, Eastham, Wellfleet, and **Truro**—served by *P&B* buses from Hyannis and Provincetown. Go to Hyannis and change buses there or take the ferry to Provincetown and catch the bus at the end of the dock.

For visitor information, call the Cape Cod Chamber of Commerce in Hyannis (508-362-3225) or the Provincetown Chamber of Commerce (508-487-3424).

Concord *(trip time: 45 min.)*

To reach this historically important town, take a *Fitchburg Line commuter train* from NORTH STATION or from PORTER *(Red Line)* in Cambridge.

Walden Pond—The pond where Thoreau lived is a 30-minute walk from the train station. Leaving the depot, turn right on Thoreau Street to its end, then right on Walden Street. After crossing Route 2, take any of the trails on the right to the pond, or continue straight on Walden Street to a small beach. Alternatively, you can take the train to Lincoln and rent a bike from Lincoln Guide Service (259-9204).

Great Meadows Wildlife Refuge—a two-mile walk from the train station; for directions call 508-443-4661. Or rent a canoe at South Bridge.

South Bridge Boat House—Canoe rentals (508-369-9438). From the depot, turn left on Thoreau Street to its end, then left on Main Street (1/2 mile).

Gloucester *(trip time: 1 hour)*

Take a *Rockport Line commuter train* from NORTH STATION; connecting local buses are operated by Cape Ann Transportation Authority (CATA), Mon.-Sat. Bikes can be rented at Giles of Gloucester (508-283-3603), near the train station. (See map, page 90.)

Pavilion Beach, Half Moon Beach, and **Stage Fort Park**—A one-mile walk from the Gloucester train station. Go south on Washington Street, then right on Middle Street (at the equestrian statue) and right again on Western Ave. (Rte. 127). The park entrance is on the left at the end of the causeway. These beaches are on the harbor and are somewhat rocky.

Good Harbor Beach—Take *CATA Red Line (Thatcher Rd.) bus* (Mon.-Sat.) from Gloucester. This is one of Cape Ann's finest beaches.

Hingham *(trip time: 1 hour, 15 min.)*

World's End—This 250-acre peninsula was landscaped by Frederick Law Olmsted. Take the *Red Line (Braintree)* to QUINCY CTR.; then *T-Bus 220 (Hingham)*. Get off at Otis and North Sts., by Hingham Harbor; walk down Summer St. past the traffic circle, then turn left on Martin's Lane (about 1 mile). Or take *People Care-iers' "Hull" bus* from Hingham to Martin's Lane. The reservation is at the end of the street.

Wompatuck State Park—*Red Line (Braintree)* to QUINCY CTR.; then *T-Bus 220A (Hingham Loop)* to Main and Union streets; walk up Union St. slightly over one mile to the park. Or take *T-Bus 220 (Hingham)* to the end of the line and walk one mile up Main Street to Union Street.

Ipswich *(trip time: 1 hour)*

Crane's Beach—Take an *Ipswich Line commuter train* from NORTH STATION, Mon.-Sat. It is four miles from the train station to the beach; bikes can be rented at the Skol Shop (508-356-5872). Taxis are also available.

Lincoln *(trip time: 40 min.)*

This town has hundreds of acres of conservation land for hiking or cross-country skiing. Also located here are the Mass. Audubon Society's Drumlin Farm and the DeCordova Museum and Park. Take a *Fitchburg Line commuter train* from NORTH STATION or PORTER. *(Red Line)* in Cambridge. The Lincoln Guide Service (259-9204), near the train station, rents bikes and skis.

Lynn

Take *T-Bus 441* or *442 (Marblehead)*, or *455 (Salem via Loring Ave.)* from HAYMARKET, or *T-Commuter Rail (Rockport/Ipswich Lines)* from NORTH STATION to downtown Lynn.

Lynn Beach and Nahant Beach—From the new Lynn train/bus station, walk 1/2 mile east on Carroll Pkwy. to the rotary and cross the parkway to the beach. Lynn Beach is to the left; Nahant Beach to the right. Both beaches are wide and sandy.

King's Beach—*T-Bus 442 (Marblehead-Haymarket via Humphrey St.)* stops 1/2 block from the beach.

Lynn Woods—This 2,200-acre park has nearly 30 miles of trails. From downtown Lynn take *T-Bus 436 (Goodwins Circle)* to Great Woods Road by Gannon Golf Course (592-8238), or take *T-Bus 429 (North Saugus)* to Penny Brook Road. (Both buses operate Mon.-Sat.) Park maps are available and skis can be rented (598-4212) at the headquarters on Great Woods Road.

Malden and Melrose

Pine Banks Park —This park has hiking and skiing trails and a picnic area with a duck pond and a small zoo. Take the *Orange Line* to *Oak Grove;* follow signs "To Buses," then walk along the driveway to the left. Near the end of the parking lot, go through the opening in the fence on your right, and cross a footbridge. Walk one block to the end of Fairlawn St.; turn left on Main Street. One block to the park entrance. Or take *T-Bus 136/137* directly to the park.

Manchester-by-the-Sea *(trip time: 50 min.)*

Take *Rockport Line Commuter Rail* from NORTH STATION to this Cape Ann town. Bicycles can be rented at Seaside Cycle (508-526-1200).

Singing Beach—This small, but excellent, beach is 1/2 mile from the station and is very popular with transit riders. You cannot get closer to the beach by driving; people with cars must park at the railroad station.

Marblehead *(trip time: 1 hour)*

Take *T-Bus 441 or 442 (Marblehead)* from HAYMARKET. Bike rentals are available at Marblehead Cycle (1-631-1570) on Bessom Street, downtown.

Devereux Beach—Get off the bus at Ocean Avenue in Marblehead; (*not* Ocean Avenue in Swampscott); walk 1/2 mile east on Ocean Avenue.

Martha's Vineyard *(trip time: 3 hours)*

The easiest way to the Vineyard is *Bonanza* bus from BACK BAY STATION in Boston to Woods Hole, then a *Steamship Authority* ferry to Vineyard Haven (year-round) or Oak Bluffs (summer only). Other ferries sail from Falmouth (Island Queen), Hyannis (Hy-Line), and New Bedford (Cape Island Express).

Summer buses on the island are operated by Island Transport, Martha's Vineyard Transportation Services, and Martha's Vineyard Transit Authority; bicycles can be rented at all of the island's ferry docks. For visitor information, call 508-693-0085.

Medford

Mystic River—*Orange Line* to WELLINGTON. Make two right turns leaving the station; walk through the parking lot, toward Boston, then through a gate and past a gravel storage area. When you reach the river's edge, turn right under the tracks. The park extends 3 miles upriver, past Medford Square (served by T-Buses 94, 95, 96, 101, and 134). (MDC)

Middlesex Fells—This 2,000-acre park can be reached by several MBTA routes. Take the *Orange Line* to OAK GROVE, make two right turns leaving the station, and walk north on Washington Street 1/2 mile, then left up Goodyear Avenue to a trailhead. Or take the *Orange Line* to MALDEN CENTER then *T-Bus 99 (Upper Highland)* to the end.

The western half of the park can be reached by the *Orange Line* to WELLINGTON, then *T-Bus 100 (Elm St.)*. Get off at the rotary and cross over the highway to Pine Hill and a lookout tower; or stay on the bus to the end of the line and walk 1 1/2 blocks north on the Fellsway to a trailhead.

Milton and Canton *(trip time: 45 min.–1 hour)*

The Blue Hills have over 500 miles of trails; Great Blue Hill, at 635 feet, is higher than the John Hancock Tower. For park information call 698-1802. There are several nearby stables for horseback riding. (MDC)

Blue Hills Reservation, west—*Red Line* to MATTAPAN, then *Hudson Bus* to Canton, Mon.-Sat. Get off at the Trailside Museum. The Skyline Trail extends eight miles to Willard St. (see "Blue Hills, east"). The **Blue Hills Ski Area** (828-5070) has a chair lift and three slopes for downhill skiing.

From the Hillside Street bus stop, it is a one-mile hike to **Houghton's Pond** where you can swim, fish, and have a cookout (a fire permit is necessary).

Blue Hills, central—*Red Line* to ASHMONT, then *T-Bus 240 (Avon Line)* or *240A (Crawford Sq.)*. The bus goes right through the park.

Blue Hills, east—*Red Line (Braintree)* to QUINCY CENTER, then *T-Bus 238 (Crawford Sq.)*. Get off at West and Willard streets by the skating rink. Or: *T-Bus 215 (Quincy Ctr.-Ashmont)* to Copeland and West streets (Boyd Sq.); follow West Street 1/2 mile.

Fowl Meadow—*Orange Line* or *T-Bus 39* to FOREST HILLS; then *T-Bus 32 (Wolcott Sq.)* to the end of the line. Walk 1/2 mile east on the Neponset Valley Pkwy. The trail begins just across the river on the right. Or hike from the Trailside Museum (see "Blue Hills Reservation, west"). (MDC)

Ponkapoag Pond—*Red Line* to MATTAPAN, then *Hudson Bus* to Canton. (Mon.-Sat.). Get off at the Ponkapoag Golf Course and hike east around the golf course. No swimming. (MDC)

Nantasket *(trip time: 1 hour)*

The big amusement park is gone, but the wide beach and some small arcades remain. The *Bay State Cruise Co.* has daily ferries from Long Wharf in summer. Or: *Red Line (Braintree)* to QUINCY CENTER, then *T-Bus 220* to Hingham, then *People Care-iers' "Hull" bus*. (MDC)

Nantucket *(trip time: 4 hours)*

Ferries to Nantucket sail from Hyannis, where the docks are a 1/2-mile walk from the bus station. (See map, page 90.) The *Steamship Authority* has year-round ferries and Hy-Line sails from May to October.

Barrett's Tours operates summer buses on the island. Bikes can be also rented near the ferry docks.

For visitor information, call 508-228-1700 or 508-228-0925.

Newton *(trip time: 30 min.–45 min.)*

Charles River—Green Line-D to RIVERSIDE; walk behind the streetcar sheds and cross an unused railroad bridge to the park. A three-mile walk along the river is possible. (MDC)

The Charles River Canoe and Kayak Center , canoe, kayak, and scull rentals and instruction, is a 20-minute walk from RIVERSIDE *(Green Line-D)*; call 965-5110 for directions.

Hemlock Gorge and Echo Bridge —Green Line-D (Riverside) to WABAN. Turn left on Beacon Street over the tracks, then left on Waban Avenue after the church, and left again on Annawan Road to the river (about 1/2 mile). Follow the river to the left. (MDC)

Hammond Pond Woods—Green Line-D (Riverside) to CHESTNUT HILL. Turn left on Hammond Street, then right before the shopping center to the park entrance on your right. No swimming. (MDC)

Quincy

Wollaston Beach —Red Line (Braintree) to WOLLASTON; walk east on Beale and Beach streets (one mile). Or take *T-Bus 217 (Wollaston Beach)*, Mon.-Sat., from Wollaston or Ashmont (Red Line). (MDC)

Neponset Marshes —Red Line to ASHMONT, then *T-Bus 217 (Wollaston Beach)*, Mon.-Sat., to Adams and Squantum streets. This is an excellent spot for birdwatching. (MDC)

Revere

Revere Beach—Blue Line to either REVERE BEACH or WONDERLAND; walk one block east to the beach. (MDC)

Rockport *(trip time: 70 min.)*

Take a *Rockport Line commuter train* from NORTH STATION to this North Shore town. (See map, page 92.)

Rockport Beach—This small, rocky beach is just north of the town center, 1/2 mile from the Rockport train station.

Halibut Point—You can walk on huge slabs of granite which lead down to the surf. Take *CATA Blue Line (Lanesville)* bus (Mon.-Sat.) from the train station in either Rockport or Gloucester to Gott Avenue; the park is at the end of Gott Avenue. Or walk a little over two miles from Rockport; go north from town on Granite Avenue, then turn right on Gott Avenue. No swimming.

Somerville

"Blessing of the Bay"—Inexpensive sailing and lessons on the Mystic River (628-9610). *Orange Line* to SULLIVAN, then *T-Bus 95 (West Medford)* to Shore Drive and walk under the highway.

Waltham and Belmont

Beaver Brook and Waverley Oaks—This small park has picnic tables, wildflowers, and a duck pond where you can ice skate in winter. *Red Line* to HARVARD, then *T-Bus 73 (Waverley)* to the end of the line; walk 1/4 mile up Trapelo Road to the park. (MDC)

Watertown

Charles River—There is a nice park on the north bank of the river, and you can bike or walk along the river all the way to downtown Boston—six miles. Take any of the following *T-Buses* to Watertown Sq.: *57 (Watertown-Kenmore); 70 (Cedarwood-Central); 70A (N. Waltham-Central);* or *71 (Watertown-Harvard).* (MDC)

Weston   *(trip time: 1 hour)*

Weston Ski Track —Cross-country skiing and rentals (891-6575). *Green Line-D* to RIVERSIDE, then a one-mile walk; call for directions.

Weymouth   *(trip time: 45 min.)*

Great Esker Park—This high gravel ridge was deposited along the shores of the Back River by glaciers in the last Ice Age. Take the *Red Line* to QUINCY CENTER, then *T-Bus 220 (Hingham).* Get off at Harborlight Mall and enter the park behind the shopping center.

Winchester

Mystic Lakes—*Lowell Line commuter rail* to Wedgemere; walk left on Mystic Valley Parkway 1/2 mile to a small fresh-water beach and park. (MDC)

Winthrop

Winthrop Beach — *Blue Line* to ORIENT HEIGHTS, then take any *Paul Revere "Winthrop Beach"* or *"Point Shirley"* bus. (MDC)

Part III

Destination Listings

First Night: Copley Square, Boston

9. Museums, Attractions, and Points of Interest
10. Theaters, Cinemas, and Auditoriums
11. Nightlife
12. Major Spectator Sports
13. Shopping Centers
14. Educational Institutions
15. Hospitals
16. Cities, Towns, and Neighborhoods

WHY PAY MORE?

➤ MBTA Monthly Pass holders are entitled to discounts at some institutions listed in this chapter (indicated by *). The Pass Program also includes discounts for participating restaurants and retail outlets. For more information, call 722-5218.

➤ If you are planning to purchase tickets for a production at one of the theaters listed in Chapter 12, check out Bostix in Faneuil Hall or Copley Square (723-5181) where half-price, same-day tickets are sold for some local shows.

➤ Many attractions offer discounts for members and special rates for families, senior citizens, and those who visit during off-peak hours. Inquire with the institution for details.

☞ In Chapters 9-16 names of MBTA rapid transit stations are capitalized (e.g., COPLEY).

Chapter 9

Museums, Attractions, and Points of Interest

Adams National Historic Site
135 Adams St., Quincy (773-1177).
- Red Line (Braintree) to MATTAPAN; 1/2-mile walk N on Burgin Pkwy. to Adams St.

African Meeting House
8 Smith Ct. (behind 46 Joy St.), Boston (742-5415).
See "Boston African-American National Historic Site."

American Jewish Historical Society
2 Thornton Rd., Waltham (891-8110).
- T-Bus 70 (Cedarwood-Central) to end of line; walk up Cedarwood Ave. to Thornton Rd.

Blue Hills Trailside Museum
1904 Canton Ave., Milton (333-0690).
- Hudson Bus (Mattapan-Canton), connects w/Red Line at MATTAPAN.

Boston African American National Historic Site/ Black Heritage Trail
46 Joy St., Boston (742-5415).
- Blue Line to BOWDOIN.
- Red Line to CHARLES/MGH.
- Green Line to GOVERNMENT CTR.

Boston Nat'l Historical Park
Visitor Center, 15 State St., Boston (242-5642).
- Orange Line or Blue Line to STATE.
- Green Line to GOVERNMENT CTR.

Boston Public Library
666 Boylston St., Boston (536-5400).
- Green Line or T-Buses to COPLEY.
- Orange Line or T-Commuter Rail to BACK BAY STA.

Boston Tea Party Ship and Museum *
Congress Street Bridge, Boston (338-1773).
- Red Line to SOUTH STA.; walk NE on

Atlantic Ave. 1 block (past Peter Pan), then right on Congress St. 1 block.

Bunker Hill Monument
Monument Sq., Charlestown (242-5641).
- Orange Line to COMMUNITY COLLEGE; 1/2-mile walk.
- T-Commuter Boat from Long Wharf to Charlestown Navy Yard; 1/2-mile walk.
- T-Bus 92 (Assembly Sq.-Downtown) to Main and Winthrop Sts.
- T-Bus 93 (Sullivan-Downtown) to Bunker Hill and Lexington Sts.

Bunker Hill Pavilion *
"The Whites of Their Eyes"
55 Constitution Rd., Charlestown (241-7575).
See "Charlestown Navy Yard."

Busch-Reisinger Museum
In same building with Fogg Art Museum
32 Quincy St., Cambridge (495-9400).
- Red Line or T-Buses to HARVARD.

Charles River Museum of Industry *
154 Moody St., Waltham (893-5410).
- T-Commuter Rail or any T-Bus to Central Sq., Waltham; walk 1 block S on Moody St.; turn left just before the river.

Charlestown Navy Yard
Charlestown (242-5601).
- T-Commuter Boat from Long Wharf; 1/4 mile walk from Charlestown dock to U.S.S. *Constitution* (Navy Yard Shuttle Bus).
- T-Bus 92 (Assembly Sq.-Downtown) to City Sq.; 1/4 mile walk.
- T-Bus 93 (Sullivan-Downtown) to the Navy Yard.
- T-Bus 111 (Woodlawn-Haymarket) to City Sq.; 1/4 mile walk.
- Green Line, Orange Line, or T-Commuter Rail to NORTH STA.; 1/4 mile walk across the Charlestown Bridge.
- In summer, Bay State Cruise Co. and

* discount offered to MBTA monthly passholders (as of February 1995)

Boston Harbor Cruises from Long Wharf allow you to get off at the Navy Yard and return on a later boat.

"Cheer's" (Bull & Finch Pub)
84 Beacon St., Boston (227-9605)
•Red Line to PARK ST.
•Green Line to ARLINGTON.

Children's Museum*
300 Congress St., Boston (426-8855).
•Red Line or T-Commuter Rail to SOUTH STA.; walk NE on Atlantic Ave. one block (past Peter Pan), then right on Congress St. two blocks, past the Tea Party Ship.

Christian Science Center
Massachusetts Ave. at Huntington Ave., Boston (450-2000).
•Green Line-E to SYMPHONY.
•T-Bus 1 (Harvard-Dudley).
•Green Line-(B, C, or D) to HYNES CONVENTION CTR./ICA; walk S on Mass. Ave. 2 blocks.
•Orange Line to MASS. AVE.; walk N on Mass. Ave. two blocks.

The Commonwealth Museum
Columbia Point, Dorchester (727-9268).
•Red Line to JFK/UMASS; take Kennedy Library shuttle bus and walk from Kennedy Library to the museum.
•T-Bus 8 (Harbor Pt.-Kenmore) to UMass.; walk to museum.
•Boston Harbor Cruises water shuttle from Long Wharf.

Computer Museum *
300 Congress St., Boston (426-2800).
Same directions as Children's Museum

U.S.S. *Constitution* (Old Ironsides) U.S.S. Constitution Museum *
Charlestown Navy Yard, Charlestown (426-1812).
See "Charlestown Navy Yard."

Danforth Museum
123 Union Ave., Framingham (508-620-0050).
•T-Commuter Rail (Framingham Line) to Framingham; 1/2-mile walk N.

The Discovery Museum
177 Main St., Acton (508-264-4200).
•T-Commuter Rail (Fitchburg Line) to S. Acton; walk 1/2 mile N on Main St.

Faneuil Hall
Merchants Row, Boston (635-3105, 242-5642).
•Orange Line or Blue Line to STATE.
•Orange Line to HAYMARKET.
•Green Line to GOVERNMENT CTR.

First Night
New Year's Eve, Boston.
•All MBTA lines operate at least one hour later than normal. No fare after 10 pm. Call MBTA for travel information, 722-3200.

Fogg Art Museum
32 Quincy St., Cambridge (495-9400).
•Red Line or T-Buses to HARVARD.

Franklin Park Zoo
Blue Hill Avenue, Dorchester (442-2002).
•Orange Line to FOREST HILLS; free shuttle bus to zoo, weekends & holidays, every 12 min.
•T-Bus 16 (Forest Hills-JFK/UMass).
•T-Bus 22 (Ashmont-Ruggles).
•T-Bus 28 (Mattapan-Ruggles).
•T-Bus 29 (Mattapan-Jackson Sq.).
•T-Bus 39 (Forest Hills-Back Bay Sta.).
•T-Bus 45 (Franklin Park Zoo-Ruggles).

Freedom Trail
Boston.
The trail begins at Boston Common; see Ch. 8.
•Red Line or Green Line to PARK ST.

Fuller Museum of Art
455 Oak St., Brockton (508-588-6000).
•From ASHMONT (Red Line) take BAT Bus 12 (Brockton); transfer to BAT Bus 4A (Westgate via N. Warren).

Isabella Stewart Gardner Museum
280 the Fenway, Boston (566-1401).
•Green Line-E to MUSEUM OF FINE ARTS.
•T-Bus 8 (Harbor Pt.-Kenmore).
•T-Bus 39 (Forest Hills-Back Bay Sta.).
•T-Bus 47 (Central-Albany St.).
Get off at MUSEUM OF FINE ARTS; walk N on Louis Prang St. (Texaco station at corner) 1-1/2 blocks to the museum.

Gibson House Museum
137 Beacon St., Boston (267-6338).
•Green Line to ARLINGTON.

Musicians at the Gardner

Glass Flowers (Botanical Museum)
495-3045.
See "Harvard University Museum of Cultural and Natural History."

Gore Place
52 Gore St., Waltham (894-2798).
•T-Bus 70 (Cedarwood-Central).
•T-Bus 70A (N. Waltham-Central).

John Hancock Observatory *
St. James Ave., Copley Sq., Boston (542-6429).
•Green Line or T-Buses to COPLEY.
•Orange Line or T-Commuter Rail to BACK BAY STA.

Harvard University Museum of Cultural and Natural History
24 Oxford St., Cambridge (495-3045).
•Red Line or T-Buses to HARVARD.

Institute of Contemporary Art (ICA) *
955 Boylston St., Boston (266-5152).
•Green Line-(B, C, or D) or T-Bus 1 (Harvard-Dudley) to HYNES CONVENTION CTR./ICA.

Jackson Homestead Newton City Museum
527 Washington St., Newton (552-7238).
•T-Buses to Newton Corner; walk 1/2 mile W on Washington St.
•T-Bus 53, 54, 56, or 58 from Newton Corner or DOWNTOWN CROSSING.

Kendall Whaling Museum
27 Everett St., Sharon (784-5642).
•T-Commuter Rail (Attleboro Line) to Sharon; walk E on Rt. 27, left at fork onto Upland Rd.; right on Everett St. (1/2 mile).

John F. Kennedy National Historic Site
Birthplace of the President
83 Beals St., Brookline (566-7937).
•Green Line-C to COOLIDGE CORNER; walk 4 blocks N on Harvard St., right 1 block on Beals St.
•T-Bus 66 (Harvard-Dudley) to Beals St.

John F. Kennedy Library And Museum *
Columbia Point, Dorchester (929-4523)
•Red Line to JFK/UMASS; free shuttle bus to the library every 20 min. (wheelchair accessible).
•T-Bus 8 (Harbor Pt.-Kenmore) to UMass.; walk to library.
•T-Bus 16 (Forest Hills-JFK/UMass).
•T-Bus 17 (Fields Corner-JFK/UMass).
•Boston Harbor Cruises water shuttle from Long Wharf.

Longfellow National Historic Site
105 Brattle St., Cambridge (876-4491).
•Red Line or T-Buses to HARVARD; 6-block walk up Brattle St.

Longyear Historical Society
(Mary Baker Eddy Museum)
120 Seaver St., Brookline (277-8943).
•Green Line-D to BROOKLINE HILLS or BEACONSFIELD; 5-block walk from either stop to top of hill; call for directions.

Mapparium
1 Norway St., Boston (450-2000).
See "Christian Science Center."

Massachusetts Historical Society
1154 Boylston St., Boston (536-1608).
•Green Line-(B, C, or D) or T-Bus 1 (Harvard-Dudley) to HYNES CONVENTION CTR./ICA.

Massachusetts State House
Beacon St., Boston (727-3676).
•Red Line or Green Line to PARK ST.

Milton Art Museum
44 Edge Hill Rd., Milton (696-1145).
•T-Bus 245 (Quincy Ctr.-Mattapan).

M.I.T. Museum
265 Massachusetts Ave., Cambridge
(253-4444).
•Red Line to CENTRAL; walk 5 blocks
S on Mass. Ave. to the museum.
•T-Bus 1 (Harvard-Dudley) to Sidney
St. or Windsor St.

Museum of Afro American History *
46 Joy St., Boston (742-1854).
See "Boston African-American National Historic Site."

Museum of Fine Arts *
465 Huntington Ave., Boston (267-9300).
•Green Line-E to MUSEUM OF FINE
ARTS.
•T-Bus 8 (Harbor Pt.-Kenmore).
•T-Bus 39 (Forest Hills-Back Bay Sta.).
•T-Bus 47 (Central-Albany St.).

Museum of Our National Heritage
33 Marrett Rd., Lexington (861-6559).
•T-Bus 62 (Bedford-Alewife).
•T-Bus 76 (Hanscom Field-Alewife).
Get off at Mass. Ave. and Marrett Rd.

Museum of Science *
Science Park, Boston (723-2500).
•Green Line (Lechmere) to SCIENCE
PARK.
•Red Line to CHARLES/MGH; walk E
along the Charles River to the museum.

Museum of the National Center of Afro-American Artists
300 Walnut Ave., Roxbury (442-8614).
•T-Bus 22 (Ashmont-Ruggles)
•T-Bus 44 (Jackson Sq.-Ruggles)
Get off at Walnut Ave. and Seaver St.

Museum of Transportation *
Larz Anderson Park, 15 Newton St.,
Brookline (522-6547).
•T-Bus 51 (Cleveland Cir.-Forest Hills)
to Newton and Clyde Sts.; walk E on
Newton St. 1/2 mile.
From Boston: Green Line-D to
RESERVOIR, then T-Bus 51 as above.

New England Aquarium *
Central Wharf, Boston (973-5200).
•Blue Line to AQUARIUM.

Old North Church (Christ Church)
193 Salem St., Boston (523-6676).
•Green Line, Orange Line, or T-Buses
to HAYMARKET; cross under the
Central Artery and walk up Salem St.

Old South Meeting-House *
310 Washington St., Boston (482-6439).
•Orange Line or Blue Line to STATE.
•Red Line to DOWNTOWN CROSSING.

Old State House *
206 Washington St., Boston (720-3290).
•Orange Line or Blue Line to STATE.
•Green Line to GOVERNMENT CTR.

Frederick Law Olmsted National Historic Site
99 Warren St., Brookline (566-1689).
•Green Line-D to BROOKLINE HILLS;
walk 2 blocks S on Cypress St., right 4
blocks on Walnut St., left 1 block on
Warren St. (after the church).
•T-Bus 60 (Chestnut Hill-Kenmore) to
Warren St.; cross Rt. 9 and walk 2
blocks S on Warren St.

Harrison Gray Otis House
141 Cambridge St., Boston (227-3956).
•Blue Line to BOWDOIN.
•Green Line to GOVERNMENT CTR.
•Red Line to CHARLES/MGH.

Peabody Museum of Archeology
495-2248.
See "Harvard University Museum."

Prudential Skywalk *
Prudential Ctr., 800 Boylston St., Boston
(236-3318).
•Green Line-E to PRUDENTIAL.
•Green Line-(B, C, or D) or T-Bus 1
(Harvard-Dudley) to HYNES CON-
VENTION CTR./ICA.

Quincy Historical Society
8 Adams St., Quincy (773-1144).
•Red Line (Braintree) to QUINCY CTR.

Paul Revere House
19 North Sq., Boston (523-2338).
•Green Line, Orange Line, or T-Buses to
HAYMARKET; follow the Freedom Trail.

Arthur M. Sackler Art Museum
485 Broadway, Cambridge (495-9400).
•Red Line or T-Buses to HARVARD.

Saugus Ironworks National Historic Site
244 Central St., Saugus (233-0050).
•T-Bus 430 (Saugus-Malden Ctr.).

Semitic Museum
6 Divinity Ave., Cambridge (495-3123).
•Red Line or T-Buses to HARVARD.

Sports Museum of New England *
CambridgeSide Galleria.
100 CambridgeSide Place, Cambridge
(577-7678).

•Green Line or T-Buses to LECHMERE.
•Free shuttle bus from KENDALL or LECHMERE.

Swan Boats
Public Garden, Boston (635-4050).
•Green Line to ARLINGTON.

Trinity Church
Copley Sq., Boston (536-0944).
•Green Line or T-Buses to COPLEY.
•Orange Line or T-Commuter Rail to BACK BAY STA.

Chapter 10

Theaters, Cinemas, and Auditoriums

Agassiz Theatre
10 Garden St., Cambridge (495-8676).
•Red Line to HARVARD.

American Repertory Theatre
See "Loeb Drama Center."

Back Alley Theatre
1253 Cambridge St., Inman Sq.,
Cambridge (576-1253).
•T-Bus 69 (Harvard-Lechmere).
•T-Bus 83 (Rindge Ave.-Central).
•T-Bus 91 (Sullivan-Central).

Bayside Exposition Center
200 Mt. Vernon St., Dorchester
(825-5151).
•Red Line to JFK/UMASS; 3-block walk.
•T-Bus 8 (Harbor Pt.-Kenmore).
•Special shuttle buses from JFK/ UMASS to some events.

Berklee Performance Center
136 Massachusetts Ave., Boston
(226-7455).
•Green Line-(B, C, or D) or T-Bus 1
(Harvard-Dudley) to HYNES CONVEN-TION CTR./ICA.

Boston Baked Theatre
255 Elm St., Somerville (628-9575).
•Red Line or T-Buses to DAVIS.

Boston Center for the Arts
539 Tremont St., Boston (426-5000).
•Orange Line to BACK BAY STA.; walk
S on Clarendon St. 5 blocks to
Tremont St. and turn left.
•Green Line to ARLINGTON; walk S on
Berkeley St. 7 blocks to Tremont St.
and turn right.
•T-Bus 39 (Forest Hills-Back Bay Sta.);
walk S on Clarendon St. 5 blocks to
Tremont St. and turn left.
•T-Bus 43 (Ruggles-Park St.).

Boston Garden/FleetCenter
150 Causeway St., Boston (227-3200).
•Green or Orange lines to NORTH STA.
•T-Commuter Rail to NORTH STA.

Boston University School for the Arts Concert Hall
855 Commonwealth Ave., Boston
(353-3349).
•Green Line-B to B.U. WEST.
See also "Tsai Performance Center."

Boston University Theatre
See "Huntington Theatre Co."

Brattle Theatre
40 Brattle St., Cambridge (876-6837).
•Red Line or T-Buses to HARVARD.

Cabot Street Theatre
286 Cabot St., Beverly (927-3677).
•T-Commuter Rail (Rockport/Ipswich Lines) to Beverly Depot; walk 3 blocks E on Railroad Ave. to Cabot St., then left 1/2 mile to the theater.

Cambridge Multicultural Arts Center
41 Second St., Cambridge (577-1400).
•Green Line or T-Buses to LECHMERE.

The Centrum at Worcester
50 Foster St., Worcester (508-798-8888).
•Peter Pan from Boston to Worcester; 1/2 mile from the Worcester Bus Terminal.
See map page 106.

Charles Playhouse
76 Warrenton St., Boston (426-6912).
•Green Line to BOYLSTON; walk S on Tremont to Stuart, right on Stuart, left on Warrenton St.
•Orange Line to N. E. MEDICAL CTR.

Charlestown Working Theatre
442 Bunker Hill St., Charlestown (242-3285).
•Orange Line or T-Buses to SULLIVAN; 4-block walk.
•T-Bus 93 (Sullivan-Downtown).

Cheri Complex 1-4
50 Dalton St., Boston (536-2870).
•Green Line-(B, C, D) to HYNES CONVENTION CTR./ICA.
•Green Line-E to PRUDENTIAL.
•T-Bus 39 (Forest Hills-Back Bay).

Cinema 57 1-2
200 Stuart St., Boston (482-1222).
•Green Line to BOYLSTON.
•Orange Line to N.E. MEDICAL CTR.
•T-Bus 43 (Ruggles-Park St.).

Colonial Theatre
106 Boylston St., Boston (426-9366).
•Green Line to BOYLSTON.
•Orange Line to CHINATOWN.

Converse Hall
Tremont Temple, 88 Tremont St., Boston (523-7320).
•Red Line or Green Line to PARK ST.

Coolidge Corner Theatre
290 Harvard St., Brookline (734-2500).
•Green Line-C or T-Bus 66 (Harvard-Dudley) to COOLIDGE CORNER.

Copley Place Cinema 1-11
100 Huntington Ave., Boston (266-1300).
•Orange Line or T-Commuter Rail to BACK BAY STA.
•Green Line or T-Buses to COPLEY.

Cyclorama
See "Boston Center for the Arts."

Double Edge Theatre
5 St. Lukes Rd., Allston (254-4228).
•Green Line-B to FORDHAM RD.

Emerson Majestic Theatre
221 Tremont St., Boston (578-8727).
•Green Line to BOYLSTON.
•Orange Line to N. E. MEDICAL CTR.

Faneuil Hall
Merchants Row, Boston (951-2555).
•Green Line to GOVT. CTR.
•Blue Line or Orange Line to STATE.

Firehouse Multicultural Arts Center
659 Centre St., Jamaica Plain (524-3816).
•T-Bus 39 (Forest Hills-Back Bay Sta.).

Foxboro Stadium
Rt. 1, Foxborough (508-543-3900).
•Special T-Commuter Rail trains to some concerts and sporting events from SOUTH STA. and BACK BAY STA.

Great Woods
S. Main St. (Rt. 140), Mansfield (508-339-2333).
•T-Commuter Rail (Attleboro Line) to Mansfield; 3-mile walk/taxi ride S of station.

John Hancock Hall
180 Berkeley St., Boston (572-7700).
•Green Line to ARLINGTON.
•Orange Line to BACK BAY STA.

Harvard Square Cinema
10 Church St., Cambridge (864-4850).
•Red Line or T-Buses to HARVARD.

Hasty Pudding Theatre
12 Holyoke St., Cambridge (496-8400).
•Red Line or T-Buses to HARVARD.

Hatch Shell Concerts on the Esplanade
Embankment Rd., Boston
(727-5114 x555).
•Red Line to CHARLES/MGH.
•Green Line to ARLINGTON; walk N
on Arlington St. along the Public
Garden to the Esplanade.

Huntington Theatre Co.
264 Huntington Ave., Boston
(266-7900).
•Green Line-E to SYMPHONY.
•Orange Line to MASS. AVE.
•T-Bus 1 (Harvard-Dudley).
•T-Bus 39 (Forest Hills-Back Bay Sta.).

Hynes Convention Ctr.
900 Boylston St., Boston (954-2000).
•Green Line-(B, C, or D) or T-Bus 1
(Harvard-Dudley) to HYNES CON-
VENTION CTR./ICA.
•T-Bus 39 (Forest Hills-Back Bay Sta.).

Janus Cinema
57 J.F. Kennedy St., Cambridge
(661-3737).
•Red Line or T-Buses to HARVARD.

Jordan Hall
30 Gainsborough St., Boston
(536-2412).
•Green Line-E to SYMPHONY.
•Orange Line to MASS AVE.
•T-Bus 1 (Harvard-Dudley) to SYM-
PHONY.
•T-Bus 39 (Forest Hills-Back Bay Sta.).

Jorge Hernandez Cultural Center at Villa Victoria
85 W. Newton St., Boston (247-7604).
•T-Bus 43 (Ruggles-Park St.).
•Green Line-E to PRUDENTIAL; walk 4
blocks S on W. Newton St.
•Orange Line to BACK BAY STA.; walk
4 blocks S on Dartmouth St.; turn right
on Tremont St. 2 blocks.
•T-Bus 39 (Forest Hills-Back Bay Sta.);
walk 4 blocks S on Dartmouth St.; turn
right on Tremont St. 2 blocks.

Killian Hall
Massachusetts Institute of Technology,
160 Memorial Drive.
•Red Line to KENDALL.
•T-Bus 1 (Harvard-Dudley).

Kresge Auditorium
Massachusetts Institute of Technology,
Massachusetts Ave., Cambridge
(253-4720).
•T-Bus 1 (Harvard-Dudley).

Symphony Hall, Boston

Loeb Drama Center
64 Brattle St., Cambridge (547-8300).
•Red Line or T-Buses to HARVARD.

Longy School of Music
1 Follen St., Cambridge (876-0952).
•Red Line and T-Buses to HARVARD;
walk 3 blocks N on Garden St. past
Sheraton Commander Hotel.

Lyric Stage
140 Clarendon St., Boston (437-7172).
•Orange Line or T-Commuter Rail to
BACK BAY STA.
•Green Line or T-Buses to COPLEY.

Mechanics Hall
321 Main St., Worcester
(508-752-0888).
•Peter Pan from Boston to Worcester; 1/2
mile from the Worcester Bus Terminal.
See map page 106.

Mobius
354 Congress St., Boston (542-7416).
•Red Line or T-Commuter Rail to
SOUTH STA.; 5-block walk.

National Ctr. of Afro-American Artists (Elma Lewis School)
300 Walnut Ave., Roxbury (442-8614).
•T-Bus 22 (Ashmont-Ruggles) to Seaver St. and Elm Hill Ave.

Newbury St. Theatre
565 Boylston St., Boston (262-7779).
•Green Line or T-Buses to COPLEY.

New Theater
565 Boylston St., Boston (247-7388).
•Green Line or T-Buses to COPLEY.

New England Hall
225 Clarendon St., Boston (266-7262).
•Green Line or T-Buses to COPLEY.
•T-Commuter Rail to BACK BAY STA.

New Repertory Theatre
54 Lincoln St., Newton Highlands (332-1646).
•Green Line-D to NEWTON HIGH-LANDS.

Nickelodeon Cinemas
34 Cummington St., Boston (424-1500).
•Green Line to first outbound stop after Kenmore (BLANDFORD ST.).

Open Door Theatre
Pinebank Park, the Jamaicaway, Jamaica Plain (524-4007).
•T-Bus 39 (Forest Hills-Back Bay Sta.) to Perkins St.; walk 3 blocks W on Perkins to the Jamaicaway and turn left.

The Opera House
539 Washington St., Boston (426-5300).
•Red Line or Orange Line to DOWN-TOWN CROSSING.
•Green Line to PARK ST.

Orpheum Theatre
Hamilton Place, off Tremont St. across from Park St. Church, Boston (482-0650).
•Red Line or Green Line to PARK ST.

Park Plaza Castle
Arlington St., Boston (426-2000).
•Green Line to ARLINGTON; walk 2 blocks S on Arlington St.

The Performance Place
277 Broadway, Somerville (625-1300).
•T-Bus 89 (Clarendon Hill-Sullivan).
•T-Bus 101 (Malden Ctr.-Sullivan, via Medford Sq.).

Providence Civic Center
1 LaSalle Sq., Providence, RI (401-331-6700).
•Bonanza from Boston/BACK BAY STA. to Providence; 1/4-mile walk from Kennedy Plaza.
•Amtrak to Providence.
See map page 106.

Puppet Showplace
30 Station St., Brookline (731-6100).
•Green Line-D or T-Buses to BROOKLINE VILLAGE.

Sanders Theatre
Memorial Hall, Kirkland St., Cambridge (496-2222).
•Red Line or T-Buses to HARVARD.

Shubert Theatre
265 Tremont St., Boston (426-4520).
•Orange Line to N. E. MEDICAL CTR.
•Green Line to BOYLSTON.

Somerville Theatre
55 Davis Sq., Somerville (625-5700).
•Red Line or T-Buses to DAVIS.

Strand Theatre
543 Columbia Rd., Uphams Corner, Dorchester (282-2000).
•T-Bus 15 (Kane Sq.-Ruggles).
•T-Bus 16 (Forest Hills-JFK/UMass).
•T-Bus 17 (Fields Corner-JFK/UMass).
•Red Line to JFK/UMASS; 15-minute walk W on Columbia Rd., or special shuttle buses from JFK/UMASS to some events.

Symphony Hall
301 Massachusetts Ave., Boston (266-1492).
•Green Line-E to SYMPHONY.
•Orange Line to MASS. AVE.
•T-Bus 1 (Harvard-Dudley) to SYMPHONY.
•T-Bus 39 (Forest Hills-Back Bay Sta.).

Tanglewood
West St. (Rt. 183), Lenox, Mass (266-1492).
See Lenox listing in Ch. 16; a 25-min. walk from the Lenox bus stop.

Terrace Room, Boston Park Plaza Hotel
64 Arlington St., Boston (426-2000).
•Green Line to ARLINGTON.

Theatre Lobby
216 Hanover St., Boston (227-9872).
•Green or Orange lines to HAYMARKET.

Triangle Theater
58 Berkeley St., Boston (426-3550).
•Orange Line to BACK BAY STA.; walk S on Clarendon St. 2 blocks, left on Chandler St., right on Berkeley.
•Green Line to ARLINGTON; walk S on Berkeley St. 6 blocks.
•T-Bus 39 (Forest Hills-Back Bay Sta.).

Trinity Repertory Co.
201 Washington St., Providence, RI (401-351-4242).
•Bonanza from Boston/BACK BAY STA. to Providence; 1/4-mile walk from Kennedy Plaza.
•Amtrak to Providence.
See map page 106.

Tsai Performance Center
Boston University,
655 Commonwealth Ave., Boston (353-8724).

•Green Line-B to B.U. CENTRAL or B.U. EAST.
•T-Bus 47 (Central-Albany St.).

Wang Center for the Performing Arts
268 Tremont St., Boston (482-9393).
•Orange Line to N. E. MEDICAL CTR.
•Green Line to BOYLSTON.

Wilbur Theatre
246 Tremont St., Boston (423-4008).
•Orange Line to N. E. MEDICAL CTR.
•Green Line to BOYLSTON.

World Trade Center Exhibition Hall
Commonwealth Pier, 164 Northern Ave., Boston (439-5000).
•Red Line to SOUTH STA.; 3/4-mile walk S on Summer St., left on Viaduct St.
•T-Bus 7 (City Pt–Franklin & Devonshire).
•Free shuttle buses from SOUTH STA., 6:00 am-8:00 pm, every 10 min.

Chapter 11
Nightlife

Billiards

Boston Billiard Club
126 Brookline Ave., Boston (536-POOL).
•Green Line (B, C, D) to KENMORE.

Jillian's Billiard Club
145 Ipswich St., Boston (437-0300).
Directly behind Fenway Park
•Green Line (B, C, D) to KENMORE.

Comedy

Comedy Connection
Faneuil Hall, Boston (248-9700).
•Green Line to GOVERNMENT CTR.; walk across City Hall Plaza to the Market.

•Blue Line to STATE or AQUARIUM.
•Orange Line to STATE.

Catch a Rising Star
4 JFK St., Harvard Square (661-0167).
Upstairs at the Wursthaus
•Red Line to HARVARD.
•T-Bus 1 (Harvard-Dudley).
•T-Bus 66 (Harvard-Dudley).

Nick's Comedy Stop
100 Warrenton St., Boston (482-0930, 800-441-5653).
•Green Line to BOYLSTON.
•Orange Line to N. E. MEDICAL CTR.

Dick Doherty's Comedy Clubs
—Comedy Vault
Remington's, 124 Boylston St., Boston (267-6626).
•Green Line to BOYLSTON.
•Orange Line to CHINATOWN.

—Comedy Campus
Aku Aku Restaurant, 109 Brookline Ave., Boston (536-0619).
•Green Line (B, C, D) to KENMORE.
•Green Line-D to FENWAY.

—Comedy Hut
Aku Aku Restaurant, 149 Alewife Brook Pkwy., Cambridge (491-2422).
•Red Line to ALEWIFE.

Comedy Cafe
Charles Playhouse, 76 Warrenton St. Boston (426-6339, 391-0022).
•Green Line to BOYLSTON.
•Orange Line to N. E. MEDICAL CTR.

Dance

Avalon
15 Lansdowne St., Boston (262-2424).
•Green Line (B, C, D) to KENMORE.

Avenue C
25 Boylston St., Boston (423-3832).
•Green Line to BOYLSTON.
•Orange Line to CHINATOWN.

Axis
13 Lansdowne St., Boston (262-2437).
•Green Line (B, C, D) to KENMORE.

Boston Beach Club
North Market, Faneuil Hall Marketplace, Boston (227-9664).
•Green Line to GOVERNMENT CTR.; walk across City Hall Plaza to the Market.
•Orange Line or Blue Line to STATE.

Club Nicole
Back Bay Hilton, 40 Dalton St. (267-2582).
•Green Line (B, C, D) to HYNES CONVENTION CTR./ICA
•Green Line-E to PRUDENTIAL.
•T-Bus 39 (Back Bay Sta.-Forest Hills)
•T-Bus 1 (Harvard-Dudley) to HYNES CONVENTION CTR./ICA.

Club M-80
969 Commonwealth Ave., Boston (351-2527).
•Green Line-B to PLEASANT ST.

Europa
51 Stuart St., Boston (423-3939).
•Green Line to BOYLSTON.
•Orange Line to N.E. MEDICAL CTR.

Jukebox/Galxc
275 Tremont St., Boston (542-1123).
•Green Line to BOYLSTON.
•Orange Line to N. E. MEDICAL CTR.

ManRay
21 Brookline St., Cambridge (864-0400).
•Red Line to CENTRAL.
•T-Bus 1 (Harvard-Dudley) to Brookline Street.

Paradise
967 Commonwealth Ave., Boston (351-2582).
•Green Line-B to PLEASANT ST.

Roxy
279 Tremont St., Boston (227-ROXY).
•Green Line to BOYLSTON.
•Orange Line to N. E. MEDICAL CTR.

Venus de Milo
11 Lansdowne St., Boston (421-9595).
•Green Line (B, C, D) to KENMORE.

Zanzibar
1 Boylston Pl., Boston (351-7000).
•Green Line to BOYLSTON.
•Orange Line to CHINATOWN.

Folk

Bookcellar Cafe
1971 Massachusetts Ave., Cambridge (864-9625).
•Red Line to PORTER; walk N on Mass. Ave. 3 blocks.

Cantab Lounge
738 Massachusetts Ave., Cambridge (354-2685).
•Red Line to CENTRAL.
•T-Bus 1 (Harvard-Dudley) to Prospect Street.

Naked City Coffeehouse
Old Cambridge Baptist Church, 1151 Massachusetts Ave., Cambridge (491-8963).
•Red Line or T-Buses to HARVARD.

Nameless Coffeehouse
First Unitarian Church, 3 Church St., Cambridge (864-1630).
•Red Line or T-Buses to HARVARD.

Passim

47 Palmer St., Cambridge (492-7679).
•Red Line or T-Buses to HARVARD.

Toad

1920 Massachusetts Ave., Cambridge
(876-9180).
•Red Line to PORTER.

Jazz/Blues

Burke's

808 Huntington Ave., Boston (232-2191).
•Green Line-E to MISSION PARK.
•T-Bus 39 (Back Bay Sta.-Forest Hills).
•T-Bus 66 (Harvard-Dudley) to
MISSION PARK.

Hampshire House

84 Beacon St., Boston (227-9600).
•Green Line to ARLINGTON; walk N
on Arlington Street past Public
Garden.

Harpers Ferry

158 Brighton Ave., Allston (492-7679).
•Green Line-B to HARVARD.AVE.;
walk N 1/3 mi. on Harvard Avenue ,
then left.on Brighton Avenue.
•T-Bus 66 (Harvard-Dudley) to
Brighton Avenue.
•T-Bus 57 (Kenmore-Watertown) to
Brighton Avenue.

House of Blues

114 Mt. Auburn St., Cambridge
(491-BLUE).
•Red Line or T-Buses to HARVARD.

Johnny D's Uptown Restaurant and Music Club

17 Holland St., Somerville (776-9667).
•Red Line to DAVIS.

Middle East Restaurant

472 Massachusetts Ave., Cambridge
(354-8238).
•Red Line to CENTRAL.
•T-Bus 1 (Harvard-Dudley) to Brookline
Avenue.

Midway Cafe

3496 Washington St., Jamaica Plain
(524-9038).
•Orange Line to GREEN; walk S on
Southwest Corridor Park to Williams
Street, then left.

Regattabar

Charles Hotel, 1 Bennett St.,
Cambridge (876-7777).
•Red Line or T-Buses to HARVARD;
walk W on Brattle Street.

Ryles

212 Hampshire St., Inman Square,
Cambridge (876-9330).
•T-Bus 69 (Harvard-Lechmere).

Sticky Mike's

21 Boylston Pl., Boston (351-2540).
•Green Line to BOYLSTON.
•Orange Line to CHINATOWN.

The Tam

1648 Beacon St., Brookline (277-0982).
•Green Line-C to WASHINGTON SQ.

Wally's

427 Massachusetts Ave., Boston
(424-1408).
•Orange Line to MASS. AVE.; walk E
to South End.
•T-Bus 1 (Harvard-Dudley) to Columbus Avenue.

Willow Jazz Club

699 Broadway, Ball Square, Somerville
(623-9874).
•Red Line to DAVIS; walk N on College
Avenue 1/2 mi. to Powderhouse
Square, then right onto Broadway.

Rock

Causeway

65 Causeway St., Boston (499-7996).
•Green or Orange line to NORTH STA.

Club 3

608 Somerville Ave., Somerville
(623-6957).
•Red Line to PORTER; walk E 1/4 mi.
on Somerville Avenue.

Great Scott

1222 Commonwealth Ave., Allston
(566-9014).
•Green Line-B to HARVARD.AVE.
•T-Bus 66 (Harvard-Dudley) to
Commonwealth Avenue.

Hard Rock Cafe Cavern

131 Clarendon St., Boston (353-1400).
•Green Line to COPLEY.
•Orange Line to BACK BAY STA.

Johnny D's Uptown Restaurant and Music Club
17 Holland St., Somerville (776-9667).
•Red Line to DAVIS.

Local 186
186 Harvard Ave., Allston (787-9722).
•Green Line-B to HARVARD AVE.;
walk N 1/4 block on Harvard Avenue.
•T-Bus 66 (Harvard-Dudley) to
Commonwealth Avenue.

Middle East Restaurant
472 Massachusetts Ave., Cambridge
(354-8238).
•Red Line to CENTRAL.
•T-Bus 1 (Harvard-Dudley) to Brookline
Avenue.

Midway Cafe
3496 Washington St., Jamaica Plain
(524-9038).
•Orange Line to GREEN; walk S on
Southwest Corridor Park to Williams
Street, then left.

Paradise
967 Commonwealth Ave., Boston
(254-2053).
•Green Line-B to PLEASANT ST.

Plough and Stars
912 Massachusetts Ave., Cambridge
(492-9653).
•Red Line to CENTRAL; walk 5/8 mi.
toward Harvard Square.
•T-Bus 1 (Harvard-Dudley) to Hancock
Street.

The Rat
528 Commonwealth Ave., Kenmore
Square, Boston (536-2750)
•Green Line or T-Buses to Kenmore

The Tam
1648 Beacon St., Brookline (277-0982).
•Green Line-C to WASHINGTON SQ.

T. T. the Bear's Place
10 Brookline St., Cambridge (492-0082).
•Red Line to CENTRAL.
•T-Bus 1 (Harvard-Dudley) to Brookline
Avenue.

Chapter 12

Major Spectator Sports

Baseball

Boston Red Sox
Fenway Park, Boston (267-8661).
•Green Line-(B, C, or D) to KENMORE.
•Green Line-D (Riverside) to FENWAY.
•T-Commuter Rail "Fenway Flyer" trains
to all *weekend* home games from: S.
Attleboro, Attleboro, Mansfield, Sharon,
Canton Jct., Rt. 128 Sta., Hyde Park.
Forge Park/495, Franklin, Norfolk,
Walpole, Windsor Gardens, Norwood
Central, Norwood Depot, Readville.
*Framingham, *W. Natick, *Natick,
*Wellesley Sq., *Wellesley Hills,
*Wellesley Farms, Auburndale, W.
Newton, Newtonville. (*service to
weekend and *weeknight* games).

Basketball

Boston Celtics
Boston Garden/FleetCenter
150 Causeway St., Boston. (227-3206,
523-6050)
•Green or Orange line to NORTH STA.
•T-Commuter Rail to NORTH STA.

Boston College (Big East)
Conte Forum (552-3014)
•Green Line-B to BOSTON COLLEGE.
*(see **Football/B.C.** for alternatives)*

Dog Racing

Raynham Greyhound Park
Raynham, MA (508-824-4071)
•Bloom Bus (Boston-Taunton) stops at
the park for afternoon races.

Wonderland Park
Revere (284-1300)
- Blue Line to WONDERLAND.
- T-Buses 441, 442 (Marblehead-Haymarket).

Football

Boston College
Alumni Stadium
Chestnut Hill (552-3004)
- Green Line-B to BOSTON COLLEGE, 2-min. walk.
- Green Line-C to CLEVELAND CIRCLE, 5-min. walk.
- Green Line-D to RESERVOIR or CHESTNUT HILL, 10-min. walk.

Boston University
Nickerson Field
Commonwealth Ave. (353-2872)
- Green Line-B to PLEASANT ST. or BABCOCK ST.

Harvard University
Harvard Stadium
N. Harvard St., Boston (495-2206)
- T-Buses 66, 86 from HARVARD.
- T-Bus 70 (Central-Cedarwood).
See map, page 26.

Holy Cross College
Fitton Field
Worcester (508-793-2572)

- Peter Pan bus to Worcester, then WRTA local bus (call 508-791-WRTA).

New England Patriots (NFL)
Foxboro Stadium
Foxborough (508-543-1776)
- Special T-Commuter Rail trains to all games from SOUTH STA., BACK BAY STA., Hyde Park, Rt. 128 Sta., Canton Jct., Sharon, Mansfield.

Northeastern University
Parsons Field
Kent Street, Brookline (373-2672)
- Green Line-D to LONGWOOD; walk up hill to Longwood Avenue, then right and first left onto Kent Street.
- Green Line-D to BROOKLINE VILLAGE; walk E on Station Street to Kent Street.

Hockey

Boston Bruins (NHL)
Boston Garden/FleetCenter
150 Causeway St. (227-3206)
- Green or Orange Lines to NORTH STA.
- T-Commuter Rail to NORTH STA.

Boston College
Conte Forum
Chestnut Hill (552-3004)
- Green Line-B to BOSTON COLLEGE
*(see **Football/B.C.** for alternatives)*

CELEBRATED ANNUAL EVENTS

The Boston Marathon is on Patriots Day in April. The finish line is at Copley Sq., but *COPLEY station is closed on Marathon day*. For the final stretch: Orange Line to BACK BAY STA.; Green Line to HYNES CONVENTION CTR./ICA, ARLINGTON, or KENMORE; or Green Line-C to any stop on Beacon Street. *To see the race earlier:* Green Line-B to BOSTON COLLEGE for "Heartbreak Hill"; Green Line-D to WOODLAND; or T-Commuter Rail (Framingham Line) to Wellesley Hills, Wellesley Sq., Natick, W. Natick, or Framingham.

The Head of the Charles Regatta (Charles River), in which hundreds of college crews row, occurs in October. Red Line to HARVARD and walk south on J. F. Kennedy St. to the Charles River. Or Green Line-B to B. U. CENTRAL and walk across the B. U. Bridge.

US Tennis Championship at Longwood. Green Line-D to CHESTNUT HILL (*not*Longwood). The Longwood Cricket Club is next to the station.

Boston University
Walter Brown Arena
285 Babcock St., Boston (353-2872)
•Green Line-B to BABCOCK ST.

Harvard University
Bright Hockey Center
60 JFK St., Cambridge (495-2206)
•Red Line to HARVARD.

Northeastern University
Matthews Arena
St. Botolph Street, Boston (373-2672)
•Orange Line to MASS. AVE.
•Green Line-E to SYMPHONY.
•T-Bus 1 (Harvard-Dudley) to St. Botolph St.
•T-Bus 39 (Forest Hills-Back Bay Sta.)
  to Gainsborough Street

Providence Bruins (AHL)
Providence Civic Center
LaSalle Sq., Providence (401-273-5000)
•Bonanza Bus from BACK BAY STA.
  to Kennedy Plaza, Providence; walk
  1/4 mi. west.
•Amtrak to Providence.
•Local RIPTA buses (call 401-781-9400).
See map, page 106

Horse Racing

Suffolk Downs
Revere (567-3900)
•Blue Line to SUFFOLK DOWNS. Free
shuttle bus to entrance.

Jai Alai

Newport Jai Alai
Newport, RI (401 849-5000).
•Bonanza Bus from BACK BAY STA. to
Newport.

Lacrosse (indoor)

Boston Blazers
Boston Garden/FleetCenter
150 Causeway St., (227-3206)
•Green or Orange lines to NORTH STA.
•T-Commuter Rail to NORTH STA.

Chapter 13

Shopping Centers

The Arsenal Marketplace
485 Arsenal St., Watertown.
•T-Bus 70 (Cedarwood-Central).
•T-Bus 70A (N. Waltham-Central).

Assembly Square Mall
133 Middlesex Ave., Somerville.
•T-Bus 90 (Davis-Wellington).
•T-Bus 92 (Assembly Sq.-
  Downtown)*before 4:00 pm (6:20 pm
  Sat) only.*
•T-Bus 95 (W. Medford-Sullivan).

The Atrium
Boylston St. (Rt. 9), Newton.
•The 9 Line free shuttle bus from
  NEWTON CENTRE and CHESTNUT
  HILL *(Green Line-D)*. Call 527-1400.

Burlington Mall
Rt. 128 & Middlesex Tpk., Burlington.
•T-Bus 350 (Burlington-Alewife).
•Burlington People Mover buses.
•Lexpress (Lexington-Burlington Mall).

CambridgeSide Galleria
First St., Cambridge.
•Green Line or T-Buses to
  LECHMERE.
•Free shuttle bus from LECHMERE or
  KENDALL.

Chestnut Hill Shopping Center
27 Boylston St. (Rt.9), Newton.
•T-Bus 60 (Chestnut Hill-Kenmore).
•Green Line-D to CHESTNUT HILL,
  walk S on Hammond St. and right on
  Boylston St. (1/2 mile).

Quincy Market, Boston

The Mall at Chestnut Hill
199 Boylston St. (Rt.9), Newton.
•T-Bus 60 (Chestnut Hill-Kenmore) to end of line at Hammond Pond Pkwy.; 1 1/2-block walk. Look for stairs to the right to get up to parking lot.

Copley Place
100 Huntington Ave., Boston.
•Orange Line or T-Commuter Rail to BACK BAY STA.
•Green Line or T-Buses to COPLEY.

Dedham Mall
300 V.F.W. Pkwy. (Rt. 1), Dedham.
•T-Bus 34E (Walpole Ctr.-Forest Hills).
•T-Bus 35 (Dedham Mall-Forest Hills).
•T-Bus 52 (Dedham Mall-Watertown).
•Dedham Local Bus.

Dedham Plaza
725 Providence Hwy. (Rt. 1), Dedham.
•T-Bus 34E (Walpole Ctr.-Forest Hills). Bus stops at back entrance to plaza.

Downtown Crossing
Summer and Washington Sts., Boston.
•Red Line or Orange Line to DOWN-TOWN CROSSING.
•Green Line to PARK ST.
•Blue Line to STATE.
See Ch. 5 for buses to Downtown Crossing.

Faneuil Hall Marketplace
Congress St., Boston.
•Green Line to GOVERNMENT CTR.; go across City Hall Plaza to the Market.
•Blue Line to STATE or AQUARIUM.
•Orange Line to STATE.

Fresh Pond Mall
186 Alewife Brook Pkwy., Cambridge.
•Red Line to ALEWIFE; 1/4-mile walk.
•T-Bus 74 (Belmont Ctr.-Harvard), *trips "via Concord Ave." only.*
•T-Bus 78 (Arlmont-Harvard).

Liberty Tree Mall
Independence Way, Danvers.
•T-Bus 435 (Lynn-Danvers).
•T-Bus 458 (Salem-Danvers).

Marketplace Center
200 State St., Boston.
•Blue Line to STATE or AQUARIUM, across Surface Artery.
•Green Line to GOVERNMENT CTR.; walk across City Hall Plaza past Faneuil Hall Market.

Meadow Glen Mall
3850 Mystic Valley Pkwy., Medford.
•Hudson Bus (Fulton St.-Meadow Glen Mall), via Medford Sq.

•T-Bus 134 (N. Woburn-Wellington) to Locust St.; 2-block walk.
•T-Bus 134 A (Medford-Wellington) to Locust St.

Mystic Mall
166 Everett Ave., Chelsea.
•T-Bus 112 (Wellington-Maverick).
•T-Commuter Rail (Rockport/Ipswich Line) to Chelsea; 4-block walk.

Natick Mall and Sherwood Plaza
1345 Worcester St. (Rt. 9), Natick.
•Peter Pan (Boston-Worcester, Rt. 9 local).
•Natick Neighborhood Bus.
•LIFT 2, 3, and 4.

Newbury Street shopping area
Back Bay, Boston.
•Green Line to ARLINGTON, COPLEY or HYNES CONVENTION CTR./ICA.
•Orange Line or T-Commuter Rail to BACK BAY STA.

New England Shopping Center
1205 Broadway (Rt. 1), Saugus.
•T-Bus 430 (Saugus-Malden Ctr.).

Northgate Shopping Center
Squire Rd., Revere.
•T-Bus 119 (Northgate-Beachmont).
•T-Bus 411 (Revere House-Malden Ctr.).

Northshore Shopping Center
Rt. 128 at Rt. 114, Peabody.
•T-Bus 435 (Lynn-Danvers).
•Michaud Buses from Peabody and Salem.

Porter Square
White St., Cambridge.
•Red Line to PORTER.
•T-Bus 77 (Arlington Hts.-Harvard).
•T-Bus 77A (N. Cambridge-Harvard).
•T-Bus 87 (Arlington Ctr.-Lechmere).

Prudential Center
800 Boylston St., Boston
•Orange Line or T-Commuter Rail to BACK BAY STATION; go through Copley Place and cross Huntington Ave. Bridge.
•Green Line or T-Buses to COPLEY, PRUDENTIAL, or HYNES CONVENTION CTR./ICA.

Quincy Market
See "Faneuil Hall Marketplace."

Shoppers World (under reconstruction)
Rt. 9, Framingham.
•Peter Pan (Boston-Worcester, Rt. 9 local).
•Peter Pan (Boston-Framingham, express).
•Gulbankian's (Framingham-Hudson), Sat. only.
•LIFT 1, 2, 3, 4, and 6.
•Natick Neighborhood Bus.

Silver City Galleria
2 Galleria Drive, Taunton.
•American Eagle bus from Boston.
•Bloom Bus lines from Boston.

South Shore Plaza
250 Granite St., Braintree.
•T-Bus 236 (Quincy Ctr.-South Shore Plaza).
•T-Bus 238 (Quincy Ctr.-Crawford Sq.).
•T-Bus 240A (Crawford Sq.-Ashmont): Some trips have through service to the mall from ASHMONT, Milton, and N. Randolph.

Swampscott Mall
Paradise Rd., Swampscott.
•T-Bus 441 (Marblehead-Haymarket).
•T-Bus 455 (Salem-Haymarket, via Loring Ave.).

Twin City Mall
264 O'Brien Hwy., Cambridge.
•T-Bus 80 (Arlington Ctr.-Lechmere).
•T-Bus 87 (Arlington Ctr.-Lechmere).
•T-Bus 88 (Clarendon Hill-Lechmere).
•T-Bus 69 (Harvard-Lechmere) to Lambert St., 1-block walk.

Watertown Mall
550 Arsenal St., Watertown.
•T-Bus 70 (Cedarwood-Central).
•T-Bus 70A (N. Waltham-Central).

Woburn Mall
300 Mishawum Rd., Woburn.
•T-Commuter Rail (Lowell Line) to Mishawum.

Chapter 14

Educational Institutions*

Amherst College
Amherst, Mass. (413-542-2000).
•Peter Pan (Boston-Amherst) to
Amherst Ctr.; 1-block walk.
•PVTA/Five Colleges shuttle buses.

Andover-Newton Theological School
210 Herrick Rd., Newton Centre
(964-1100).
•Green Line-D (Riverside) to NEWTON
CENTRE.
•T-Bus 52 (Dedham Mall-Watertown).

Aquinas Junior College
—Milton
303 Adams St., Milton (696-3100).
•T-Bus 217 (Wollaston Beach-Ashmont).
—Newton
15 Walnut Park, Newton (969-4400).
•Any T-Bus or Express Bus to Newton
Corner; walk 1/2 mile W on Washington St. to Walnut Park.
•T-Buses 53, 54, 56, 58 from Newton
Corner or DOWNTOWN CROSSING
to Washington St. and Walnut Park.

Art Institute of Boston
700 Boylston St., Boston (262-1223).
•Green Line (B, C, or D) or T-Buses to
KENMORE.

Babson College
Forest St. and Wellesley Ave., Wellesley
(235-1200).
•T-Commuter Rail (Framingham Line)
to Wellesley Hills; walk 1 mile S on
Forest St.
•Babson College student government
bus from WOODLAND *(Green Line-
D)*, Fri-Sat-Sun; call 239-4330.

Bay State College
122 Commonwealth Ave., Boston
(236-8000).
•Green Line to COPLEY.

Bentley College
Forest and Beaver Sts., Waltham
(891-2000).
•T-Bus 54 (Waverley-Newton Corner).

•T-Bus 73 (Waverley-Harvard) to
Waverley, transfer to T-Bus 54.
•Bentley College shuttle bus from Harvard
Sq., nights, weekends; call 891-2148.

Berklee College of Music
1140 Boylston St., Boston (266-1400).
•Green Line-(B, C, or D) or T-Bus 1
(Harvard-Dudley).to HYNES CONVENTION CTR./ICA.

Boston Architectural Center
320 Newbury St., Boston (536-3170).
•Green Line-(B, C, or D) or T-Bus 1
(Harvard-Dudley) to HYNES CONVENTION CTR./ICA.

Boston Center for Adult Education
5 Commonwealth Ave., Boston
(267-4430).
•Green Line or T-Buses to ARLINGTON.

Boston College
140 Commonwealth Ave., Chestnut Hill
(Newton) (552-8000).
•Green Line-B (Boston College) to end of
line. Stop is at north edge of campus.
•Green Line-D (Riverside) to
CHESTNUT HILL; 1/2-mile walk N on
Hammond St. to south edge of campus.
•Boston College shuttle bus from
CLEVELAND CIR. and Commonwealth Ave., daily; call 552-3060.
—Newton Campus
885 Centre St., Newton. (552-8550)
•T-Bus 52 (Dedham Mall-Watertown).
•Green Line-D (Riverside) to NEWTON
CENTRE; then T-Bus 52 (Watertown).
•Any T-Bus to Watertown Sq. or
Newton Corner; then T-Bus 52
(Dedham Mall).
•Boston College shuttle bus from main
campus and CLEVELAND CIR., daily;
call 552-3060.

Boston Conservatory of Music
8 the Fenway, Boston (536-6340).
•Green Line-(B, C, or D) or T-Bus 1
(Harvard-Dudley) to HYNES CONVENTION CTR./ ICA.

* For experimental crosstown buses, see pages 138-139.

Boston University
Charles River Campus
Commonwealth Ave., Boston (353-2000).
•Green Line-B (Boston College) to
 BLANFORD ST., B.U. EAST, B.U.
 CENTRAL, and B.U. WEST stops.
•T-Bus 47 (Central-Albany St.).
-Medical School
88 E. Newton St., Boston (638-8000)
See "Boston University Medical Center"
in Chapter 15.

Bradford College
320 S. Main St., Bradford (Haverhill)
(508-372-7161).
•T-Commuter Rail (Haverhill) to
 Bradford.

Brandeis University
415 South St., Waltham (736-2000).
•T-Commuter Rail (Fitchburg Line) to
 Brandeis/Roberts.
•T-Bus 53/304 (Roberts-Newton
 Corner-Downtown).
•T-Bus 70 (Cedarwood-Central) to end
 of line; walk up Cedarwood Ave., left
 on Thornton Rd. to campus.

Bridgewater State College
100 State St., Bridgewater
(508-697-1200).
•Interstate (Boston-Middleborough).

Brown University
45 Prospect St., Providence, RI
(401-863-1000).
•Amtrak, T-Commuter Rail, or Bonanza
 to Providence; 1/2-mile walk from train
 station or Kennedy Plaza, or take one of
 the following buses:
•RIPTA Bus 38 (Rumford/Tunnel).
•RIPTA Bus 40 (Butler/Tunnel).
•RIPTA Bus 41 (Elmgrove/Tunnel).
•RIPTA Bus 42 (Hope/Tunnel).

Bunker Hill Community College
Rutherford Ave., Charlestown
(241-8600).
•Orange Line to COMMUNITY
 COLLEGE.

Cambridge Center for Adult Education
42 Brattle St., Cambridge (547-6789).
•Red Line or T-Buses to HARVARD.

Cambridge College
44B Brattle St., Cambridge (492-5108).
•Red Line or T-Buses to HARVARD.

Clark University
950 Main St., Worcester (508-793-7711).
•Peter Pan to Worcester, then
•WRTA Bus 19S (Cherry Valley or
 Leicester Ctr.)
•WRTA Bus 26S (Auburn Mall).

Curry College
1071 Blue Hill Ave., Milton (333-0500).
•Hudson Bus (Mattapan-Canton).

Eastern Nazarene College
23 E. Elm Ave., Wollaston (Quincy)
(773-6350).
•Red Line (Braintree) to WOLLASTON;
 1/2-mile walk.
•T-Bus 212 (Quincy Ctr.-N. Quincy, via
 Billings Rd.).
•T-Bus 217 (Wollaston Beach-Ashmont).

Emerson College
100 Beacon St., Boston (578-8600).
•Green Line to ARLINGTON.

Emmanuel College
400 the Fenway, Boston (277-9340).
•Green Line-D (Riverside) to FENWAY.
•T-Bus 8 (Harbor Pt.-Kenmore).
•T-Bus 47 (Central-Albany St.)
•T-Bus 60 (Chestnut Hill-Kenmore).
•T-Bus 65 (Brighton Ctr.-Kenmore).
•LMA Shuttle (Cambridge-Longwood
 Med. Area).

Fisher Junior College
118 Beacon St., Boston (236-8800).
•Green Line to ARLINGTON.

Framingham State College
100 State St., Framingham
(508-620-1220).
•Peter Pan (Boston-Worcester, Rt. 9
 local).
•Peter Pan (Boston-Framingham,
 express).
•LIFT 2, 2X, and 3 (connect with T-
 Commuter rail from Boston).

Hampshire College
Route 116, Amherst (413-549-4600).
•Peter Pan (Boston-Amherst), 3 trips
 daily stop at the college.
•Peter Pan (Boston-Amherst) to
 Amherst Ctr. or UMass., transfer to
 PVTA.
•PVTA/Amherst Bus 301 (Mt. Holyoke).
•PVTA/Five Colleges shuttle buses.

Harvard University
Harvard Sq., Cambridge (495-1000).
•Red Line or T-Buses to HARVARD.
•LMA Shuttle (Cambridge-Longwood Med. Area).
—Business School
Soldiers Field Rd., Allston (495-6800).
(Across Charles River from Harvard Sq.).
•Red Line or T-Buses to HARVARD; walk across river (1/2 mile) or T-Bus 66 or 86.
•T-Bus 66 (Harvard-Dudley).
•T-Bus 70 (Cedarwood-Central) to Western Ave.
•T-Bus 86 (Sullivan-Cleveland Cir.).
—Medical Area
25 Shattuck St., Boston (432-1000).
•Green Line-E to LONGWOOD/ HOSPITALS.
•T-Bus 8 (Harbor Pt.-Kenmore).
•T-Bus 39 (Forest Hills-Back Bay Sta.).
•T-Bus 47 (Central-Albany St.).
•T-Bus 66 (Harvard-Dudley) to BRIGHAM CIR.
•LMA Shuttle (Cambridge-Longwood Med. Area).

Holy Cross College
College St., Worcester (508-793-2011).
•Peter Pan bus to Worcester, then
•WRTA Bus 10 (College Hill).
•WRTA Bus 4 (Millbury Line) to McKeon Rd., 1/2-mile walk.

Laboure College
2120 Dorchester Ave., Dorchester (296-8300)
See "Carney Hospital" in Chapter 15.

Lasell Junior College
1844 Commonwealth Ave., Newton (243-2000).
•Green Line-D (Riverside) to RIVER-SIDE, walk 1/2-mile E on Grove St., turn right on Woodland Rd. to back of campus.

Lesley College
29 Everett St., Cambridge (868-9600).
•Red Line and T-Buses to HARVARD; walk 3 blocks N on Mass. Ave. to Everett St.
•T-Bus 77 (Arlington Heights-Harvard).
•T-Bus 77A (N. Cambridge-Harvard).

Longy School of Music
1 Follen St., Cambridge (876-0956).
•Red Line and T-Buses to HARVARD; walk 3 blocks N. on Garden St. past the Sheraton Commander Hotel.

Massachusetts Bay Community College
50 Oakland St., Wellesley (237-1100)
•Shuttle bus from RIVERSIDE (Green Line-D), Mon-Fri, Sept-May.
•Peter Pan (Boston-Worcester, Rt. 9 local) to Oakland St., then one-block walk.

Massachusetts College of Art
621 Huntington Ave., Boston (232-1555)
•Green Line-E to LONGWOOD/ HOSPITALS.
•T-Bus 8 (Harbor Pt.-Kenmore).
•T-Bus 39 (Forest Hills-Back Bay).
•T-Bus 47 (Central-Albany St.).
•T-Bus 66 (Harvard-Dudley) to BRIGHAM CIR., two-block walk.

Massachusetts College of Pharmacy
179 Longwood Ave., Boston (732-2800).
•Green Line-E to LONGWOOD/ HOSPITALS.
•T-Bus 8 (Harbor Pt.-Kenmore).
•T-Bus 39 (Forest Hills-Back Bay).
•T-Bus 47 (Central-Albany St.).
•T-Bus 66 (Harvard-Dudley) to BRIGHAM CIR., two-block walk.
•LMA Shuttle (Cambridge-Longwood Med. Area).

Massachusetts Institute of Technology
77 Massachusetts Ave., Cambridge (253-1000)
•Red Line to KENDALL. Station is at east end of campus.
•T-Bus 1 (Harvard-Dudley).
•LMA Shuttle (Cambridge-Longwood Med. Area).

Middlesex Community College
Springs Road, Bedford (275-8910)
•T-Bus 62 (Bedford-Alewife) to ALEWIFE.

Mount Holyoke College
South Hadley (413-538-2000)
•Peter Pan (Boston-Amherst), 3 trips daily stop at the college.
•Peter Pan (Boston-Amherst) to Amherst Ctr. or UMass, transfer to PVTA.
•PVTA/Amherst Bus 301 (Mt. Holyoke).
•PVTA/Five Colleges shuttle buses.
•PVTA/Holyoke Bus 211 (S. Hadley Ctr.).

Mount Ida College
777 Dedham St., Newton Centre
(969-7000).
•T-Bus 52 (Dedham Mall-Watertown).
•Green Line-D (Riverside) to NEWTON
CENTRE, then T-Bus 52 (Dedham Mall).
•Shuttle bus from NEWTON CENTRE
(Green Line-D). Call 928-4588.

New England Conservatory of Music
290 Huntington Ave., Boston (262-1120).
•Green Line-E to SYMPHONY.
•Orange Line to MASS. AVE.
•T-Bus 1 (Harvard-Dudley).
•T-Bus 39 (Forest Hills-Back Bay).

New England School of Art and Design
28 Newbury St., Boston (536-0383).
•Green Line to ARLINGTON.

New England School of Law
154 Stuart St., Park Plaza, Boston
(451-0010).
•Green Line to BOYLSTON.
•Orange Line to N.E MED. CTR.
•T-Bus 43 (Ruggles-Park St.).

Newbury College
-Boston Campus
291 Boylston St. (730-7044).
•Green Line-(B, C, or D) or T-Bus 1
(Harvard-Dudley) to HYNES CONVEN-
TION CTR./ICA.
-Brookline Campus
129 Fisher Ave., (730-7000).
•Green Line-D (Riverside) to RESER-
VOIR, six-block walk.
•Shuttle van from RESERVOIR, Mon-
Fri during the school year.

Northeastern University
360 Huntington Ave., Boston (437-
2000).
•Green Line-E to NORTHEASTERN.
•Orange Line or T-Buses to
RUGGLES.
•T-Bus 1 (Harvard-Dudley) to SYM-
PHONY.
•T-Bus 39 (Forest Hills-Back Bay).
•T Commuter Rail (Needham, Franklin,
Attleboro/Stoughton lines) to Ruggles.

North Shore Community College
3 Essex St., Beverly (508-927-9374).
College Annex, Sohier Rd., Beverly.
•T-Bus 451 (North Beverly-Salem).

—Lynn Campus
300 Broad St., Lynn
•T-Commuter Rail (Rockport/Ipswich
Lines) and all T-Buses to Lynn/Central
Sq.; 2-block walk.

Pine Manor College
400 Heath St., Chestnut Hill (Brookline)
(731-7000).
•T-Bus 60 (Chestnut Hill-Kenmore) to
Randolph Rd., walk up Randolph to
Heath St.
•Shuttle bus from CHESTNUT HILL
(Green Line-D), Star Market, Chestnut
Hill, The Atrium.

Providence College
River Ave. at Eaton St., Providence
(401-865-1000) .
•Amtrak, Bonanza, Greyhound and T-
Commuter Rail to Providence, then
•RIPTA Bus 50 (Douglas) to Admiral St.
and River Ave.
•RIPTA Bus 57 (Smith) to Smith St.
and River Ave.

Quincy Junior College
34 Coddington St., Quincy (773-2406).
•Red Line (Braintree) or T-Buses to
QUINCY CTR.

Radcliffe College
Garden St., Cambridge (495-8601).
•Red Line or T-Buses to HARVARD.

Regis College
235 Wellesley St., Weston (893-1820).
•Daily shuttle buses from RIVERSIDE
(Green Line-D) during the school year.

Roxbury Community College
1234 Columbus Ave., Roxbury
(445-1927).
•Orange Line to ROXBURY CROSSING.
•T-Bus 66 (Harvard-Dudley).
•Also served by T-Buses 15, 19, 22,
23, 28, 29, 42, 44, 45.

Salem State College
352 Lafayette St., Salem
(508-741-6000).
•T-Bus 455 (Salem-Haymarket, via
Loring Ave.).

Simmons College
300 the Fenway, Boston (521-2000)
•Green Line-D to FENWAY (dormitories).
•Green Line-E to MUSEUM OF FINE
ARTS (academic buildings).

•T-Bus 8 (Harbor Pt.-Kenmore).
•T-Bus 47 (Central-Albany St.).
•T-Bus 60 (Chestnut Hill-Kenmore).
•T-Bus 65 (Brighton Ctr.-Kenmore).
•LMA Shuttle (Cambridge-Longwood Med. Area).

Smith College
Elm St., Northampton (413-584-2700).
•Peter Pan (Boston-Amherst) to Northampton; 3-block walk.
•PVTA/Five Colleges shuttle buses.

Stonehill College
320 Washington St., North Easton (238-1081).
•BAT Bus 9 (Pearl St.).

Suffolk University
41 Temple St., Beacon Hill, Boston (573-8000).
•Red Line and Green Line to PARK ST.
•Blue Line to BOWDOIN.

Tufts University
Boston Ave., Medford (628-5000).
•Red Line to DAVIS; 3/4-mile walk, or take T-Bus 94 or 96 (Medford Sq.).
•T-Bus 80 (Arlington Ctr.-Lechmere, via Medford Hillside).
•T-Bus 94 (Medford Sq.-Davis).
•T-Bus 96 (Medford Sq.-Harvard).
•T-Bus 89 (Clarendon Hill-Sullivan). *This bus stops at the edge of the campus; the others go through the middle of the campus.*
—**Medical School**
136 Harrison Ave., Boston (956-7000).
See "Tufts-New England Medical Center" in Chapter 15.

University of Massachusetts
—**Amherst** (413-545-0111).
•Peter Pan (Boston-Amherst), stops at the campus.
•PVTA/Five Colleges shuttle buses.
—**Boston: Harbor Campus**
Dorchester (287-5000).
•Red Line to JFK/UMASS; then UMass shuttle bus to the campus, daily. Buses operate every 15 min. or less, until at least 10:20pm Mon-Thurs, 7:00pm Fri, and 5:45pm weekends and school vacations. Call 287-5040.
•T-Bus 8 (Harbor Pt.-Kenmore).
•T-Bus 16 (Forest Hills-JFK/UMass), rush hours only.
•T-Bus 17 (Fields Corner-JFK/UMass)

—**Dartmouth**
Old Westport Rd., N. Dartmouth.
•SRTA (Fall River-New Bedford).
—**Lowell: North Campus**
1 University Ave., Lowell.
•LRTA Bus 11 (Pawtucketville).
—**Lowell: South Campus**
Broadway, Lowell.
•LRTA Bus 10 (U. of Lowell S.).
—**Medical School**
55 Lake Ave. N., Worcester (508-856-0011).
•WRTA Bus 24 (Belmont St./Lake Ave.).
•Peter Pan (Boston-Worcester, Rt. 9 local)—from Boston/Peter Pan, Park Plaza, Copley Sq., and Brigham Cir.

University of Rhode Island
Kingston, RI (401-792-1000).
•Amtrak (Shore Line) to Kingston, RI; then RIPTA Bus (Newport or Galilee), Mon-Sat; or 2-mile walk or taxi.
•Bonanza or Greyhound to Providence (Kennedy Plaza), then RIPTA Bus (Kingston), 4-6 trips daily.

Wellesley College
106 Central St., Wellesley (283-1000).
•T-Commuter Rail (Framingham Line) to Wellesley Sq., 10-minute walk.
•Wellesley and MIT operate a bus between the schools for cross-registered students, Mon-Fri. If space is available, others from the Wellesley and MIT communities may ride. Call 253-1668.
•Wellesley Senate bus from Harvard Sq., MIT, Mass. Ave. & Beacon St., and WOODLAND *(Green Line-D),* Fri night-Sat-Sun. Call 235-0320 x2670.

Wentworth Institute
550 Huntington Ave., Boston (442-9010).
•Green Line-E to MUSEUM OF FINE ARTS
•Orange Line or T-Buses to RUGGLES.
•T-Bus 8 (Harbor Pt.-Kenmore).
•T-Bus 39 (Forest Hills-Back Bay Sta.).
•T-Bus 47 (Central-Albany St.).

Wheaton College
E. Main St., Norton (508-285-7722).
•GATRA (Attleboro-Taunton), *connects w/T-Commuter Rail (Attleboro Line) at Attleboro,* Mon-Fri.
•Wheaton College shuttle bus from Mansfield and Attleboro, *connects w/ T-Commuter Rail (Attleboro Line),* Mon-Thurs nights.
•Wheaton College shuttle bus from Boston, Fri nights.

Wheelock College
200 the Riverway, Boston (734-5200).
- Green Line-D to FENWAY or LONGWOOD.
- T-Bus 8 (Harbor Pt.-Kenmore).
- T-Bus 47 (Central-Albany St.).
- T-Bus 60 (Chestnut Hill-Kenmore).
- T-Bus 65 (Brighton Ctr.-Kenmore).
- LMA Shuttle (Cambridge-Longwood Med. Area).

Williams College
Williamstown, Mass. (413-597-3131).
- Peter Pan (Boston-Bennington, VT) stops at the college

Women's Educational & Industrial Union
356 Boylston St., Boston (536-5651).
- Green Line or T-Buses to ARLINGTON or COPLEY.

Worcester Polytechnic Institute
100 Institute Rd., Worcester (508-831-5000).
- Peter Pan bus to Worcester, then
- WRTA Bus 6N (Holden/Chaffins).
- WRTA Bus 32 (Holden/Jefferson).
- Or take any of these WRTA Buses to Lincoln Sq. (1/2-mile walk): 17, 19N, 21, 23, 24, 26N, 30N.

Worcester State College
486 Chandler St., Worcester (508-793-8000).
- Peter Pan bus to Worcester, then
- WRTA Bus 6S (Chandler/Dawson Rd.).

Chapter 15
Hospitals*

Angell Memorial Animal Hospital
350 So. Huntington Ave., Jamaica Plain (522-7282).
- T-Bus 39 (Forest Hills-Back Bay Sta.) to Perkins St. (Call the MBTA for current pet policy).

Atlanticare Medical Center Lynn Hospital Division
212 Boston St., Lynn (598-5100).
- T-Bus 429 (Lynn-N. Saugus).
- T-Bus 435 (Lynn-Danvers).
- T-Bus 450 (Salem-Haymarket)
- Lynn East/West Loop buses.

Beth Israel Hospital
330 Brookline Ave., Boston (735-2000).
- Green Line-D to LONGWOOD; 4-block walk.
- T-Bus 8 (Harbor Pt.-Kenmore).
- T-Bus 47 (Central-Albany St.).
- T-Bus 60 (Chestnut Hill-Kenmore).
- T-Bus 65 (Brighton Ctr.-Kenmore).
- LMA Shuttle (Cambridge-Longwood Med. Area).

Boston City Hospital
818 Harrison Ave., Boston (534-5000).
- T-Bus 1 (Harvard-Dudley).

- T-Bus 8 (Harbor Pt.-Kenmore).
- T-Bus 10 (City Pt.-Copley).
- T-Bus 47 (Central-Albany St.).
- T-Bus 49 (Dudley-Downtown) to Mass. Ave., 1-block walk.

Boston Specialty and Rehabilitation Hospital
249 River St., Mattapan (534-2000).
- T-Bus 27 (Mattapan-Ashmont).

Boston University Medical Center Hospital
88 E. Newton St., Boston (638-8000).
- T-Bus 8 (Harbor Pt.-Kenmore).
- T-Bus 10 (City Pt.-Copley).
- T-Bus 47 (Central-Albany St.).
- T-Bus 49 (Dudley-Downtown) to E. Newton St., 1-block walk.
- T-Bus 1 (Harvard-Dudley) to Boston City Hosp., 3-block walk.

Brigham & Women's Hospital
75 Francis St., Boston (732-5500).
- Green Line-E to BRIGHAM CIRCLE.
- T-Bus 39 (Forest Hills-Back Bay Sta.) to BRIGHAM CIRCLE.
- T-Bus 60 (Chestnut Hill-Kenmore) to Francis St.

* For experimental crosstown buses, see pages 138-139.

• T-Bus 65 (Brighton Ctr.-Kenmore) to Francis St.
• T-Bus 66 (Harvard-Dudley) to BRIGHAM CIRCLE.
• LMA Shuttle (Cambridge-Longwood Med. Area).

—Ambulatory Care Center
850 Boylston St., Chestnut Hill (278-0880).
• T-Bus 60 (Chestnut Hill-Kenmore) to Eliot St.

Cambridge Hospital
1493 Cambridge St., Cambridge (498-1000).
• T-Bus 69 (Harvard-Lechmere).
• T-Bus 83 (Rindge Ave.-Central) to Beacon & Cooney Sts.; 1-block walk.

Carney Hospital
2100 Dorchester Ave., Dorchester (296-4000).
• Red Line to ASHMONT; walk 1/2 mile S on Dorchester Ave.
• T-Bus 27 (Mattapan-Ashmont).
• T-Bus 217 (Wollaston Beach-Ashmont).
• T-Bus 240 (Avon Line-Ashmont).
• T-Bus 240A (Crawford Sq.-Ashmont).
The following T-Buses stop 2 blocks from the hospital:
• T-Bus 21 (Ashmont-Forest Hills).
• T-Bus 215 (Quincy Ctr.-Ashmont).

Central Hospital
26 Central St., Somerville (625-8900).
• T-Bus 83 (Rindge Ave.-Central).
• T-Bus 87 (Arlington Ctr.-Lechmere).

Children's Hospital
300 Longwood Ave., Boston (735-6000).

• Green Line-D to LONGWOOD; 4-block walk.
• Green Line-E to LONGWOOD/ HOSPITALS; 4-block walk.
• T-Bus 8 (Harbor Pt.-Kenmore).
• T-Bus 47 (Central-Albany St.).
• T-Bus 60 (Chestnut Hill-Kenmore).
• T Bus 65 (Brighton Ctr.-Kenmore).
• T-Bus 39 (Forest Hills-Back Bay Sta.) to LONGWOOD/HOSPITALS; 4-block walk.
• LMA Shuttle (Cambridge-Longwood Med. Area).

Dana-Farber Cancer Institute
44 Binney St., Boston (632-3000).
Same directions as Children's Hospital.

Faulkner Hospital
1153 Centre St., Jamaica Plain (522-5800).
• T-Bus 38 (Wren St.-Forest Hills).

Fernald State School
200 Trapelo Rd., Waltham (894-3600).
• T-Bus 73 (Waverley-Harvard) to Waverley Sq.
• T-Bus 54 (Waverley-Newton Corner) to Waverley Sq.
Daily shuttle buses from Waverley Sq. (1 mile); call 894-3600 x2175.

Franciscan Children's Hospital
30 Warren St., Brighton (254-3800).
• Green Line-B to WARREN ST., 2-block walk.
• T-Bus 57 (Watertown-Kenmore) to Warren St.; 1/2 block walk.

Deaconess Glover Hospital
148 Chestnut St., Needham (444-5600).
• T-Bus 59 (Needham Jct.-Watertown).

Hahnemann Hospital
1515 Commonwealth Ave., Brighton (254-1100).
• Green Line-B to WASHINGTON ST.
• T-Bus 65 (Brighton Ctr.-Kenmore).

Hebrew Rehabilitation Center
1200 Centre St., Roslindale (325-8000).
• T-Bus 38 (Wren St.-Forest Hills).

Jewish Memorial Hospital
59 Townsend St., Roxbury (442-8760).
• T-Bus 42 (Forest Hills-Ruggles) to Townsend St.

Joslin Diabetes Center
1 Joslin Pl. (off 437 Brookline Ave.),
Boston (732-2400).
Same directions as Beth Israel Hospital.

Lahey Clinic Medical Center
41 Mall Rd., Burlington (273-5100).
•T-Bus 350 (Burlington-Alewife).
•T-Bus 353 (Burlington Ind. Area-
Haymarket).

Lawrence Memorial Hospital
170 Governors Ave., Medford
(396-9250).
•T-Buses to Medford Sq.; 3/4 mile walk.

Malden Hospital
Hospital Rd., Malden (322-7560).
•T-Bus 99 (Upper Highland-Wellington).

Massachusetts Eye and Ear Infirmary
243 Charles St., Boston (523-7900).
•Red Line to CHARLES/MGH.

Massachusetts General Hospital
55 Fruit St., Boston (726-2000).
•Red Line to CHARLES/MGH.

McLean Hospital
115 Mill St., Belmont (855-2000).
•T-Bus 54 (Waverley-Newton Corner)
to Waverley Sq.
•T-Bus 73 (Waverley-Harvard) to
Waverley Sq.
•T-Commuter Rail (Fitchburg Line)—
from NORTH STA. to Waverley.
Hospital is mile 1/4 walk up a steep hill
from Waverley Sq. *Do not follow the
signs "To McLean Hospital";* this is the
auto route which is considerably longer.
Shuttles from Waverley Sq.; call 855-
2121.

Medical Center at Symmes
39 Hospital Rd., Arlington (646-1500).
•T-Bus 67 (Turkey Hill-Alewife) to
Hospital Rd.
•T-Bus 77 (Arlington Hts.-Harvard) to
Brattle St.; walk 1/2 mile up hill.

Melrose-Wakefield Hospital
585 Lebanon St., Melrose (979-3000).
•T-Buses 136/137 (Reading-Malden Ctr.).
•T-Commuter Rail (Reading/Haverhill
Line) to Melrose/Cedar Pk.; 1/2-mile.

Milton Hospital
92 Highland St., Milton (696-4600).
•T-Bus 240 (Avon Line-Ashmont).
•T-Bus 240A (Crawford Sq.-Ashmont).
•T-Bus 245 (Quincy Ctr.-Mattapan); *trips
"via Shadowlawn" do not serve the
hospital.*

Mount Auburn Hospital
330 Mt. Auburn St., Cambridge
(492-3500).
•T-Bus 71 (Watertown-Harvard).
•T-Bus 73 (Waverley-Harvard).

New England Baptist Hospital
125 Parker Hill Ave., Roxbury
(738-5800).
•Green Line-E to PARKER HILL AVE.
•T-Bus 39 (Forest Hills-Back Bay Sta.)
to PARKER HILL AVE.
•T-Bus 66 (Harvard-Dudley) to
PARKER HILL AVE.
•Mission Hill Link Bus—all routes.
Parker Hill Ave. has a very steep hill.
You may wish to take Mission Hill Link
(or a cab) from BRIGHAM CIRCLE.

New England Deaconess Hospital
185 Pilgrim Rd., Boston (732-7000).
Same directions as Beth Israel Hospital.

New England Medical Center
See "Tufts-New England Medical Ctr."

New England Rehabilitation Hospital
Rehabilitation Way, Woburn
(935-5050).
•T-Bus 350 (Burlington-Alewife).

Newton-Wellesley Hospital
2014 Washington St., Newton Lower Falls
(243-6000).
•Green Line-D to WOODLAND.

Quincy City Hospital
114 Whitwell St., Quincy (773-6100).
•T-Bus 245 (Quincy Ctr.-Mattapan).

St. Elizabeth's Hospital
736 Cambridge St., Brighton
(878-9901).
•T-Bus 57 (Watertown-Kenmore).
•T-Bus 65 (Brighton Ctr.-Kenmore).
•T-Bus 86 (Sullivan-Cleveland Cir.) to
Brighton Ctr., 3-block walk.

Sancta Maria Hospital
799 Concord Ave., Cambridge
(868-2200).
- T-Bus 74 (Belmont Ctr.-Harvard), *trips "via Concord Ave." only.*
- T-Bus 78 (Park Cir.-Harvard).

Lemuel Shattuck Hospital
170 Morton St., Jamaica Plain
(522-8110).
- Orange Line or T-Bus 39 to FOREST HILLS; 1/2 mile walk.
- T-Bus 21 (Ashmont-Forest Hills).
- T-Bus 31 (Mattapan-Forest Hills).

Shriners Burns Institute and Hospital for Crippled Children
51 Blossom St., Boston (722-3000).
- Red Line to CHARLES/MGH.

Somerville Hospital
230 Highland Ave., Somerville
(666-4400).
- T-Bus 88 (Clarendon Hill-Lechmere)
- T-Bus 90 (Davis-Wellington).

Spaulding Rehabilitation Hospital
125 Nashua St., Boston (720-6400).
- Green Line (Lechmere) to SCIENCE PARK.
- T-Commuter Rail to NORTH STA.

Tufts-New England Medical Center
750 Washington St., Boston
(956-5000).
- Orange Line to N. E. MEDICAL CTR.
- Green Line to BOYLSTON; 4-block walk.
- T-Bus 11 (City Pt.-Downtown).
- T-Bus 43 (Ruggles-Park St.).
- T-Bus 49 (Dudley-Downtown).

Veterans Administration Clinic
251 Causeway St., Boston (248-1010).
- Green Line, Orange Line, or T-Commuter Rail to NORTH STA.

Veterans Administration Hospital
200 Springs Rd., Bedford (275-7500).
- T-Bus 62 (Bedford-Alewife), *before 7:00 pm only.*

Veterans Administration Hospital
150 S. Huntington Ave., Jamaica Plain
(739-5476).
- Green Line-E to HEATH ST.
- T-Bus 39 (Forest Hills-Back Bay Sta.).
- T-Bus 46 (Heath St.-Dudley).

Veterans Administration Hospital
1400 V.F.W. Parkway, West Roxbury
(323-7700).
- T-Bus 36A (V.A. Hospital-Forest Hills).
- T-Bus 52 (Dedham Mall-Watertown).

Waltham-Weston Hospital
Hope Ave., Waltham (647-6000).
- T-Bus 53 (Roberts-Newton Corner).
- T-Bus 70 (Cedarwood-Central) to Main & South Sts.; walk 1/2 mile S on South St. to Hope Ave.
- T-Commuter Rail or any T-Bus to Central Sq./Waltham; 3/4-mile walk or take T-Bus 53 (Roberts).

Whidden Memorial Hospital
103 Garland St., Everett (389-6270).
- T-Bus 110 (Wonderland-Wellington) to Woodlawn St.; 1/2 mile walk via Woodlawn St., left on Garland St.

Winthrop Hospital
40 Lincoln St., Winthrop (846-2600).
- Paul Revere Bus (Orient Hts.-Winthrop Beach via Highlands).
- Paul Revere Bus (Orient Hts.-Winthrop Beach via Centre).
Get off at Main & Pleasant Sts.; walk 2 blocks S on Pleasant St. to Lincoln St.

Youville Hospital
1575 Cambridge St., Cambridge
(876-4344).
- T-Bus 69 (Harvard-Lechmere).

Chapter 16

Cities, Towns, and Neighborhoods

This chapter covers every city and town in Massachusetts directly served from Boston by public transportation, plus a number of towns in the Greater Boston area that are near transit, but are not directly served.

Stations on Boston's rapid transit system (e.g. RIVERSIDE, NORTH STA.) have been capitalized.

🅿 indicates selected park-and-ride facilities near major highways. For more parking information, call 800-392-6100 or 722-3200.

Abington
- Carey's (Boston-Whitman), 2 rush hour trips serve Abington Ctr. and N. Abington.

Acton
- T-Commuter Rail (Fitchburg Line)— from NORTH STA. to S. Acton.
- Yankee Line (Boston-Littleton), 1 rush hour trip.
- 🅿 Off Main St. (Rt. 27), S of Rts. 2 and 111 (S. Acton).

Allston (Boston)
- Green Line-B (Boston College), serves Commonwealth Ave.
- T-Bus 57 (Watertown-Kenmore).
- T-Bus 64 (Oak Sq.-Central).
- T-Bus 66 (Harvard-Dudley, via Brookline).
- T-Bus 70 (Cedarwood-Central).
- T-Bus 86 (Sullivan-Cleveland Cir.).
- *Union Sq.:* T-Buses 57, 64, 66.
- *Western Ave.:* T-Buses 70, 86.

Amesbury
- The Coach Co. (Boston-Amesbury), rush hour only.
- MVRTA (Haverhill-Newburyport).

Amherst
- Peter Pan (Boston-Greenfield)—from Boston/Peter Pan and RIVERSIDE. Stops at Amherst Ctr. and UMass.; 3 trips/day also stop at Hampshire College.
- PVTA local buses.
- GMTA local bus to UMass. from Greenfield and Montague.

Andover
- T-Commuter Rail (Haverhill Line)—from NORTH STA. to Ballardvale and Andover.

- Trombly (Boston-Andover)—from Park Plaza and Essex St, rush hour only.
- Flight Line—from Logan Airport.
- MVRTA local buses.

Arlington
- T-Bus 62 (Bedford-Alewife).
- T-Bus 67 (Turkey Hill-Alewife).
- T-Bus 77 (Arlington Hts.-Harvard).
- T-Bus 78 (Arlmont-Harvard).
- T-Bus 79 (Arlington Hts.-Alewife).
- T-Bus 80 (Arlington Ctr.-Lechmere, via Medford Hillside).
- T-Bus 84 (Alewife-Arlmont)
- T-Bus 87 (Arlington Ctr.-Lechmere, via Somerville Ave.).
- T-Bus 350 (Burlington-Alewife).
- *Primary service:* T-Bus 77 from Harvard.
- *Arlington Ctr.:* T-Buses 67, 77, 79, 80, 87, 350.
- *Arlington Hts.:* T-Buses 62, 77, 79.

Ashland
- LIFT 6 (Framingham-Milford), *connects w/T-Commuter Rail and Boston buses in Framingham.* Serves Rt.126.
- LIFT 5 (Framingham-Hopkinton), *connects w/T-Commuter Rail at Framingham.* Serves Rt.135.

Attleboro & So. Attleboro
- T-Commuter Rail (Attleboro Line)— from SOUTH STA. and BACK BAY STA. to Attleboro and S. Attleboro.
- Mass Limousine—from Logan Airport to S. Attleboro.
- GATRA local buses.
- 🅿 Main St. (Rt. 152), S of Rt. 123 (downtown).

Auburn
- Peter Pan (Boston-Worcester, express), rush hour only.
- WRTA local bus from Worcester.

YOU CAN GET THERE, BUT...

The following Massachusetts towns (mostly small) do not have direct public transportation service from Boston. A transfer to a local transit line is required. Sometimes this is easy; sometimes, not. For more information see the indicated Regional Transit Authority (RTA) entry in Chapter 20.

See **BRTA** for: Adams, Cheshire, Dalton, Great Barrington, Hinsdale, Lanesborough, Sheffield, Stockbridge.

See **CCRTA** for: Centerville, Cotuit, Marstons Mills, Mashpee, Osterville.

See **FRTA** for: Bernardston, Charlemont, Gill, Northfield, Shelburne Falls.

See **GATRA** for: Plainville, Rehoboth, Seekonk.

See **GMTA** for: Conway, Leverett, Millers Falls, Montague, Turners Falls.

See **LRTA** for: Dracut, Tyngsborough.

See **PVTA** for: Agawam, Belchertown, Easthampton, East Longmeadow, Granby, Hadley, Longmeadow, Ludlow, Sunderland, West Springfield, Wilbraham, Williamsburg.

See **SRTA** for: Acushnet, Dartmouth, Mattapoisett, Somerset, Swansea, Westport.

See **WRTA** for: Boylston, Brookfield, Clinton, Douglas, East Brookfield, Holden, Leicester, Spencer, West Boylston.

Auburndale (Newton)
- T-Commuter Rail (Framingham Line)- from SOUTH STA. & BACK BAY STA.
- T-Express Bus 305 (Waltham-Downtown), rush hour only.
- T-Bus 58 (Auburndale-Newton Corner-Downtown), via Waltham.
- Green Line-D (Riverside) to RIVERSIDE; 1/2-mile walk.

Avon
- T-Bus 240 (Avon Line-Ashmont).
- BAT Bus 12 (Ashmont-Brockton)— from ASHMONT (Red Line).

Ayer
See also Fort Devens.
- T-Commuter Rail (Fitchburg Line)—from NORTH STA.

Back Bay (Boston)
See Chapter 5 for subway, bus, and train service to Back Bay and map. See "Logan Airport" for service to the airport from Back Bay.

Barnstable
See also Hyannis.
- Plymouth & Brockton (Boston-Hyannis)—from Park Plaza, Boston/ Peter Pan, and Logan Airport.
- **P** Route 132 at Route 6, exit 6.

Bay Village (Boston)
- Green Line to ARLINGTON.
- Orange Line to N. E. MEDICAL CTR.
- T-Bus 9 (City Pt.-Copley, via Broadway).
- T-Bus 43 (Ruggles-Park St.).

Beacon Hill (Boston)
- Red Line to CHARLES/MGH and PARK ST.
- Blue Line to BOWDOIN.
- Green Line to PARK ST.
- T-Bus 43 (Ruggles-Park St.).
- T-Bus 55 (Queensberry St.-Park St.).

Bedford
- T-Bus 62 (Bedford-Alewife).
- T-Express Bus 353 (Burlington Ind. Area-Haymarket), rush hour "reverse commute" only.

•LRTA local bus from Lowell.
🅿 Mt. Pleasant St. off Billerica Ave. (N. Billerica)

Boston
See Chapter 5 for service to downtown Boston and Back Bay.
See "Logan Airport" for service to the airport from downtown and Back Bay.
Transit service to Boston's neighborhoods is listed alphabetically under the following: Allston, Bay Village, Beacon Hill, Brighton, Charlestown, Chinatown, Dorchester, East Boston, the Fenway, Fort Point Channel, Hyde Park, Jamaica Plain, Mattapan, Mission Hill, North End, Readville, Roslindale, Roxbury, South Boston, South End, West Roxbury.

Bourne
See also Buzzards Bay, Otis A.F.B.
•Bonanza (Boston-Woods Hole)—from BACK BAY STA. and Logan Airport.

Boxford
•The Coach Co. (Boston-Haverhill), rush hour only.

Bradford
See Haverhill.

Braintree
•Red Line (Braintree) to BRAINTREE.
•Carey's (Boston-Whitman), 2 rush hour trips serve E. Braintree.
•T-Bus 225 (Quincy Ctr.-Weymouth Landing), serves Quincy Ave.
•T-Bus 230 (Quincy Ctr.-Holbrook), serves Washington St.
•T-Bus 236 (Quincy Ctr.-South Shore Plaza), serves E. Braintree, Franklin St.
•T-Bus 238 (Quincy Ctr.-Crawford Sq.), serves Granite and Pond Sts.
•Green Harbor Transp.—from Logan Airport to Susse Chalet.
•Logan Express—from Logan Airport to Forbes Rd., off Granite St.

Brewster
•Plymouth & Brockton (Hyannis-Provincetown), *connects w/Boston buses at Hyannis.*

Bridgewater and W. Bridgewater
•Interstate (Boston-Middleborough), serves Bridgewater Ctr., West Bridgewater, Elm Sq., Hockomock, and Correctional Complex.

BAT bus depot, Brockton

•T-Bus 353A (Burlington Ind. Area-Dudley), rush hour "reverse commute" only.
•M & L Transp.—from Logan Airport.

Bellingham
*See **Franklin** for trains to Boston.*

Belmont
•T-Commuter Rail (Fitchburg Line)—from NORTH STA. to Belmont Ctr. and Waverley.
•T-Bus 54 (Waverley-Newton Corner-Downtown), via Waltham.
•T-Bus 73 (Waverley-Harvard).
•T-Bus 74 (Belmont Ctr.-Harvard).
•T-Bus 78 (Arlmont-Harvard).

Beverly
•T-Commuter Rail (Rockport Line)—from NORTH STA. to Beverly Depot, Montserrat, Prides Crossing (rush hour only), and Beverly Farms.
•T-Commuter Rail (Ipswich Line)—from NORTH STA. to Beverly Depot and N. Beverly.
•T-Bus 451 (N. Beverly-Salem).
•Beverly Shoppers' Shuttle.

Billerica
•T-Commuter Rail (Lowell Line)—from NORTH STA. to N. Billerica.

Brighton (Boston)
- Green Line-B (Boston College), serves Commonwealth Ave.
- Green Line-C (Cleveland Circle) to CLEVELAND CIRCLE.
- Green Line-D (Riverside) to RESERVOIR.
- T-Express Bus 301 (Brighton Ctr.-Downtown).
- T-Bus 57 (Watertown-Kenmore).
- T-Bus 64 (Oak Sq.-Central).
- T-Bus 65 (Brighton Ctr.-Kenmore).
- T-Bus 70 (Cedarwood-Central).
- T-Bus 86 (Sullivan-Cleveland Cir.).

Brighton Ctr.: T-Buses 57, 65, 86, 301.
Oak Sq.: T-Buses 57, 64, 301.
Western Ave.: T-Buses 70, 86.

Brockton
- BAT Buses 12 and 12X (Ashmont-Brockton)—from Ashmont *(Red Line)*.
- Plymouth & Brockton (Boston-Brockton)—from Park Plaza and SOUTH STA.
- BAT local buses.
- P Westgate Mall by Cinema 1 & 2, Route 27 at Route 24, exit 18A.

Brookline
- Green Line-B (Boston College), serves Commonwealth Ave. in adjacent Allston and Brighton.
- Green Line-C (Cleveland Circle), serves Beacon St., COOLIDGE CORNER.
- Green Line-D (Riverside) to LONGWOOD, BROOKLINE VILLAGE, BROOKLINE HILLS, BEACONSFIELD and RESERVOIR.
- T-Bus 51 (Cleveland Cir.-Forest Hills).
- T-Bus 60 (Chestnut Hill-Kenmore), serves Boylston St. (Rt.9).
- T-Bus 65 (Brighton Ctr.-Kenmore), serves Washington St.
- T-Bus 66 (Harvard-Dudley), serves Harvard St.
- T-Bus 86 (Sullivan-Cleveland Cir.).
- Peter Pan (Boston-Worcester, Rt. 9 local), stops at BROOKLINE VILLAGE and Chestnut Hill.

See Brookline Village map, page 24.

Burlington
- T-Bus 350 (Burlington-Alewife).
- T-Express Bus 352 (Burlington-Boston), rush hour only.
- T-Express Bus 353 (Burlington Ind. Area-Haymarket), rush hour "reverse commute" only.
- T-Bus 353A (Burlington Ind. Area-Dudley), rush hour "reverse commute" only.
- M & L Transp.—from Logan Airport to hotels.
- Lexpress (Lexington-Burlington Mall).
- Burlington B Line local buses.

Buzzards Bay
- Bonanza (Boston-Wareham)—from BACK BAY STA., 2 rush hour trips.

Byfield (Newbury)
- The Coach Co. (Boston-Amesbury), rush hour only.

Cambridge
See Chapter 5 and maps of CENTRAL and HARVARD Squares for coverage of core transit lines in Cambridge.
E. Cambridge: Green Line (LECHMERE) and T-Bus 69
Inman Sq.: T-Buses 69, 83, 91.
Mass. Ave.: Red Line (CENTRAL, HARVARD, PORTER); T-Bus 1 (CENTRAL, HARVARD) and T-Buses 77, 77A (HARVARD, PORTER).
Mt. Auburn St.: T-Buses 71, 73.
N. Cambridge: Red Line (PORTER, DAVIS, and ALEWIFE); Commuter Rail; and T-Buses 77, 77A, 83.
P Route 2, junction Rt. 16 and U.S. 3 (Alewife).

Canton
- T-Commuter Rail (Stoughton Line)—from SOUTH STA. and BACK BAY STA. to Canton Jct. and Canton Ctr.
- T-Commuter Rail (Attleboro Line)—from SOUTH STA. and BACK BAY STA. to Canton Jct.
- Hudson Bus (Mattapan-Canton)—from MATTAPAN (Red Line).
- P Sherman St., between Chapman and Washington Sts. (Canton Junction).

Charlestown (Boston)
- Orange Line to COMMUNITY COLLEGE and SULLIVAN SQ.
- T-Commuter Boat—from Long Wharf.
- T-Bus 92 (Assembly Sq.-Downtown), serves Main St.
- T-Bus 93 (Sullivan-Downtown), serves Bunker Hill St.
- T-Bus 111 (Woodlawn-Haymarket).
- Navy Yard Shuttle Bus.

Charlestown Navy Yard: T-Commuter Boat; T-Bus 93; and shuttle bus.
See Orange Line maps (pages 114-115) for other buses to SULLIVAN SQ.

Chelmsford
- LRTA local buses from **Lowell.**
- Flight Line—from Logan Airport.
- M & L Transp.—from Logan Airport.
See Lowell for train service to Boston.

Chelsea
- T-Commuter Rail (Rockport/Ipswich Line)—from NORTH STA.
- T-Bus 111 (Woodlawn-Haymarket).
- T-Bus 112 (Wellington-Maverick).
- T-Buses 116/117 (Wonderland-Maverick).

Chestnut Hill (Brookline/ Newton)
- Green Line-B (Boston College) to BOSTON COLLEGE.
- Green Line-D (Riverside) to CHESTNUT HILL.
- T-Bus 51 (Cleveland Cir.-Forest Hills).
- T-Bus 60 (Chestnut Hill-Kenmore).
- Peter Pan (Boston-Worcester, Rt. 9 local), stops in Chestnut Hill.

Chicopee
- Peter Pan (Boston-Springfield).
- PVTA local buses from Springfield and Holyoke.

Chinatown (Boston)
- Orange Line to CHINATOWN and N. E. MEDICAL CTR.
- Green Line to BOYLSTON, cross Tremont St., walk 1 block on Boylston St.
- T-Bus 3 (Chinatown-Marine Ind. Pk.).
- T-Bus 11 (City Pt.-Downtown, via Bayview).
- T-Bus 49 (Dudley-Downtown).

Cohasset
- Plymouth & Brockton (Boston-Scituate)—from Park Plaza, Boston/ Peter Pan and SOUTH STA.

Concord
- T-Commuter Rail (Fitchburg Line)— from NORTH STA.and PORTER to Concord and W. Concord.
- Yankee Line (Boston-Littleton), 1 rush hour trip.
- Concord Free Bus local buses.
- P Main St. (Rt. 62) and Common-wealth Ave. (W. Concord).

Cuttyhunk (Elizabeth Islands)
- American Eagle to New Bedford, then
- Cuttyhunk Boat from New Bedford.

Danvers
- T-Bus 435 (Lynn-Danvers).

- T-Bus 458 (Haymarket-Danvers), rush hour only.
- The Coach Co. (Boston-Haverhill), rush hour only. Serves Danvers Plaza.

Dedham
- T-Commuter Rail (Franklin Line)— from SOUTH STA. and BACK BAY STA. to Endicott & Dedham Corp. Ctr.
- T-Commuter Rail (Attleboro/Stoughton Lines)—from SOUTH STA. and BACK BAY STA. to Route 128 Sta.
- T-Bus 34E (Walpole Ctr.-Forest Hills), serves Washington St. and Dedham Sq.
- T-Bus 35 (Dedham Mall-Forest Hills).
- T-Bus 52 (Dedham Mall-Watertown).
- Amtrak (Boston-New York, Shore Line) stops at Route 128 Sta.
- Dedham Local Bus.
From Boston: Orange Line or T-Bus 39 to FOREST HILLS, then T-Bus 34E; or Commuter Rail.
- P Allied Dr., off rotary at Route 128/I-95, exit 14 (Dedham Corporate Center).

Deerfield
- Peter Pan (Boston- Benningon, VT)— from Boston/Peter Pan and RIVER-SIDE.
- FRTA local bus from Greenfield.
- PVTA from Amherst to S. Deerfield.

Dennis
- Plymouth & Brockton (Hyannis-Provincetown), *connects w/Boston buses at Hyannis.* Serves Dennis and E. Dennis.

Dorchester (Boston)
- Red Line (Ashmont) to JFK/UMASS, SAVIN HILL, FIELDS CORNER, SHAWMUT, and ASHMONT.
- Red Line (Mattapan) to CEDAR GROVE, BUTLER ST., MILTON, and CENTRAL AVE.
- T-Commuter Rail (Fairmount Line)— from South Sta. to Uphams Corner and Morton St.
- BAT Bus 12 (Ashmont- Brockton.
- T-Bus 8 (Harbor Pt.-Kenmore).
- T-Bus 14 (Roslindale-Dudley).
- T-Bus 15 (Kane Sq.-Ruggles).
- T-Bus 16 (Forest Hills-JFK/UMass).
- T-Bus 17 (Fields Corner-Andrew).
- T-Bus 18 (Ashmont-Andrew).
- T-Bus 19 (Fields Corner-Ruggles, via Grove Hall).
- T-Bus 20 (Fields Corner-Neponset & Adams).
- T-Bus 21 (Ashmont-Forest Hills).

•T-Bus 22 (Ashmont-Ruggles, via Jackson Sq.).
•T-Bus 23 (Ashmont-Ruggles, via Dudley Sq.).
•T-Bus 26 (Norfolk St.-Ashmont).
•T-Bus 27 (Mattapan-Ashmont).
•T-Bus 28 (Mattapan-Ruggles).
•T-Bus 29 (Mattapan-Jackson Sq.).
•T-Bus 44 (Jackson Sq.-Ruggles, via Humboldt Ave.).
•T-Bus 45 (Franklin Park-Ruggles, via Grove Hall).
•T-Bus 210F (Fields Corner-Quincy Ctr.).
•T-Bus 215 (Quincy Ctr.-Ashmont).
•T-Bus 217 (Wollaston Beach-Ashmont).
•T-Bus 240 (Avon Line-Ashmont).
•T-Bus 240A (Crawford Sq.-Ashmont.).
Codman Sq.: T-Buses 22, 23, 26; or walk from Shawmut, 3 blocks.
Edward Everett Sq.: T-Buses 8, 16, 17; or walk from JFK/U.MASS., 4 blocks.
Four Corners: T-Bus 23.
Grove Hall: T-Buses 14, 19, 23, 28, 45.
Lower Mills: Mattapan Line (MILTON) and T-Buses 27, 217, 240, 240A.
Meeting House Hill: T-Buses 15, 17.
Neponset: T-Buses 20, 210F.
Uphams Corner: T-Buses 15, 16, 17; or walk from Commuter Rail, 3 blocks.

Dover
•Brush Hill (Boston-Milford), rush hour only. Serves Rt.109.
See **Needham** *for train service to Boston.*

Duxbury
•Plymouth & Brockton (Boston-Plymouth Ctr.)—from Park Plaza, Boston/Peter Pan and SOUTH STA. Serves Rt. 53.
•Plymouth & Brockton (Boston-S. Duxbury), rush hour only. Serves Millbrook, Snug Harbor, Hall's Corner, S. Duxbury.
•H. T. Drummond commuter vans.

East Boston
See also Logan Airport.
•Blue Line to MAVERICK, AIRPORT, WOOD ISLAND, ORIENT HTS., and SUFFOLK DOWNS.
•T-Bus 112 (Wellington-Maverick).
•T-Buses 116/117 (Wonderland-Maverick).
•T-Bus 120 (Orient Hts.-Maverick).
•T-Bus 121 (Wood Island-Maverick).
•T-Bus 400 (Lynn-Haymarket).
•T-Bus 455 (Salem-Haymarket, via Loring Ave.).

Eastham
•Plymouth & Brockton (Hyannis-Provincetown), *connects w/Boston buses at Hyannis.*

Easton
•Interstate (Boston-Middleborough), 1 trip Mon.-Fri.
•BAT Local bus from Brockton.
See **Stoughton** *for train service to Boston.*

Everett
•T-Bus 97 (Malden Ctr.-Wellington, via Hancock St.).
•T-Bus 99 (Upper Highland-Wellington).
•T-Bus 104 (Malden Ctr.-Sullivan, via Ferry St.).
•T-Bus 105 (Malden Ctr.-Sullivan, via Faulkner).
•T-Bus 106 (Lebanon St.-Wellington).
•T-Bus 109 (Linden Sq.-Sullivan).
•T-Bus 110 (Wonderland-Wellington).
•T-Bus 111 (Woodlawn-Haymarket).
•T-Bus 112 (Wellington-Maverick).
Everett Sq.: T-Buses 97, 104, 109, 110, 112.
Glendale Sq.: T-Buses 104, 109.
Main St.: T-Buses 99, 105, 106.

Fairhaven
•American Eagle from Boston/Peter Pan.
•SRTA local buses from New Bedford.

Fall River
•Bonanza (Boston-Newport, RI)—from BACK BAY STA. and Logan Airport.
•Bloom Bus, Fall River-Taunton.
•SRTA local buses.

Falmouth
See also Woods Hole.
•Bonanza (Boston-Woods Hole)—from BACK BAY STA. and Logan Airport.
•Bonanza from New York, NY.
•CCRTA (from Hyannis-Woods Hole).
•Island Queen—ferry to Martha's Vineyard, May-Oct.
See map, page 88.

The Fenway (Boston)
•Green Line-D (Riverside) to FENWAY and LONGWOOD.
•Green Line-E (Heath St.) to SYM-PHONY and stops along Huntington Ave.
•T-Bus 8 (Harbor Pt.-Kenmore).
•T-Bus 39 (Forest Hills-Back Bay Sta.).
•T-Bus 47 (Central-Albany St.).

Falmouth/Woods Hole

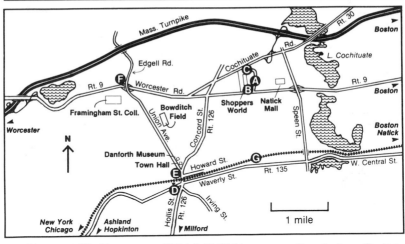

* to/from Boston
** to/from Logan Airport

Ⓐ Falmouth Station
Depot Ave.
508-548-7588
Bonanza to Boston &
New York
Peter Pan to Springfield
CCRTA
(Hyannis-Woods Hole)

Ⓑ Falmouth Harbor
Falmouth Heights Rd.
508-548-4800
Island Queen to Martha's
Vinyard (May-Oct.)

Ⓒ Woods Hole Terminal
508-548-3788 (ferry)
Steamship Authority to
Martha's Vinyard
(year-round)
Bonanza to Boston &
New York
CCRTA
(Hyannis-Woods Hole)

Framingham

Shoppers World
[The exact locations of "A","B" & "C"
will vary during Shoppers World
reconstruction]

Ⓐ Commuter Lot
Peter Pan: (ℙ)
—Boston-Framingham
express*
LIFT 2, 3 & 6
Natick Neighborhood Bus

Ⓑ Bus Shelter-Rt. 9
Peter Pan:
—Boston-Worcester, Rt. 9
local*
—Boston-Framingham
express* (some trips)
—Boston-Worcester
express* (some trips)

LIFT 1, 2, 3 & 6Natick
Neighborhood Bus
Gulbankian bus to Hudson

Ⓒ Massport Terminal (ℙ)
Logan Express**
Natick Neighborhood Bus

Downtown Framingham

Ⓓ Railroad Station (ℙ)
443 Waverly St.
T-Commuter Rail*
(Framingham Line)
Amtrak to New York & Chicago
LIFT 5 to Hopkinton

Ⓔ Concord & Howard Sts.
All LIFT routes

Ⓕ Framingham Center
Rt. 9 & Edgell Rd.
Peter Pan:
—Boston-Worcester,
Rt. 9 local*
—Boston-Framingham
express* (some trips)
—Boston-Worcester
express* (some trips)
LIFT 1, 2 & 3

Ⓖ West Natick station
Rt. 135 @ Boden Lane (ℙ)
T-Commuter Rail*
(Framingham Line)

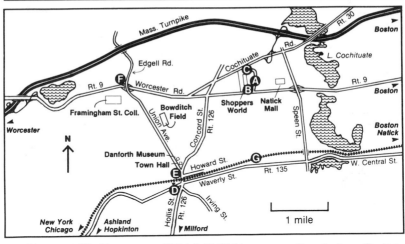

88

•T-Bus 55 (Queensberry St.-Park St.).
•T-Bus 60 (Chestnut Hill-Kenmore).
•T-Bus 65 (Brighton Ctr.-Kenmore).
•Peter Pan (Boston-Worcester, Rt. 9 local), stops at BRIGHAM CIRCLE. *See map, page 20.*

Fitchburg
•T-Commuter Rail (Fitchburg Line)— from NORTH STA and PORTER.
•Vermont Transit (Boston-Rutland, VT)—from SOUTH STA,Logan Airport, and RIVERSIDE to "Fitchburg Jct.," 3-4 trips daily.
•MART local buses.
P Main St. (Rt. 2A), E of Rt. 12 (downtown).

Fort Devens (Ayer)
•T-Commuter Rail (Fitchburg Line)— from NORTH STA. and PORTER to Ayer and Shirley.
•MART local bus from Leominster.

Fort Point Channel (South Boston)
•Red Line to SOUTH STA.
•T-Bus 3 (Chinatown-Marine Ind. Pk.).
•T-Bus 6 (Haymarket-Marine Ind. Pk.).
•T-Bus 7 (City Point-Otis & Summer).

Foxborough
•Bonanza (Logan Airport-Providence, RI). *This bus does not stop in down-town Boston.*
•Mass Limousine—from Logan Airport. *See Chapter 12 for service to Patriots games; Chapter 10 for service to concerts at Foxboro Stadium.*
See **Sharon** *for regular train service to Boston.*

Framingham
•T-Commuter Rail (Framingham Line)— from SOUTH STA. and BACK BAY STA.
•Peter Pan (Boston-Framingham, express)—from Boston/Peter Pan, Park Plaza, and Copley Sq.
•Peter Pan (Boston-Worcester, Rt. 9 local)—from Boston/Peter Pan, Park Plaza, Copley Sq., BRIGHAM CIR. and BROOKLINE VILLAGE.
•Logan Express—from Logan Airport.
•Amtrak—Trains to New York and Chicago stop at Framingham station.
•Gulbankian's (Framingham-Hudson), Sat. only.
•Natick Neighborhood Bus.
•LIFT local buses to Ashland, Holliston, Hopkinton and Milford.

Downtown Framingham: T-Commuter Rail; Amtrak; and all LIFT routes.
Framingham Ctr.: Peter Pan (express and local); LIFT 1, 2, and 3.
Shoppers World: Peter Pan (express and local); Logan Express; Crystal Transport; Gulbankian's; LIFT 1, 2, 3, 4 and 6; and Natick Neighborhood Bus.
Waterview: Peter Pan (express and local); LIFT 1.
P Rt. 135, W of Rt. 126 (downtown). Rt. 9 (Shoppers World).
See map, page 88

Franklin
•T-Commuter Rail (Franklin Line)— from SOUTH STA. and BACK BAY STA. to Franklin and Forge Park/495.
P Route 140, 1/2 mile W of I-495, exit 17 (Forge Park/495).

Gardner
•Vermont Transit (Boston-Rutland, VT)—from SOUTH STA, Logan Airport, and RIVERSIDE, 3-4 trips daily.
•MART local buses.

Georgetown
•The Coach Co. (Boston-Haverhill), rush hour only.

Gloucester
•T-Commuter Rail (Rockport Line)— from NORTH STA. to W. Gloucester and Gloucester.
•AC Cruises—from Boston/Pier 1 to Rocky Neck, summer only.
•CATA local buses.
See map, page 90.

Greenfield
•Peter Pan (Boston-Greenfield)—from Boston/Peter Pan.
•GMTA and FRTA local buses.

Groveland
•The Coach Co. (Boston-Haverhill), rush hour only. Serves So.Groveland.

Hamilton
•T-Commuter Rail (Ipswich Line)—from NORTH STA. to Hamilton/Wenham.

Hanover
•Plymouth & Brockton (Boston-Plymouth Ctr.)—from Park Plaza, Boston/Peter Pan. Serves Rt. 53, Hanover Mall.

Gloucester

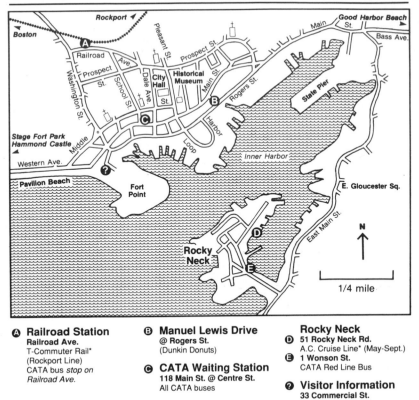

Ⓐ Railroad Station
Railroad Ave.
T-Commuter Rail*
(Rockport Line)
CATA bus *stop on
Railroad Ave.*

Ⓑ Manuel Lewis Drive
@ Rogers St.
(Dunkin Donuts)

Ⓒ CATA Waiting Station
118 Main St. @ Centre St.
All CATA buses

Rocky Neck
Ⓓ 51 Rocky Neck Rd.
A.C. Cruise Line* (May-Sept.)
Ⓔ 1 Wonson St.
CATA Red Line Bus

❓ Visitor Information
33 Commercial St.

Hyannis

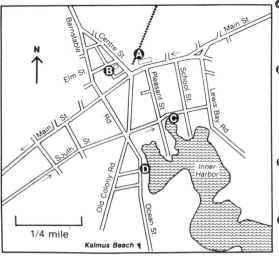

Ⓐ Railroad Station
252 Main St.
Amtrak to New York
(June-Sept.)
Cape Cod Scenic RR
excursions (June-Oct.)

Ⓑ Bus Terminal
Elm & Center Sts.
508-775-5524
Plymouth & Brockton to
Boston, Chatham &
Provincetown
Bonanza to New York
Peter Pan to Springfield
CCRTA (Hyannis-Woods Hole)

Ⓒ South St. Dock
508-771-4000
Steamship Authority to
Nantucket *(year-round)*
CCRTA (Hyannis-Woods Hole)

Ⓓ Ocean St. Dock
508-778-2600
Hy-Line to Nantucket &
Martha's Vineyard *(May-Oct.)*

90

•Plymouth & Brockton (Braintree-Marshfield)—from BRAINTREE (*Red Line*) to Hanover Mall, rush hour only.
•H. T. Drummond commuter vans.
🅿 Rt. 53 at Rt. 3, exit 13 (Hanover Mall).

Haverhill
•T-Commuter Rail (Haverhill Line)—from NORTH STA. to Bradford and Haverhill.
•The Coach Co. (Boston-Haverhill), rush hour only. Serves Bradford and Washington Sq.
•Flight Line—from Logan Airport.
•MVRTA local buses.

Hingham
•T-Commuter Boat—from Boston/Rowes Wharf.
•Plymouth & Brockton (Boston-Scituate)—from Park Plaza, Boston/Peter Pan and SOUTH STA. Serves Rt. 228, East St.
•T-Bus 220 (Quincy Ctr.-Hingham).
•T-Bus 220A (Hingham Loop).
•People Care-iers (Hingham-Hull), connects w/T-Bus 220 from QUINCY CTR..
See Rockland for service to Rt.3/228 interchange.

Holbrook
•T-Bus 230 (Quincy Ctr.-Holbrook).

Holliston
•*Lift 6 (Framingham-Milford), connects w/Boston buses and trains in Framingham.*

Holyoke
•Peter Pan (Boston-Amherst)—from Boston/Peter Pan and RIVERSIDE, 13 trips daily.
•PVTA—buses from Springfield.
•PVTA local buses.

Hopkinton
•LIFT 5 (Framingham-Hopkinton), *connects w/ T-Commuter Rail at Framingham.*

Hudson
•Gulbankian's (Boston-Hudson)—from Park Plaza and Copley Sq.
•Gulbankian's (Framingham-Hudson)—from Shoppers World, Sat. only.

Hull
•People Care-iers (Hingham-Hull), *connects w/T-Bus 220 at Hingham and with Bay State Cruise Co. ferry service at Point Pemberton.*

•Bay State Cruise Co. (Boston-Pemberton)—from Long Wharf, year-round, rush hour only.

Hyannis
•Plymouth & Brockton (Boston-Hyannis)—from Park Plaza, Boston/Peter Pan, and Logan Airport.
•Plymouth & Brockton (Hyannis-Provincetown).
•CCRTA (Hyannis-Woods Hole).
•Amtrak from New York, NY, summer only.
•Bonanza from New York, NY.
•Steamship Authority—ferry to Nantucket, year-round.
•Hy-Line—ferries to Nantucket and Martha's Vineyard, May-Oct.
See map, page 90.

Hyde Park (Boston)
See also Readville.
•T-Commuter Rail (Attleboro/Stoughton/Franklin Lines)—from SOUTH STA. and BACK BAY STA. to Hyde Park.
•T-Commuter Rail (Fairmount Line)—from SOUTH STA. to Fairmount.
•T-Bus 24 (Wakefield Ave.-Mattapan).
•T-Bus 32 (Wolcott Sq.-Forest Hills).
•T-Bus 33 (Dedham Line-Mattapan).
•T-Bus 40 (Georgetowne-Forest Hills).
•T-Bus 50 (Cleary Sq.-Forest Hills, via Roslindale).
Cleary Sq.: T-Buses 32, 33, 50; and T-Commuter Rail (Hyde Park).
From Boston: Orange Line or T-Bus 39 to FOREST HILLS, then T-Bus 32; or T-Commuter Rail.

Ipswich
•T-Commuter Rail (Ipswich Line)—from NORTH STA.
•The Coach Co. (Boston-Newburyport), rush hour only. Serves Rt.1.
🅿 Topsfield Rd., S of Market St., off Rt. 1A.

Jamaica Plain (Boston)
•Orange Line to JACKSON SQ., STONY BROOK, GREEN, and FOREST HILLS.
•Green Line-E (Heath St.), serves S. Huntington Ave.
•T-Bus 39 (Forest Hills-Back Bay Sta.), serves S. Huntington Ave., Centre St., South St.
•T-Commuter Rail (Needham Line)—from SOUTH STA. and BACK BAY STA. to FOREST HILLS.
•T-Bus 38 (Wren St.-Forest Hills).
•T-Bus 41 (Centre & Eliot Sts.-Dudley).

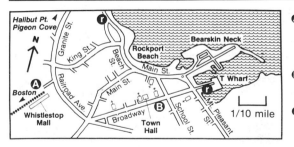

Lowell

City Hall
Whistler House
Merrimack St.
Paige
Bridge St.
Market St.
Broadway
Worthen St.
Dutton St.
Market Mills
National Park HQ
Quilt Museum
Pawtucket Canal
Fletcher St.
Prescott St.
Central St.
George
Middlesex St.
Church St.
Appleton St.
Summer St.
Gorham St.
Thorndike St.
South Common
Highland St.
Court House
Boston ◀
1/10 mile
N ↑

Ⓐ Gallagher Terminal
145 Thorndyke St.
508-459-7101
T-Commuter Rail*
(Lowell Line)
Vermont Transit* **
Greyhound
Peter Pan
LRTA Downtown Shuttle

Ⓑ LRTA Transit Center
Paige & Merrimack Sts.
All LRTA buses
MVRTA to Lawrence

Ⓒ Lowell Sheraton
Hudson Airporter**
M & L Transportation**
LRTA Downtown Shuttle

Ⓣ Lowell Natl. Park
trolley stops

❓ Visitor Information
246 Market St.
National Park Service tours

New Bedford

Middle St.
Elm St.
City Hall
William St.
Glass Museum
Whaling Museum
Seamen's Bethel
Union St.
Spring St.
Zeiterion Theatre
School St.
Sixth St.
Pleasant St.
Purchase St.
Acushnet Ave
Second St.
Johnny Cake Hill
Water St.
Kennedy Hwy.
Front St.
Acushnet River
Pier 3 Ⓒ
State Pier
N ↑
1/10 mile

Ⓐ SRTA Terminal
Elm & Pleasant Sts.
508-990-0000
American Eagle*
Bonanza
All SRTA Buses

Ⓑ Elm St. Garage
Shuttle buses to
Billy Woods Warf

Ⓒ Pier 3
Cuttyhunk Boat

Ⓓ Billy Woods Warf
Cove Rd.
1 1/4 mi. south of downtown
Cape Island Express to
Martha's Vinyard (May-Oct.)
Shuttle bus from
Elm St. Garage

❓ Visitor Information
47 N. Second St.

Rockport

Halibut Pt. ◀
Pigeon Cove
N ↑
Granite St.
King St.
Beach St.
Rockport Beach
Main St.
Bearskin Neck
T Wharf
Railroad Ave.
Main St.
Boston
Whistlestop Mall
Broadway
Town Hall
School St.
Mt. Pleasant St.
1/10 mile

Ⓐ Railroad Station
T-Commuter Rail*
(Rockport Line)
CATA Blue Line bus *on
Railroad Ave.*

Ⓑ Richdale Store
21 Broadway
All CATA buses

🅡 Public Rest Rooms

• T-Bus 42 (Forest Hills-Ruggles).
• T-Bus 46 (Heath St.-Dudley).
• T-Bus 48 (Jamaica Plain Loop).
Centre St./The Monument: T-Buses 38, 39, 41, 48.
Washington St.: T-Bus 42; and Orange Line (GREEN, FOREST HILLS).
See Orange Line map for other buses to FOREST HILLS

Kingston
• Plymouth & Brockton (Boston-Plymouth Ctr.)—from Park Plaza, Boston/Peter Pan and SOUTH STA.
• H. T. Drummond commuter vans.
• Green Harbor Transp.—from Logan Airport to Howard Johnson's.

Lawrence
• T-Commuter Rail (Haverhill Line)—from NORTH STA.
• Trombly (Boston-Andover)—from Park Plaza and Essex St, rush hour only.
• Flight Line—from Logan Airport.
• MVRTA local buses.

Lee
• Peter Pan (Boston-Albany, NY)—from Boston/Peter Pan and RIVERSIDE, 5 trips daily.
• Greyhound (Boston-Albany, NY)—from SOUTH STA. and RIVERSIDE, 1 trip daily.
• BRTA local bus.

Lenox
• Peter Pan (Boston-Bennington, VT)—from Boston/Peter Pan and RIVER-SIDE, 1 trip daily.
• BRTA local bus.

Leominster
• T-Commuter Rail (Fitchburg Line)—from NORTH STA. and PORTER to N. Leominster.
• Vermont Transit (Boston-Rutland, VT)—from SOUTH STA., Logan Airport, and RIVERSIDE to "Fitchburg Jct.," 3-4 trips daily.
• MART local buses.

Lexington
• T-Bus 62 (Bedford-Alewife).
• T-Bus 76 (Hanscom Field-Alewife).
• Lexpress local buses.
• 128 Transportation Council shuttle from ALEWIFE (*Red Line*) to participating employers.

Lincoln
• T-Commuter Rail (Fitchburg Line)—from NORTH STA.
🅿 Lincoln Rd., N of Route 117.

Littleton
• T-Commuter Rail (Fitchburg Line)—from NORTH STA. to Littleton/495.
• Yankee Line (Boston-Littleton), rush hour only.

Logan Airport
Service from downtown Boston and Back Bay:
• Blue Line to AIRPORT.
• Airport Water Shuttle—from Rowes Wharf.
• City Transp.—from downtown and Back Bay hotels.
• Peter Pan—from Boston/Peter Pan.
Other Logan Airport service is listed by city or town in this chapter.

Lowell
• T-Commuter Rail (Lowell Line)—from NORTH STA.
• Vermont Transit (Boston-White River Jct.-Burlington, VT)—from SOUTH STA. and Logan Airport, 4 trips daily.
• Flight Line—from Logan Airport.
• M & L Transp.—from Logan Airport.
• MVRTA local bus from Lawrence.
• LRTA local buses.
🅿 145 Thorndike St. (Route 3A).

Lynn
• T-Commuter Rail (Rockport/Ipswich Line)—from NORTH STA. to Lynn/Central Sq. and GE River Works.
• T-Bus 426 (Lynn-Haymarket, via Cliftondale).
• T-Bus 429 (Lynn-N. Saugus).
• T-Bus 433 (Lynn-Pine Hill).
• T-Bus 435 (Lynn-Danvers).
• T-Bus 436 (Lynn-Goodwins Cir.).
• T-Bus 436 (Haymarket-Goodwins Cir.), rush hour only.
• T-Bus 437 (Lynn-Lake Shore Park).
• T-Bus 439 (Lynn-Nahant).
• T-Buses 441/442 (Marblehead-Haymarket).
• T-Bus 450 (Salem-Haymarket, via Western Ave.)
• T-Bus 455 (Salem-Haymarket, via Loring Ave).
• Lynn East/West Loop local buses.
Central Sq.: all of the above buses and trains except T-Bus 450.

West Lynn: T-Buses 426, 450 and West Lynn Loop.
From Boston: T-Bus 450 from HAYMARKET or T-Commuter Rail from NORTH STA.
🅿 Broad St. (Rt. 1A) and Market St. (downtown garage).

Lynnfield
• The Coach Company (Boston-Newburyport, Boston -Plaistow, NH) rush hour only. Some trips serve Logan Airport.
• T-Bus 436 (Lynn-Goodwins Cir.).
• T-Bus 436 (Haymarket-Goodwins Cir.), rush hour only.

Malden
• Orange Line to MALDEN CTR. and OAK GROVE.
• T-Commuter Rail (Reading/Haverhill Line), stops at MALDEN CTR.
• T-Bus 97 (Malden Ctr.-Wellington), serves Commercial St.
• T-Bus 99 (Upper Highland-Wellington).
• T-Bus 101 (Malden Ctr.-Sullivan, via Medford Sq.), serves Pleasant St.
• T-Bus 104 (Malden Ctr.-Sullivan, via Ferry St.).
• T-Bus 105 (Malden Ctr.-Sullivan, via Faulkner).
• T-Bus 106 (Lebanon St.-Wellington).
• T-Bus 108 (Linden Sq.-Wellington), serves Highland Ave.
• T-Bus 109 (Linden Sq.-Sullivan).
• T-Bus 119 (Northgate-Beachmont).
• T-Bus 130 (Lebanon St./Melrose-Malden Ctr.).
• T-Bus 130A (Wyoming Sq.-Malden Ctr.).
• T-Bus 131 (Melrose Highlands-Malden Ctr.).
• T-Buses 136/137 (Reading-Malden Ctr.).
• T-Bus 411 (Revere House-Malden Ctr.).
• T-Bus 426 (Lynn-Haymarket, via Cliftondale).
• T-Bus 426 (Granada Highlands-Haymarket), rush hour only.
• T-Bus 430 (Saugus-Malden Ctr.).
Granada Highlands: T-Bus 411; also T-Bus 426 in rush hour.
Linden Sq.: T-Buses 108, 109, 119, 411, 426.
Main St.: T-Buses 99, 106 (south of Malden Sq.); T-Buses 130, 131, 136, 137 (north of Malden Sq.).
Maplewood Sq./Salem St.: T-Buses 106, 108, 411, 430.
🅿 Entrance from Main St. at Malden/Melrose line or from Winter St. E of Washington St. (OAK GROVE).

Manchester-by-the-Sea
• T-Commuter Rail (Rockport Line)—from NORTH STA.

Mansfield
• T-Commuter Rail (Attleboro Line)—from SOUTH STA. and BACK BAY STA.
• Mass Limousine—from Logan Airport.
See Chapter 10 for service to Great Woods
🅿 Crocker St., off Main St., 1 block N of Route of Rt. 106 (downtown).

Marblehead
• T-Bus 441 (Marblehead-Haymarket, via Paradise Rd.).
• T-Bus 442 (Marblehead-Haymarket, via Humphrey St.).
*See **Swampscott** for train service to Boston.*

Marlborough
• Cavalier Coach (Boston-Northborough), 1 rush hour trip. Serves Rt. 20.
• Gulbankian's (Boston-Hudson)—from Park Plaza and Copley Sq.
• Gulbankian's (Framingham-Hudson)—from Shoppers World, Sat. only.

Marshfield
• Plymouth & Brockton (Boston-S. Duxbury), rush hour only. Serves Furnace Brook School., Marshfield Ctr., Brant Rock, Green Harbor.
• Plymouth & Brockton (Braintree-Marshfield)—from BRAINTREE *(Red Line)* to Furnace Brook Schl., rush hour only.
• H. T. Drummond commuter vans.
*See **Pembroke** for service to Rt.3/139 interchange.*

Martha's Vineyard
Ferries to Vineyard Haven:
• Steamship Authority—from Woods Hole, year-round.
• Cape Island Express—from New Bedford, May-Oct.
Ferries to Oak Bluffs:
• Steamship Authority—from Woods Hole, May-Sept.
• Island Queen—from Falmouth, May-Oct.
• Hy-Line—from Hyannis, May-Oct.
• Hy-Line—from Nantucket, June-Sept.
Service on the island:
• Island Transport and Martha's Vineyard Transportation Services local buses, summer only.

•VTA local buses, summer only.
•Chappaquiddick Ferry—from Edgartown to Chappaquiddick, year-round, frequent service, daily.

Mattapan (Boston)
•Red Line (Mattapan) to MATTAPAN.
•T-Commuter Rail (Fairmount Line)—from SOUTH STA. to Morton St.
•T-Bus 21 (Ashmont-Forest Hills).
•T-Bus 24 (Wakefield Ave.-Mattapan).
•T-Bus 26 (Norfolk St.-Ashmont).
•T-Bus 27 (Mattapan-Ashmont).
•T-Bus 28 (Mattapan-Ruggles).
•T-Bus 29 (Mattapan-Jackson Sq.).
•T-Bus 30 (Mattapan-Roslindale).
•T-Bus 31 (Mattapan-Forest Hills).
•T-Bus 33 (Mattapan-Dedham Line).
•Hudson Bus (Mattapan-Canton).
Mattapan Sq.: Red Line; T-Buses 24, 27, 28, 29, 30, 31, 33, and Hudson Bus.
From Boston: Red Line; or: Orange Line to FOREST HILLS, then T-Bus 31; or: Orange Line to RUGGLES, then T-Bus 28.

Maynard
See Acton and Concord for train service to Boston.

Medfield
•Brush Hill (Boston-Milford), rush hour only.

Medford
•Orange Line to WELLINGTON.
•T-Commuter Rail (Lowell Line)—from NORTH STA. to W. Medford.
•T-Express Bus 325 (Elm St.-Haymarket), rush hour only.
•T-Express Bus 326 (W. Medford-Haymarket), rush hour only.
•T-Bus 80 (Arlington Ctr.-Lechmere, via Medford Hillside).
•T-Bus 90 (Davis-Wellington).
•T-Bus 94 (Medford Sq.-Davis).
•T-Bus 95 (W. Medford-Sullivan).
•T-Bus 96 (Medford Sq.-Harvard).
•T-Bus 99 (Upper Highland-Wellington).
•T-Bus 100 (Elm St.-Wellington).
•T-Bus 101 (Malden Ctr.-Sullivan, via Medford Sq.).
•T-Bus 108 (Linden Sq.-Wellington).
•T-Bus 134 (N. Woburn-Wellington).
•T-Bus 134A (Medford-Wellington).
•Hudson Bus (Meadow Glen Mall-Fulton St.).
Fellsway: T-Buses 100, 325.
Medford Hillside:T-Buses 80, 94, 96.

Medford Sq.:T-Buses 94, 95, 96, 101, 134, 134A, 326.
W. Medford:T-Commuter Rail; T-Buses 80, 94, 95, 326.
🅿Revere Beach Pkwy. (Route 16) E. of Route 28 (Wellington).

Medway
•Brush Hill (Boston-Milford), rush hour only. Serves W. Medway.

Melrose
•T-Commuter Rail (Reading/Haverhill Line)—from NORTH STA. to Wyoming Hill, Melrose/Cedar Park, and Melrose Highlands.
•T-Bus 130 (Lebanon St./Melrose-Malden Ctr.).
•T-Bus 130A (Wyoming Sq.-Malden Ctr.).
•T-Bus 131 (Melrose Hlnds-Malden Ctr.).
•T-Buses 136/137 (Reading-Malden Ctr.).

Methuen
•MVRTA local buses from Lawrence, Lowell, and Haverhill.
•Flight Line—from Logan Airport.
See Lawrence for train service to Boston.

Middleborough
•Interstate (Boston-Middleborough)—from Park Plaza and SOUTH STA.
•Mass Limousine—from Logan Airport.

Milford
•Brush Hill (Boston-Milford), rush hour only.
•LIFT 6 (Framingham-Milford), *connects w/Boston buses and trains in Framingham.*

Millbury
•Peter Pan (Boston-Worcester, express)—from Boston/Peter Pan.
•WRTA local buses from Worcester.

Millis
•Brush Hill (Boston-Milford), rush hour only.

Milton
•Red Line (Mattapan) to MILTON, CENTRAL AVE, VALLEY RD. and CAPEN ST.
•Hudson Bus (Mattapan-Canton)—from MATTAPAN (Red Line).
•T-Bus 215 (Quincy Ctr.-Ashmont).
•T-Bus 217 (Wollaston Beach-Ashmont).
•T-Bus 240 (Avon line-Ashmont).
•T-Bus 240A (Crawford Sq.-Ashmont).
•T-Bus 245 (Quincy Ctr.-Mattapan).
•BAT local bus from Brockton.
Blue Hill Ave.: Hudson Bus.
E. Milton Sq.: T-Buses 215, 217, 245.

Newton Corner/Watertown Sq.

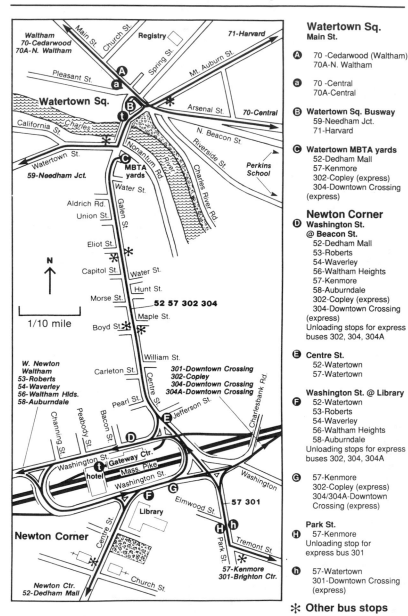

Watertown Sq.
Main St.

Ⓐ   70 -Cedarwood (Waltham)
      70A-N. Waltham

ⓐ   70 -Central
      70A-Central

Ⓑ **Watertown Sq. Busway**
      59-Needham Jct.
      71-Harvard

Ⓒ **Watertown MBTA yards**
      52-Dedham Mall
      57-Kenmore
      302-Copley (express)
      304-Downtown Crossing
(express)

Newton Corner
Ⓓ **Washington St.**
@ Beacon St.
      52-Dedham Mall
      53-Roberts
      54-Waverley
      56-Waltham Heights
      57-Kenmore
      58-Auburndale
      302-Copley (express)
      304-Downtown Crossing
(express)
Unloading stops for express
buses 302, 304, 304A

Ⓔ **Centre St.**
      52-Watertown
      57-Watertown

Washington St. @ Library
Ⓕ   52-Watertown
      53-Roberts
      54-Waverley
      56-Waltham Heights
      58-Auburndale
Unloading stops for express
buses 302, 304, 304A

Ⓖ   57-Kenmore
      302-Copley (express)
      304/304A-Downtown
      Crossing (express)

Park St.
Ⓗ   57-Kenmore
      Unloading stop for
      express bus 301

ⓗ   57-Watertown
      301-Downtown Crossing
(express)

✳ **Other bus stops**

❶ **Taxi Stands**

Milton Village:Red Line; T-Buses 217, 240, 240A; BAT.
Town Ctr.:T-Buses 240, 240A, 245.

Mission Hill (Boston)
• Green Line-E (Heath St.), serves Huntington Ave., S. Huntington Ave.
• Orange Line to ROXBURY CROSS ING.
• T-Bus 39 (Forest Hills-Back Bay Sta.).
• T-Bus 66 (Harvard-Dudley, via Brookline).
• Peter Pan (Boston-Worcester, Rt. 9 local), stops at BRIGHAM CIR.
• Mission Hill Link Bus.

Nahant
• T-Bus 439 (Lynn-Nahant). Through service from Haymarket on most trips.
See Lynn for train service to Boston.

Nantasket
See Hull.

Nantucket
• Steamship Authority—ferry from Hyannis, year-round.
• Hy-Line—ferry from Hyannis, May-Oct.
• Hy-Line—ferry from Martha's Vineyard, June-Sept.
• Barrett's Tours local buses, Summer only.

Natick
• T-Commuter Rail (Framingham Line)—from SOUTH STA. and BACK BAY STA. to Natick and W. Natick.
• Peter Pan (Boston-Worcester, Rt. 9 local)—from Boston/Peter Pan, Park Plaza, Copley Sq., and BRIGHAM CIRCLE.
• Natick Neighborhood Bus.
• LIFT local buses from Framingham to Rt.9 malls.

Needham
• T-Commuter Rail (Needham Line)— from SOUTH STA. and BACK BAY STA. to Hersey (Birds Hill), Needham Jct., Needham Ctr., and Needham Hts.
• T-Bus 59 (Needham Jct.-Watertown), via Newton Highlands.
🅿 Chestnut St., 1/2 mile S of Route 135 (Needham Jct.); Great Plain Ave. (Rt. 135, 3/4 mile W of Route 128/I-95, exit 18 (Hersey).

New Bedford
• American Eagle (Boston-New Bedford)—from Boston/Peter Pan.

• Cape Island Express—ferry to Martha's Vineyard, May-Oct.
• Cuttyhunk Boat—ferry to Cuttyhunk I.
• SRTA local buses.
🅿 Elm and Pleasant Sts. (downtown); U.S. 6 at Rt. 140 exit 1; Kings Hwy at Rt. 140 exit 4.
See map, page 92.

Newbury
Also see Byfield.
• The Coach Co. (Boston-Newburyport), rush hour only.

Newburyport
• C & J Trailways (Boston-Durham, NH)—from Boston/Peter Pan, 13 trips daily. *(Some trips serve Logan Airport)*
• Vermont Transit (Boston-Portland, ME-Bangor, ME)—from SOUTH STA., 2 trips daily.
• The Coach Co. (Boston-Amesbury, Boston-Newburyport) rush hour only.
• MVRTA (Haverhill-Newburyport).
Downtown: The Coach Co. (Boston-Newburyport); and MVRTA.
🅿 Rt. 113, east of I-95, exit 57.

Newton
• Newton is served by Green Line-D, T-Commuter Rail (Framingham Line), T-Express Buses, Peter Pan (Boston-Worcester, Rt. 9 local),Peter Pan, Greyhound and Vermont Transit intercity buses. For more information, see the following neighborhoods: Auburndale; Chestnut Hill; Newton Centre; Newton Corner; Newton Highlands; Newton Upper Falls; Newtonville; Nonantum; Riverside; West Newton.

Newton Centre
• Green Line-D (Riverside) to NEWTON CENTRE.
• T-Bus 52 (Dedham Mall-Watertown).

Newton Corner
• T-Express Bus 301 (Brighton Ctr.-Downtown).
• T-Express Bus 302 (Watertown-Copley).
• T-Express Bus 304 (Watertown-Downtown).
• T-Express Bus 304A (Newton Corner-Downtown), through service to Roberts and Waverley.
• T-Bus 52 (Dedham Mall-Watertown).
• T-Bus 53 (Roberts-Newton Corner)
• T-Bus 54 (Waverley-Newton Corner), via Waltham.

•T-Bus 56 (Waltham Highlands-Newton
Corner).
•T-Bus 57 (Watertown-Kenmore).
•T-Bus 58 (Auburndale-Newton
Corner), via Waltham.
From Boston: Green Line to
KENMORE, then T-Bus 57; or any T-
Express Bus.
See map page 96.

Newton Highlands
•Green Line-D (Riverside) to NEWTON
HIGHLANDS and ELIOT.
•T-Bus 52 (Dedham Mall-Watertown).
•T-Bus 59 (Needham Jct.-Watertown).
•T-Bus 59A (Needham St.-Watertown).
•Peter Pan (Boston-Worcester, Rt. 9
local)—from Boston/Peter Pan, Park
Plaza, Copley Sq., and Brigham Cir.

Newton Upper Falls
•T-Bus 59 (Needham Jct.-Watertown).
•Peter Pan (Boston-Worcester, Rt. 9
local)—from Boston/Peter Pan, Park
Plaza, Copley Sq., and BRIGHAM
CIRCLE.

Newtonville
•T-Commuter Rail (Framingham Line)—
from SOUTH STA. and BACK BAY STA.
•T-Bus 53 (Roberts-Newton Corner-
Downtown).
•T-Bus 54 (Waverley-Newton Corner-
Downtown).
•T-Bus 56 (Waltham Highlands-Newton
Corner-Downtown).
•T-Bus 59 (Needham Jct.-Watertown).

Nonantum (Newton)
•T-Bus 56 (Waltham Highlands-Newton
Corner-Downtown).
•T-Bus 58 (Auburndale-Newton Corner-
Downtown).
•T-Bus 59 (Needham Jct - Watertown).

Norfolk
•T-Commuter Rail (Franklin Line)—
from SOUTH STA. and BACK BAY
STA.

North Adams
•Peter Pan (Boston-Bennington, VT)—
from Boston/Peter Pan and RIVER-
SIDE.
•BRTA local buses.

Northampton
•Peter Pan (Boston-Amherst)—from
Boston/Peter Pan and RIVERSIDE.
•PVTA local buses.

North Andover
*See **Andover** and **Lawrence** for train
service to Boston.*

Northborough
•Peter Pan (Boston-Worcester, Rt. 9
local)—from Boston/Peter Pan, Park
Plaza, Copley Sq., and BRIGHAM
CIRCLE.
•Cavalier Coach (Boston-
Northborough), 1 rush hour trip.
Serves Rt.20.

North End (Boston)
•Green and Orange lines to
HAYMARKET.
•T-Bus 6 (Marine Ind. Pk.-Haymarket).
*See Green Line map on page 119 for
other buses at HAYMARKET.*

Norton
•GATRA local bus from Attleboro and
Taunton, *connects w/T-Commuter Rail
at Attleboro.*

Norwell
•Plymouth & Brockton (Boston-Plymouth
Ctr.)—from Park Plaza, Boston/Peter
Pan and SOUTH STA., serves Rt. 53.

Norwood
•T-Commuter Rail (Franklin Line)—
from SOUTH STA. and BACK BAY
STA. to Norwood Depot, Norwood
Central, and Windsor Gardens.
•T-Bus 34E (Walpole Ctr.-Forest Hills).

Orleans
•Plymouth & Brockton (Hyannis-
Provincetown), *connects w/Boston
buses at Hyannis.*

Otis A.F.B. (Bourne)
•Bonanza (Boston-Woods Hole)—from
BACK BAY STA. and Logan Airport.

Palmer
•Peter Pan (Boston-Springfield)—from
Boston/Peter Pan and RIVERSIDE, 4
trips daily.

Peabody
•T-Bus 435 (Lynn-Danvers).
•T-Bus 458 (Salem-Danvers).
•T-Bus 458 (Danvers-Haymarket), rush
hour only.
•Michaud (Lake Shore-Northshore•T-
Shopping Ctr.).
•Michaud (Salem-Northshore Shop. Ctr.).

Pembroke
• Plymouth & Brockton (Boston-Plymouth Ctr.)—from Park Plaza, Boston/Peter Pan and SOUTH STA. Serves Rt. 53.
• Plymouth & Brockton (Boston-Pembroke Ctr.), rush hour only.
• II. T. Drummond commuter vans.
• Green Harbor Transp.—from Logan Airport to Rts. 3/139.

Pittsfield
• Peter Pan (Boston-Albany, NY)—from Boston/Peter Pan and RIVERSIDE, 5 trips daily.
• Greyhound (Boston-Albany, NY)—from Park Plaza, Boston/Peter Pan and RIVERSIDE, 1 trip daily.
• Amtrak (Lake Shore Ltd.)—from SOUTH STA., BACK BAY STA. and Framingham, 1 trip daily.
• BRTA local buses.

Plymouth
• Plymouth & Brockton (Boston-Hyannis)—from Park Plaza, Boston/Peter Pan and Logan Airport.Express, stops at N. Plymouth (Industrial Park). Seasonal connecting service to Plymouth Ctr.
• Plymouth & Brockton (Boston-Plymouth Ctr.)—from Park Plaza, Boston/Peter Pan and SOUTH STA. Local via Rt.53, Plymouth Ctr.
• H. T. Drummond commuter vans.
• Green Harbor Transp.—from Logan Airport.

Providence, RI
• Amtrak or T-Commuter Rail—from SOUTH STA. and BACK BAY STA.
• Bonanza bus from BACK BAY STA.
• Greyhound bus from SOUTH STA.
• RIPTA buses
🅿 Gaspee St., opposite State House; parking off Canal St. (downtown); 1 Bonanza Way, off Cemetery St., off North Main St. (north).
See map, page 106.

Provincetown
• Bay State Cruise Co.—from Boston/Commonwealth Pier, summer only.
• Plymouth & Brockton (Hyannis-Provincetown), connects w/Boston buses at Hyannis.
• Lower Cape Bus—local bus in summer.

Quincy
• Red Line (Braintree) to N. QUINCY, WOLLASTON, QUINCY CTR., and QUINCY ADAMS.
• T-Bus 210 (Quincy Ctr.-N. Quincy)
• T-Bus 210F (Quincy Ctr.-Fields Corner), via N. QUINCY, rush hour only.
• T-Bus 211 (Quincy Ctr.-Squantum).
• T-Bus 212 (Quincy Ctr.-N. Quincy, via Billings Rd.).
• T-Bus 214 (Quincy Ctr.-Germantown).
• T-Bus 215 (Quincy Ctr.-Ashmont).
• T-Bus 216 (Quincy Ctr.-Houghs Neck).
• T-Bus 217 (Wollaston Beach-Ashmont).
• T-Bus 220 (Quincy Ctr.-Hingham).
• T-Bus 221 (Quincy Ctr.-Fort Point).
• T-Bus 222 (Quincy Ctr.-E. Weymouth).
• T-Bus 225 (Quincy Ctr.-Weymouth Landing).
• T-Bus 230 (Quincy Ctr.-Holbrook).
• T-Bus 236 (Quincy Ctr.-South Shore Plaza, via E. Braintree).
• T-Bus 238 (Quincy Ctr.-Crawford Sq.).
• T-Bus 245 (Quincy Ctr.-Mattapan).

Randolph
• T-Bus 238 (Quincy Ctr.-Crawford Sq.).
• T-Bus 240 (Avon line-Ashmont).
• T-Bus 240A (Crawford Sq.-Ashmont).
• BAT local bus from Brockton.

Raynham
• Bloom (Boston-Taunton)—from Boston/Peter Pan.

Reading
• T-Commuter Rail (Reading/Haverhill Line)—from NORTH STA.
• T-Bus 136 (Reading-Malden Ctr., via Lakeside).
• T-Bus 137 (Reading-Malden Ctr., via North Ave.).

Readville (Hyde Park)
• T-Commuter Rail (Franklin Line)—from SOUTH STA. and BACK BAY STA.
• T-Commuter Rail (Fairmount Line)—from SOUTH STA.
• T-Bus 32 (Wolcott Sq.-Forest Hills).
• T-Bus 33 (Dedham Line-Mattapan).

Revere
• Blue Line to SUFFOLK DOWNS, BEACHMONT, REVERE BEACH and WONDERLAND.
• T-Bus 110 (Wonderland-Wellington).
• T-Bus 116 (Wonderland-Maverick, via Revere St.).
• T-Bus 117 (Wonderland-Maverick, via Beach St.).

•T-Bus 119 (Northgate-Beachmont).
•T-Bus 400 (Lynn-Haymarket, via Lynn Common), serves American Legion Hwy.
•T-Bus 411 (Revere House-Malden Ctr.).
•T-Bus 426 (Lynn-Haymarket, via Cliftondale), serves Salem St.
•T-Buses 441/442 (Marblehead-Haymarket).
•T-Bus 450 (Salem-Haymarket, via Western Ave.), serves American Legion Hwy.
Bus 455 (Salem-Haymarket, via Loring Ave.).
Revere Ctr.:T-Buses 110, 116, 117, 119, 411.
🅿 Rt. 1A, N. of Bell Circle, Rt.60 (Wonderland).

Riverside (Newton)
•Green Line-D (Riverside) to RIVERSIDE.
•T-Express Bus 300 (Riverside-Downtown).
•T-Bus 353A (Burlington Ind. Area-Dudley), via Waltham.
•Greyhound to New York, NY, Islip, NY, and Albany, NY.
•Vermont Transit to Rutland, VT.
•Peter Pan to New York, NY, Albany, NY, Springfield, Amherst, and Worcester.
🅿 Grove St. at Rt. 128/I-95 exit 22.

Rockland
•Carey's (Boston-Whitman), 1 rush hour trip.
•Plymouth & Brockton (several routes)—from Park Plaza, Boston/ Peter Pan and SOUTH STA. to Rts. 3 & 228, frequent service Mon-Fri.
•H. T. Drummond commuter vans.
•Green Harbor Transp.—from Logan Airport to Rt.228 hotels.
🅿 Rt. 228 at Rt. 3, exit 14, on Hingham/Norwell line.

Rockport
•T-Commuter Rail (Rockport Line)— from NORTH STA.
•CATA local buses.
See map, page 92.

Roslindale (Boston)
•T-Commuter Rail (Needham Line)— from SOUTH STA. and BACK BAY STA.
•T-Bus 14 (Roslindale-Dudley).
•T-Bus 30 (Mattapan-Roslindale).

•T-Bus 32 (Wolcott Sq.-Forest Hills), serves Hyde Park Ave.
•T-Bus 34 (Dedham Line-Forest Hills).
•T-Bus 34E (Walpole Ctr.-Forest Hills).
•T-Bus 35 (Dedham Mall-Forest Hills, via Stimson).
•T-Bus 36 (Charles River-Forest Hills).
•T-Bus 36A (V.A. Hospital-Forest Hills).
•T-Bus 37 (Baker & Vermont-Forest Hills).
•T-Bus 38 (Wren St.-Forest Hills).
•T-Bus 40 (Georgetowne-Forest Hills).
•T-Bus 50 (Cleary Sq.-Forest Hills, via Roslindale).
•T-Bus 51 (Cleveland Cir.-Forest Hills).
*Roslindale Sq.:*T-Commuter Rail; and all of the above T-Buses *except* 32 and 38.
From Downtown Boston: Orange Line T-Bus 39 to FOREST HILLS; then any of the T-Buses; or T-Commuter. Rail.

Rowley
•The Coach Co. (Boston-Newburyport), 1 rush hour trip. Serves Rt.1.
See Ipswich for train service to Boston.

Roxbury (Boston)
See also Mission Hill and West Roxbury.
•Orange Line to RUGGLES, ROXBURY CROSSING and JACKSON SQ.
•T-Bus 1 (Harvard-Dudley, via Mass. Ave.).
•T-Bus 8 (Harbor Pt.-Kenmore).
•T-Bus 14 (Roslindale-Dudley).
•T-Bus 15 (Kane Sq.-Ruggles).
•T-Bus 19 (Fields Corner-Ruggles, via Grove Hall).
•T-Bus 22 (Ashmont-Ruggles, via Jackson Sq.).
•T-Bus 23 (Ashmont-Ruggles, via Dudley Sq.).
•T-Bus 28 (Mattapan-Ruggles).
•T-Bus 29 (Mattapan- Jackson Sq.).
•T-Bus 41 (Centre & Eliot Sts.-Dudley).
•T-Bus 42 (Forest Hills-Ruggles).
•T-Bus 44 (Jackson Sq.-Ruggles, via Humboldt Ave.).
•T-Bus 45 (Franklin Park-Ruggles, via Grove Hall), serves Blue Hill Ave.
•T-Bus 46 (Heath St.-Dudley).
•T-Bus 47 (Central-Albany St.).
•T-Bus 48 (Jamaica Plain Loop).
•T-Bus 49 (Dudley-Downtown).
•T-Bus 66 (Harvard-Dudley, via Brookline).
•T-Bus 353A (Burlington Ind. Area-Dudley), via Waltham.
Dudley Sq.: T-Buses 1, 8, 14, 15, 19, 23, 28, 41, 42, 44, 45, 46, 47, 49, 66, 353A.

From Boston: T-Bus 49 from Downtown; or: Orange Line to Mass. Ave., then T-Bus 1 (free transfer); or: Orange Line to RUGGLES, then T-Bus 8, 15, 19, 23, 28, 42, 44, 45, or 47.
Egleston Sq.: T-Buses 22, 29, 42, 44.
Warren St.: T-Buses 19, 23, 28.

Sagamore
• Plymouth & Brockton (Boston-Hyannis)—from Park Plaza, Boston/Peter Pan and Logan Airport.
🅿 at rotary, Rt. 3, exit 1.

Salem
• T-Commuter Rail (Rockport/Ipswich Line)—from NORTH STA.
• T-Bus 450 (Salem-Haymarket, via Western Ave.).
• T-Bus 451 (N. Beverly-Salem).
• T-Bus 455 (Salem-Haymarket, via Loring Ave.).
• T-Bus 458 (Salem-Danvers).
• Michaud (Salem Belt Line).
• Michaud (Salem-Northshore Shop. Ctr.).
🅿 Bridge St. at North St. (Rts. 107 & 114)
See map, page 102.

Saugus
• T-Bus 426 (Lynn-Haymarket, via Cliftondale).
• T-Bus 426 (Oaklandvale-Haymarket), rush hour only.
• T-Bus 429 (Lynn-N. Saugus).
• T-Bus 430 (Saugus-Malden Ctr.).

Scituate
• Plymouth & Brockton (Boston-Scituate)—from Park Plaza, Boston/Peter Pan and SOUTH STA. Serves Scituate, N. Scituate, Egypt, and Greenbush.

Sharon
• T-Commuter Rail (Attleboro Line)—from SOUTH STA. and BACK BAY STA.

Sherborn
See Framingham, Natick, or Wellesley for train service to Boston.

Shirley
• T-Commuter Rail (Fitchburg Line)—from NORTH STA.

Shrewsbury
• Peter Pan (Boston-Worcester, Rt. 9 local)—from Boston/Peter Pan, Park Plaza, Copley Sq., and BRIGHAM CIR. Serves Fairlawn, South St., Levitz's.
• WRTA local buses from **Worcester.**

Somerville
• Red Line to PORTER and DAVIS.
• Orange Line to SULLIVAN.
• T-Bus 80 (Arlington Ctr.-Lechmere, via Medford Hillside).
• T-Bus 83 (Rindge Ave.-Central).
• T-Bus 85 (Spring Hill-Kendall).
• T-Bus 86 (Sullivan-Cleveland Cir.).
• T-Bus 87 (Arlington Ctr.-Lechmere, via Somerville Ave.).
• T-Bus 88 (Clarendon Hill-Lechmere, via Highland Ave.).
• T-Bus 89 (Clarendon Hill-Sullivan).
• T-Bus 90 (Davis-Wellington), via SULLIVAN.
• T-Bus 91 (Sullivan-Central).
• T-Bus 92 (Assembly Sq.-Downtown).
• T-Bus 94 (Medford Sq.-Davis).
• T-Bus 95 (W. Medford-Sullivan).
• T-Bus 96 (Medford Sq.-Harvard).
• T-Bus 101 (Malden Ctr.-Sullivan, via Medford Sq.).
Ball Sq./Magoun Sq.: T-Buses 80, 89.
E. Somerville/Winter Hill: T-Buses 89, 101.
Highland Ave./City Hall: T-Buses 88, 90.
Powderhouse Sq.: T-Buses 80, 89, 94, 96; or walk from DAVIS, 1/2 mile.
Union Sq.: T-Buses 85, 86, 87, 91.
W. Somerville/Teele Sq.: T-Buses 87, 88, 89; or walk from DAVIS, 1/2 mile.
See Davis Sq. map, page 25.

Southborough
• Peter Pan (Boston-Worcester, Rt. 9 local)—from Boston/Peter Pan, Park Plaza, Copley Sq., and BRIGHAM CIR. Serves Fayville, White's Corner.
• Gulbankian's (Boston-Hudson)—from Park Plaza and Copley Sq. Serves Central St., Rt.30, Rt.85.
• Gulbankian's (Framingham-Hudson)—from Shoppers World, Sat. only.
See Framingham for additional service.

South Boston
• Red Line to BROADWAY and ANDREW.
• T-Bus 3 (Chinatown-Marine Ind. Pk.).
• T-Bus 5 (City Pt.-McCormack Hsg.).
• T-Bus 6 (Marine Ind. Pk.-Haymarket).
• T-Bus 7 (City Pt.-Otis & Summer)
• T-Bus 9 (City Pt.-Copley, via Broadway).
• T-Bus 10 (City Pt.-Copley, via Andrew).
• T-Bus 11 (City Pt.-Downtown).
Perkins Sq.: T-Buses 5, 9, 10.

Salem

* to/from Boston
** to/from Logan Airport

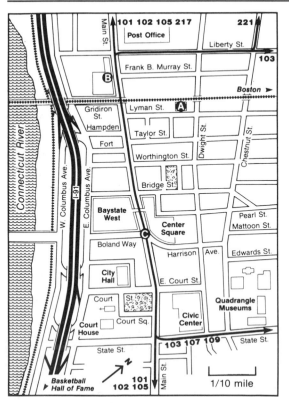

Ⓐ **Railroad Station**
Washington & Bridge Sts.
T-Commuter Rail*
(Rockport/Ipswitch Lines)
  450-Haymarket*
  451-N. Beverly
  455-Haymarket*
  458-Danvers

Ⓑ **Washington &**
  New Derby St.
Michaud Bus

Ⓒ **New Derby St.**
  450-Haymarket*
  451-N. Beverly
  455-Haymarket*
  458-Danvers

❷ **Visitor Information**
National Park Service
Visitors Center (Liberty St.)
Central Warf (Derby St.)

Springfield

Ⓐ **Railroad Station**
66 Lyman St.
413-788-477
Amtrak*

Ⓑ **Bus Treminal**
1776 Main St.
413-781-332
  Peter Pan/Bonanza
413-781-1500
  Greyhound/Vt. Transit
Peter Pan * **
Greyhound
Bonanza
Vermont Transit
PVTA Buses 101, 102, 103,
105, 107, 109, 217, 221 (on
Main St.)

Ⓒ **Baystate West**
Main St. & Boland Way
All PVTA buses

See Red Line map for other buses to ANDREW.

South End (Boston)
• Orange Line to BACK BAY STA. and MASS AVE.
• Green Line (all trains) to ARLINGTON and COPLEY, walk 3 blocks S.
• Green Line-E (Heath St.) to PRUDEN-TIAL and SYMPHONY, walk 2 blocks South.
• T-Bus 1 (Harvard-Dudley, via Mass. Ave.).
• T-Bus 8 (Harbor Pt.-Kenmore).
• T-Bus 9 (City Pt.-Copley, via Broadway).
• T-Bus 10 (City Pt.-Copley, via Andrew).
• T-Bus 43 (Ruggles-Park St.), serves Tremont St.
• T-Bus 47 (Central-Albany St.).
• T-Bus 49 (Dudley-Downtown), serves Washington St.

South Hadley
• Peter Pan (Boston-Amherst)—from Boston/Peter Pan and RIVERSIDE, 3 trips daily.
• PVTA local buses from Holyoke and Amherst.
• PVTA/Five Colleges buses to Mt. Holyoke College.

Springfield
• Peter Pan (Boston-Springfield)—from Boston/Peter Pan and RIVERSIDE, 18 trips daily.
• Greyhound (Boston-Albany NY)—from SOUTH STA. and RIVERSIDE, 2 trips daily.
• Amtrak (Inland Route and Lake Shore Ltd.)—from SOUTH STA and BACK BAY STA., and Framingham, 3 trips daily.
• PVTA local buses.
See map, page 102.

Stoneham
*See **Malden, Medford, Melrose, Wakfield & Winchester** for train service to Boston.*

Stoughton
• T-Commuter Rail (Stoughton Line)—from SOUTH STA. and BACK BAY STA.
• Interstate (Boston-Middleboro), 1 trip Mon.-Fri.
• Hudson Bus (Mattapan-Canton). Serves Cobbs Corner.
• BAT local bus.

Stow
*See **Acton** for train service to Boston.*

Sturbridge
• Peter Pan (Boston-Sturbridge)—from Boston/Peter Pan.

Sudbury
• Cavalier Coach (Boston-Northborough), 1 rush hour trip. Serves Rt. 20.
*See **Lincoln** and **Weston** for train service to Boston.*

Swampscott
• T-Commuter Rail (Rockport/Ipswich Line)—from NORTH STA.
• T-Bus 441 (Marblehead-Haymarket, via Paradise Rd.).
• T-Bus 442 (Marblehead-Haymarket, via Humphrey St.).

Taunton
• American Eagle from Boston/Peter Pan to Silver City Galleria.
• Bloom (Boston-Taunton)—from Boston/Peter Pan.
• Bloom (Fall River-Taunton).
• Mass Limousine—from Logan Airport.
• GATRA local buses.

Tewksbury
• Flight Line—from Logan Airport.
• LRTA local bus from Lowell.
*See **Lowell** for train service to Boston.*

Topsfield
• The Coach Co. (Boston-Newburyport), rush hour only. Serves Rt.1.

Truro
• Plymouth & Brockton (Hyannis-Provincetown). *Connects w/Boston buses at Hyannis; connects w/Boston ferry at Provincetown.*

Waban (Newton)
• Green Line-D (Riverside) to WABAN.

Wakefield
• T-Commuter Rail (Reading/Haverhill Line)—from NORTH STA. to Greenwood and Wakefield.
• T-Bus 136 (Reading-Malden Ctr., via Lakeside).
• T-Bus 137 (Reading-Malden Ctr., via North Ave.).

Walpole
- T-Commuter Rail (Franklin Line)—from SOUTH STA and BACK BAY STA. to Plimptonville (rush hour only) and Walpole.
- T-Bus 34E (Walpole Ctr.-Forest Hills).
- **P** West St., W of Route 1A (downtown).

Waltham
- T-Commuter Rail (Fitchburg Line)—from NORTH STA. and PORTER to Waltham (Central Sq.) and Brandeis/Roberts.
- T-Express Bus 305 (Waltham-Downtown), rush hour only.
- T-Bus 53 (Roberts-Newton Corner-Downtown).
- T-Bus 54 (Waverley-Newton Corner-Downtown).
- T-Bus 56 (Waltham Highlands-Newton Corner-Downtown).
- T-Bus 58 (Auburndale-Newton Corner-Downtown).
- T-Bus 70 (Cedarwood-Central).
- T-Bus 70A (N. Waltham-Central).
- T-Bus 353A (Burlington Ind. Area-Dudley), via RIVERSIDE. Serves Waltham Ind. Area, rush hour only, "reverse commute."

Waltham-Lexington Express—from ALEWIFE to participating employers. *Central Sq.:* T-Commuter Rail; and T-Buses 53, 54, 56, 58, 70, 70A, 305. *From Boston:*T-Commuter Rail; or T-Buses 53, 54, 56, 58, 305. *From Cambridge:* T-Commuter Rail from PORTER.; or T-Bus 70 from CENTRAL. Or go to Watertown Sq. and transfer to T-Bus 70.

Wareham
- Bonanza (Boston-Wareham)—from BACK BAY STA.
- **P** U.S. 6 at junction Rts. 28 and 25.

Watertown
- T-Express Bus 302 (Watertown-Copley).
- T-Express Bus 304 (Watertown-Downtown).
- T-Bus 52 (Dedham Mall-Watertown).
- T-Bus 54 (Waverley-Newton Corner-Downtown), via Waltham.
- T-Bus 57 (Watertown-Kenmore).
- T-Bus 58 (Auburndale-Newton Corner-Downtown).
- T-Bus 59 (Needham Jct.-Watertown).
- T-Bus 70 (Cedarwood-Central).
- T-Bus 70A (N. Waltham-Central).
- T-Bus 71 (Watertown-Harvard).
- T-Bus 73 (Waverley-Harvard).

Watertown Sq.: T-Buses 52, 57, 59, 70, 70A, 71, 302, 304. *from Boston:* T-Buses 302, 304; or Green Line to KENMORE, then T-Bus 57. *From Cambridge:* T-Bus 70 from CENTRAL. or T-Bus 71 from HARVARD. *See Watertown Sq. map, page 96.*

Wayland
- Cavalier Coach (Boston-Northborough), 1 rush hour trip. Serves Rt. 20.
*See **Lincoln** and **Weston** for train service to Boston.*

Wellesley
- T-Commuter Rail (Framingham Line)—from SOUTH STA. and BACK BAY STA. to Wellesley Farms, Wellesley Hills, and Wellesley Sq.
- Peter Pan (Boston-Worcester, Rt. 9 local)—from Boston/Peter Pan, Park Plaza, Copley Sq., and BRIGHAM CIR. Serves Wellesley Hills, Rt.9.
- **P** Washington St. at Jct. Routes 135 and 16, next to Post Office (Wellesley Sq.).

Wellfleet
- Plymouth & Brockton (Hyannis-Provincetown). *Connects w/ Boston buses at Hyannis; connects w/ Boston ferry at Provincetown.*

Wenham
- T-Commuter Rail (Ipswich Line)—from NORTH STA. to Hamilton/Wenham.

Westborough
- Peter Pan (Boston-Worcester, Rt. 9 local)—from Boston/Peter Pan, Park Plaza, Copley Sq., and BRIGHAM CIR. Serves Rt. 9, Lyman St.
- Peter Pan (Boston-Westborough), rush hours only.
- Peter Pan (Logan Airport-Worcester), 4-6 trips daily.

West Bridgewater
See Bridgewater.

Westfield
- Peter Pan (Boston-Westfield), Sun only, no summer service.
- PVTA local buses from Springfield and Holyoke.

West Newton

- •T-Commuter Rail (Framingham Line)— from SOUTH STA. and BACK BAY STA.
- •T-Express Bus 305 (Waltham-Downtown), rush hour only.
- •T-Bus 53 (Roberts-Newton Corner-Downtown).
- • I-Bus 54 (Waverley-Newton Corner-Downtown).

Weston

- •T-Commuter Rail (Fitchburg Line)— from NORTH STA. to Kendal Green, Hastings, and Silver Hill. (Silver Hill: rush hour only.)
- •Cavalier Coach (Boston-Northborough), serves Rt.20, 1 rush hour trip.

West Roxbury (Boston)

- •T-Commuter Rail (Needham Line)—from SOUTH STA. and BACK BAY STA. to Bellevue, Highland, and West Roxbury.
- •T-Bus 34 (Dedham Line-Forest Hills).
- •T-Bus 34E (Walpole Ctr.-Forest Hills).
- •T-Bus 35 (Dedham Mall-Forest Hills, via Stimson).
- •T-Bus 36 (Charles River-Forest Hills).
- •T-Bus 36A (V.A. Hospital-Forest Hills).
- •T-Bus 37 (Baker & Vermont-Forest Hills).
- •T-Bus 38 (Wren St.-Forest Hills).
- •T-Bus 40 (Georgetowne-Forest Hills).
- •T-Bus 51 (Cleveland Cir.-Forest Hills).
- •T-Bus 52 (Dedham Mall-Watertown).

Centre St.: T-Commuter Rail; T-Buses 35, 36, 36A, 37.

Washington St.: T-Buses 34, 34E, 40.

From Downtown Boston: Orange Line or T-Bus 39 to FOREST HILLS; then any of the above buses; or T-Commuter Rail.

Westwood

- •T-Commuter Rail (Attleboro/Stoughton Lines)—from SOUTH STA. and BACK BAY STA. to Rt.128 Sta.
- •T-Commuter Rail (Franklin Line)— from SOUTH STA. and BACK BAY STA. to Islington.
- •T-Bus 34E (Walpole Ctr.-Forest Hills), serves Washington St. (Rt.1A).
- •Brush Hill (Boston-Milford), rush hour only. Serves Rt.109.
- •Amtrak (Boston-New York, Shore Line) stops at Rt.128 Sta.
- **P** University Ave. (Rt 128 Sta.)

Weymouth

- •Carey's (Boston-Whitman), rush hour only; 5 trips serve S. Weymouth, 2 trips serve Weymouth Landing.
- •T-Bus 220 (Quincy Ctr.-Hingham).
- •T-Bus 221 (Quincy Ctr.-Fort Point).
- •T-Bus 222 (Quincy Ctr.-E. Weymouth).
- •T-Bus 225 (Quincy Ctr.-Weymouth Landing).

Whitman

- •Carey's (Boston-Whitman), rush hour only.

Williamstown

- •Peter Pan (Boston-Bennington, VT)— from Boston/Peter Pan.
- •BRTA local bus.

Wilmington

- •T-Commuter Rail (Lowell Line)—from NORTH STA. to Wilmington.
- •T-Commuter Rail (Haverhill Line)— from NORTH STA. to N. Wilmington.
- **P** Rt. 62, west of I-93, exit 40 (North Wilmington).

Winchendon

- •Vermont Transit (Boston-Rutland, VT)—from SOUTH STA., Logan Airport, and RIVERSIDE.

Winchester

- •T-Commuter Rail (Lowell Line)—from NORTH STA. to Wedgemere and Winchester Ctr.
- •T-Bus 134 (N. Woburn-Wellington), serves Main St., Winchester Ctr.
- •T-Bus 350 (Burlington-Alewife),

Winthrop

- •Paul Revere "B" bus local buses from ORIENT HEIGHTS *(Blue Line).*Three routes:
- —Orient Hts.-Winthrop Beach, via Highlands.
- —Orient Hts.-Winthrop Beach, via Centre.
- —Winthrop Beach-Point Shirley.

Woburn

- •T-Commuter Rail (Lowell Line) to Mishawum and Lechmere Sales office.
- •T-Express Bus 353 (Burlington Ind. Area-Haymarket), rush hour "reverse commute" only.
- •T-Express Bus 354 (Woburn Sq.-Haymarket), rush hour only.

Providence RI

* to/from Boston
** to/from Logan Airport

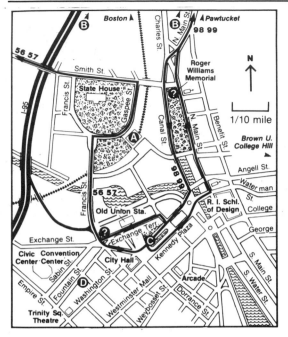

Ⓐ Railroad Station
100 Gaspee St.
401-727-7382
T-Commuter Rail*
(Attleboro Line)
Amtrak*
RIPTA Buses 56, 57
 (on Gaspee St.)

Ⓑ Bonanza Terminal
1 Bonanza Way
2 miles north of downtown
401-751-8800
Bonanza* **
RIPTA Buses 98, 99 (on
N. Main St., 4 blocks from
Bonanza terminal)

Ⓒ Kennedy Plaza
All RIPTA buses
Bonanza* to Bonanza
terminal & Boston
GATRA to Taunton, MA

Ⓓ Greyhound Terminal

❓ Visitor Information
Visitors Bureau
30 Exchange Terrace
National Park Service
N. Main St. @ Smith St.

*Not all RIPTA routes are
shown on this map*

Worcester

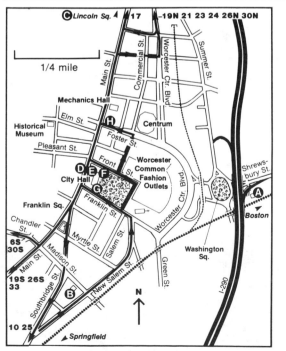

Ⓐ Railroad Station
45 Shrewsbury St.
508-755-0356
Amtrak*
T-Commuter Rail*

Ⓑ Bus Terminal
75 Madison St.
508-754-4600 Peter Pan
508-754-3247 Greyhound
Peter Pan * **
Greyhound *

Ⓒ Lincoln Sq.
Peter Pan* from Marriot Hotel
WRTA Buses 17, 19N, 21,
23, 24, 26N, 30N

Ⓓ City Hall Plaza
Main St.
WRTA Buses 19S,25, 26S, 30S

Ⓔ WRTA Buses 1, 6N, 11, 12, 15,
17, 19N, 23, 24, 26N, 30N, 33
Fox Bus to Burrillville RI

Ⓕ Front St. WRTA Buses 4, 5E,
18, 21, 22, 28, 40, 41

Ⓖ Franklin St.
WRTA Buses 1, 6S, 10, 15,
19N, 30N, 33, 40

Ⓗ Foster St.
WRTA Buses 2, 5W, 21, 32, 41

*Not all WRTA routes are
shown on this map*

106

•T-Bus 134 (N. Woburn-Wellington), serves Main St., Woburn Sq.
•T-Bus 350 (Burlington-Alewife)
•M & L Transp.—from Logan Airport to Rt.128 hotels.
•Logan Express—from Logan Airport to Washington St. (exit 36 off 128) next to Michawum commutor rail station.

Woods Hole
•Bonanza (Boston-Woods Hole)—from BACK BAY STA. and Logan Airport.
•Bonanza from New York NY.
•CCRTA (Hyannis-Woods Hole).
•Steamship Authority—ferries to Martha's Vineyard (year-round).

Worcester
•T-Commuter Rail (Framingham Line) from SOUTH STA., rush hour only-am: to Boston; pm: to Worcester. (new service).
•Peter Pan (Boston-Worcester, express)—from Boston/Peter Pan and RIVERSIDE, 20 trips daily.

•Peter Pan (Boston-Worcester, Rt. 9 local)—from Boston/Peter Pan, Park Plaza, Copley Sq., and BRIGHAM CIR.., 9 trips Mon.-Fri.
•Greyhound (Boston-New York NY, Boston-Albany, NY)—from SOUTH STA. and RIVERSIDE, 7 trips daily.
•Amtrak (Inland Route, Lake Shore Ltd.)—from SOUTH STA., BACK BAY STA., and Framingham, 3 trips daily.
•Peter Pan from Logan Airport, 9-15 trips daily.
•WRTA local buses.
See map, page 106.

Wrentham
*See **Franklin** or **Norfolk** for train service from Boston.*

Yarmouth
•Plymouth & Brockton (Hyannis-Provincetown), *connects w/Boston buses at Hyannis.*

Worcester City Hall

Part IV
Routes and Schedules

South Station, Boston

17. MBTA Rapid Transit and Buses
18. MBTA Commuter Rail and Boats
19. Other Trains, Ferries, Buses
20. Regional Transit Authorities
21. Transit in New England

FIRST & LAST RAPID TRANSIT TRAINS

Except Red Line trains to Braintree, the last trains on all lines wait at Park Street, Government Center, and Downtown Crossing for the last trains on connecting lines, so riders can transfer between lines.

The last trains to all Green Line and Red Line destinations (except Braintree) leave Park Street at 12:45 am. Last trains on the Blue and Orange lines depart Government Center and Downtown Crossing after the arrival of the last trains from Park Street.

Buses scheduled to leave subway stations after 12:45 am wait for the last train before departing.

	First Train Mon.-Sat.	Sun.	Last Train Every Day
Blue Line			
Wonderland-Government Ctr.	5:25	5:58	12:17[1]
Orient Heights-Government Ctr.	5:13	6:04	12:25
Government Ctr. - Wonderland	5:27	6:18	12:48[2]
Green Line			
B–Boston College-Government Ctr	5:01	5:40	12:10
B–Government Ctr.-Boston College	5:30	6:07	12:45
C–Cleveland Circle-North Station	5:01	5:40	12:10
C–North Station-Cleveland Circle	5:34[3]	6:10	12:40
D–Riverside-Government Ctr.	5:01	5:40	12:10[4]
D–Government Ctr.-Riverside	5:36	6:16	12:45
E–Heath St.-Lechmere	5:30	6:15	12:14[5]
E–Lechmere-Heath St.	5:01	5:40	12:30[6]
E–Forest Hills-Back Bay Sta. (bus)	5:01	5:45	11:58[7]
E–Back Bay Sta.-Forest Hills (bus)	5:29[3]	6:13	1:00
Orange Line			
Oak Grove-Forest Hills	5:16	6:00	12:26
Forest Hills-Oak Grove	5:16	6:00	12:22
Red Line			
Alewife-Ashmont & Mattapan	5:16	6:00	12:22
Alewife-Braintree	5:24	6:08	12:14[8]
Ashmont-Alewife	5:16	6:00	12:30
Braintree-Alewife	5:16	6:00	12:18
Mattapan-Ashmont & Alewife	5:05	5:51	12:19[9]

1 On Sat. & Sun., last train leaves Wonderland at 12:20.
2 Connecting buses from Orient Heights to Wonderland on Mon.-Fri.; last through train to Wonderland leaves Government Ctr. at 11:32 pm.
3 Saturday service begins 1-2 minutes earlier.
4 On Sat. & Sun., last train leaves Riverside at 12:05.
5 Last train connecting to other lines leaves Heath St. at 12:14; other trains operate until 12:45.
6 On Sat. & Sun., last train connecting to other lines leaves Lechmere at 12:15; another train leaves at 12:30.
7 Last bus connecting to trains at Heath St. leaves Forest Hills at 11:58; other buses operate until 12:30. (Bus to train connections are not guaranteed.)
8 For later service to N. Quincy, Wollaston, and Quincy Ctr., take the last Ashmont train to Fields Corner and then a connecting bus.
9 Last train connecting to trains at Ashmont leaves Mattapan at 12:19 Mon.-Fri., 12:15 Sat.-Sun.; other trains operate until 12:50.

Chapter 17

MBTA Rapid Transit and Buses

The charts on the following pages show the approximate frequency (time between trains or buses), in minutes, of all MBTA bus and rapid transit routes as of February 1995. Trip time is approximately how long it takes to go from one end of the route to the other.

Rush hour figures show service *to* Boston (inbound) in the morning and *away from* Boston in the evening; service in the other direction may be less frequent.

A dash (—) means there is no service at the time indicated.

Listings for bus routes also show the major streets which the route serves; some minor streets have been omitted. A slash (/) between two street names means that inbound buses operate via one street and outbound buses use the other street.

For precise schedules and route information, **call the MBTA at 722-3200 or 800-392-6100;** or see the printed schedules issued for all MBTA routes. Schedules are available from some bus drivers and T employees; at Park Street station; and at other locations listed in Chapter 1.

For new crosstown bus service see page 138,

MBTA Rapid Transit	Trip Time	Mon.-Fri. frequency (min.)			Sat. Freq.	Sun. Freq.
		Rush	Midday	Night		

Blue Line

Wonderland—Bowdoin	18	4	8	11	9	11

Stations: Wonderland, Revere Beach, Beachmont, Suffolk Downs, Orient Hts., Wood Island, Airport, Maverick, Aquarium, State, Government Ctr., Bowdoin.
Nights & weekends: Wonderland—Government Ctr. only, **Bowdoin closed.**
Trip times from Gov't Ctr.: Airport 7 min., Orient Hts. 11 min., Wonderland 17 min.

Orange Line

Oak Grove—Forest Hills	33	5	8	13	10	14

Stations: Oak Grove, Malden Ctr., Wellington, Sullivan, Community College, North Sta., Haymarket, State, Downtown Crossing (Washington), Chinatown, New England Medical Ctr., Back Bay Sta., Massachusetts Ave., Ruggles, Roxbury Crossing, Jackson Sq., Stony Brook, Green, Forest Hills.
Trip times from Downtown Crossing: Sullivan 8 min., Oak Grove 16 min.; Back Bay Sta. 5 min., Ruggles 8 min., Forest Hills 17 min.

Red Line

Alewife—Ashmont	37	8	12	12	13	15

Stations: Alewife, Davis, Porter, Harvard, Central, Kendall, Charles/MGH, Park St., Downtown Crossing (Washington), South Sta., Broadway, Andrew, JFK/UMass, Savin Hill, Fields Corner, Shawmut, Ashmont.
Trip times from Park St.: Kendall 5 min., Harvard 10 min., Alewife 18 min.; Andrew 7 min., Fields Corner 14 min., Ashmont 19 min.

Alewife—Braintree	44	8	12	12	13	15

Stations: Alewife, Davis, Porter, Harvard, Central, Kendall, Charles/MGH, Park St., Downtown Crossing , South Sta., Broadway, Andrew, JFK/UMass, N. Quincy, Wollaston, Quincy Ctr., Quincy Adams, Braintree.
Trip times from Park St.: N. Quincy 14 min., Quincy Ctr. 19 min., Braintree 26 min.

Ashmont—Mattapan	9-10	4	8	11	8	11

Stations: Ashmont, Cedar Grove, Butler St., Milton, Central Ave., Valley Rd., Capen St., Mattapan. *Connects w/Alewife-Ashmont trains at Ashmont.*

MBTA Rapid Transit	Trip Time	Mon.–Fri. frequency (min.)			Sat. Freq.	Sun. Freq.
		Rush	Midday	Night		

Green Line

B **Boston College—Gov't Ctr.**   27-39   5   5   10   7   5-10
Brighton, Allston: Commonwealth Ave.
Stations: Kenmore, Hynes Convention Ctr./ICA, Copley, Arlington, Boylston, Park St., Government Ctr.
Trip times from Park St.: Copley 5 min., Kenmore 10 min., Harvard Ave. 18-33 min., Boston College 26-37 min.

C **Cleveland Circle–North Sta.**   25-40   7   5   10   5-8   7-10
Brookline: Beacon St.
Stations: Kenmore, Hynes Convention Ctr./ICA, Copley, Arlington, Boylston, Park St., Government Ctr., Haymarket, North Sta.
Trip times from Park St.: Coolidge Cor. 13-21 min., Cleveland Cir. 20-33 min.

D **Riverside–Government Ctr.**   35-45   8   10   10   6   7-10
Stations: Riverside, Woodland, Waban, Eliot, Newton Highlands, Newton Centre, Chestnut Hill, Reservoir, Beaconsfield, Brookline Hills, Brookline Village, Longwood, Fenway, Kenmore, Hynes Convention Ctr./ICA, Copley, Arlington, Boylston, Park St., Government Ctr.
Trip times from Park St.: Reservoir 18-25 min., Riverside 33-43 min.

E **Heath St.–Lechmere**   25-31   8   9   10   7-10   7-10
Jamaica Plain: S. Huntington Ave; *Mission Hill, Fenway:* Huntington Ave.
Stations: Symphony, Prudential, Copley, Arlington, Boylston, Park St., Government Ctr., Haymarket, North Sta., Science Park, Lechmere.
Trip times from Park St.: North Sta. 6 min., Lechmere 9 min.;
Brigham Cir. 13-16 min., Heath St. 16-22 min.

Arborway—Heath St.   Service temporarily suspended.

Entertainment on the Red Line, Park St. station

Blue Line

RAPID TRANSIT STATIONS

STREET ADDRESS & CONNECTING SERVICES

P **Wonderland**

1300 North Shore Rd. (Rt. 1A), opposite dog track/Revere
110-Wellington
116-Maverick, via Revere St.
117-Maverick, via Beach St.
411-Revere House-Malden Ctr.
441-Marblehead-Haymarket, via Paradise Rd.
442-Marblehead-Haymarket, via Humphrey St. (Mon.-Sat.)

Revere Beach

220 Shirley Ave. and 300 Ocean Ave./Revere
110-Wonderland-Wellington
117-Wonderland-Maverick, via Beach St.
411-Revere House-Malden

&♿ **P** **Beachmont**

630 Winthrop Ave. at 1 Bennington St./Revere
119-Northgate
119-Beachmont Loop

P **Suffolk Downs**

1230 Bennington St. and Walley St./East Boston
Does not open until 9:30 am on Sat.; 10:45 am on Sun.

P **Orient Heights**

1000 Bennington St., north of 990 Saratoga St./East Boston
Paul Revere buses:
—Winthrop Beach via Centre
—Winthrop Beach via
Highlands
120-Maverick
120-Orient Hts. Loop

Wood Island

450 Bennington St., north of Rt. 1A/East Boston
120-Orient Hts.-Maverick
121-Maverick (AM rush)

Airport

Airport access road and Porter St./East Boston
Airport shuttle buses to airline terminals

Maverick

220 Sumner St. at Chelsea and Meridian Sts./East Boston
112-Wellington
116-Wonderland, via Revere St.
117-Wonderland, via Beach St.
120-Orient Hts.
120-Jeffries Point Loop
121-Wood Island, via Eagle Sq.

Aquarium

200 Atlantic Ave. at 300 State St./Boston
Commuter Boats
6-Marine Ind. Park-Haymarket
Long Wharf ferries*
Rowes Wharf ferries*

♿ **State**

200 Washington St. at 1 State St./Boston
Wheelchair access only for outbound platform (to Wonderland). Wheelchair users coming inbound should go to Government Ctr., then cross platform and come back to State.
Orange Line
92-Assembly Sq., via Main St.
93-Sullivan, via Bunker Hill St.

Government Center
Scollay Sq.

1 Cambridge St. at Court and Tremont Sts./Boston
Green Line

Bowdoin

Cambridge St. at New Chardon and Bowdoin Sts./Boston
Open Mon.-Fri. 5:15 am-6:30 pm. Closed Sat. & Sun.

*See "Boston Terminals" map for complete list of carriers.

113

Orange Line

Oak Grove–State

RAPID TRANSIT STATIONS	STREET ADDRESS & CONNECTING SERVICES

Oak Grove ♿ 🅿️

Washington St. at Winter St./Malden

130A-Wyoming Sq.-Malden Ctr.
131-Melrose Highlands-
  Malden Ctr.
136-Reading-Malden Ctr.,
  via Lakeside
137-Reading-Malden Ctr.,
  via North Ave.

Malden 🅿️

230 Pleasant St. at Summer and Commercial St./Malden

Commuter Rail—Reading/
  Haverhill Line
97-Wellington, via Hancock St.
99-Upper Highland-Wellington,
  via Main St.
101-Sullivan, via Medford Sq.
104-Sullivan, via Ferry St.
105-Sullivan, via Faulkner
106-Lebanon. St.-Wellington,
  via Main St.
108-Linden Sq.-Wellington,
  via Highland Ave.
130-Lebanon St., Melrose
130A-Wyoming Sq.
131-Melrose Highlands
136-Reading, via Lakeside
137-Reading, via North Ave.
411-Revere House
  (Wonderland)
430-Saugus

Wellington ♿ 🅿️

Revere Beach Pkwy. (Rt. 16), east of Rt. 28/Medford

90-Davis, via Sullivan
97-Malden Ctr., via Hancock St.
99-Upper Highland, via Main St.
  & Malden Ctr.
100-Elm St., Medford
106-Lebanon St., via Main St. &
  Malden Ctr.
108-Linden Sq., via
  Highland Ave. & Malden
  Ctr.
110-Wonderland
112-Maverick
134-N. Woburn
134M-Medford

Sullivan ♿ 🅿️

1 Broadway and 1 Cambridge St./Charlestown

86-Cleveland Cir., via Harvard
89-Clarendon Hill-Lechmere
90-Davis-Wellington
91-Central
92-Assembly Sq.-Downtown, via
  Main St.
93-Downtown, via Bunker Hill St.
95-W. Medford
101-Malden Ctr., via
  Medford Sq.
104-Malden Ctr., via Ferry St.
105-Malden Ctr., via Faulkner
109-Linden Sq.

Community College

Austin St., west of Rutherford Ave./Charlestown

North Station

135 Causeway St. at Canal St./Boston

Commuter Rail   Green Line

Haymarket

Congress St. at New Sudbury St./Boston

Green Line
Commuter buses*
6-Marine Ind. Park, via South Sta.
92-Assembly Sq.-Downtown,
  via Main St.
93-Sullivan-Downtown, via
  Bunker Hill St.
111-Woodlawn (Chelsea)
325-Elm St., Medford (express)
326-W. Medford (express)
352-Burlington (express)
353-Burlington Ind. Area
354-Woburn (express)
426-Lynn, via Cliftondale
441-Marblehead, via
  Paradise Rd.
442-Marblehead, via
  Humphrey St.
450-Salem, via Highland Ave.
455-Salem, via Loring Ave.
Special rush hour service:
426-Granada Highlands or
  Oaklandvale
436-Happy Valley
439-Nahant
458/468-Danvers

State ♿

200 Washington St. at 1 State St./Boston

Blue Line
92-Assembly Sq., via Main St.
93-Sullivan, via Bunker Hill
  St.

*See "Boston Terminals"
map for complete list of
carriers.

To Forest Hills via Downtown Crossing

RAPID TRANSIT STATIONS	STREET ADDRESS & CONNECTING SERVICES

To Oak Grove via State

♿ Downtown Crossing
Washington

450 Washington St. at 1 Summer St./Boston

Red Line
Green Line via walkway to
  Park St.
7-City Pt., via Summer St.
11-City Pt., via Bayview
49-Dudley
53-Roberts, via Waltham &
  Newton Corner
54-Waverley, via Waltham &
  Newton Corner
92-Assembly Sq., via Main St.

93-Sullivan, via Bunker Hill St.
300-Riverside (express)
301-Brighton Ctr. (express)
304-Watertown (express)
304A-Newton Corner
  (express)
305-Waltham (express)
Special rush hour service:
56-Waltham Highlands or
  Cedarwood
58-Auburndale

♿ Chinatown
Essex

640 Washington St. at 1 Boylston St./Boston
11-City Pt., via Bayview   49-Dudley

♿ New England Med. Ctr.
South Cove

750 Washington St., south of Stuart St./Boston
3-Marine Ind. Pk.   43-Ruggles
11-City Pt., via Bayview   49-Dudley

♿ Back Bay Station
/South End

145 Dartmouth St., south of Stuart St./Boston
Commuter Rail   10-City Pt., via Andrew
Amtrak   39-Forest Hills (free transfer)
Bonanza

♿ Massachusetts Ave.

380 Massachusetts Ave., south of St. Botolph St./Boston
1-Harvard-Dudley (free transfer to/from Dudley)
CT1-Central -B.U. Medical Center

♿ Ruggles

800 Columbus Ave. at Melnea Cass Blvd./Roxbury

Commuter Rail—Attleboro/
  Stoughton, Franklin,
  Needham Lines (Ltd Svc.)
8-Harbor Pt.-Kenmore
15-Kane Sq.
19-Fields Corner, via Grove
  Hall
22-Ashmont, via Jackson Sq.
23-Ashmont, via Dudley Sq.

28-Mattapan, via Dudley Sq.
42-Forest Hills
43-Park St.
44-Jackson Sq., via
  Humboldt Ave.
45-Franklin Park Zoo
47-Central-Albany St.
CT2-Kendal-Ruggles
CT3-Beth Israel-Andrew

♿ Roxbury Crossing

1400 Tremont St., west of 1200 Columbus Ave./Roxbury
66-Harvard-Dudley, via   Mission Hill Link Bus, Blue
  Brookline   Route

♿ Jackson Sq.

1500 Columbus Ave. at 240 Centre St./Jamaica Plain
22-Ashmont-Ruggles   44-Ruggles, via Humboldt Ave.
29-Mattapan-Jackson Sq.   46-Heath St.-Dudley
41-Centre & Eliot Sts.-Dudley 48-Jamaica Plain Loop

♿ Stony Brook

100 Boylston St. at 180 Lamartine St./Jamaica Plain
48-Jamaica Plain Loop

♿ Green

150 Green St. at 380 Amory St./Jamaica Plain
48-Jamaica Plain Loop

♿ 🅿 Forest Hills

3700 Washington St., south of Morton St./Jamaica Plain

Commuter Rail—Needham Line
Franklin Park Zoo bus
  (weekends)
16-JFK/UMass
21-Ashmont
31-Mattapan
32-Wolcott Sq., via Hyde Park
  Ave.
34-Dedham Line (Washington
  St.)
34E-Walpole Ctr.

35-Dedham Mall, via Stimson
36-Charles River
36A-V.A. Hospital
37-Baker & Vermont Sts.
38-Wren St.
39-Back Bay Sta.
40-Georgetowne
42-Ruggles
50-Cleary Sq., via Roslindale
51-Cleveland Circle

Red Line

RAPID TRANSIT STATIONS	STREET ADDRESS & CONNECTING SERVICES

& **P** **Alewife** ○
Alewife Brook Pkwy. at Rindge Ave. and Rt. 2/Cambridge

Waltham-Lexington Express	79-Arlington Hts.
62-Bedford	83-Central
67-Turkey Hill	84-Arlmont Village
76-Hanscom Field	350-Burlington

& **Davis** ○
Tufts U.
1 College Ave. and 1 Holland St./Somerville

87-Arlington Ctr.-Lechmere, via	90-Wellington, via Sullivan
Somerville Ave.	94-Medford Sq., via W. Medford
88-Clarendon Hill-Lechmere,	96-Medford Sq.-Harvard, via
via Highland Ave.	George St.

& **Porter** ○
1900 Massachusetts Ave. at 830 Somerville Ave./Cambridge

Commuter Rail—Fitchburg Line	83-Rindge Ave.-Central
77-Arlington Hts.-Harvard	96-Medford Sq.-Harvard
77A-N. Cambridge-Harvard	

& **Harvard** ○
1400 Massachusetts Ave. at 1 Brattle St./Cambridge

1-Dudley, via Mass. Ave.	74-Belmont Ctr.
66-Dudley, via Brookline	77-Arlington Hts.
69-Lechmere	77A-N. Cambridge
71-Watertown	78-Arlmont
72-Huron Ave.	86-Sullivan-Cleveland Circle
73-Waverley	96-Medford Sq.

& **Central** ○
650 Massachusetts Ave. at 1 Prospect St./Cambridge

Metrobus to Longwood Ave.	70A-N. Waltham
1-Harvard-Dudley	83-Rindge Ave.
47-Albany St.	91-Sullivan
64-Oak Sq.	CT1-Central-B. U. Med. Ctr.
64-Kendall (rush hours)	CT2-Kendall-Ruggles
70-Cedarwood (Waltham)	

& **Kendall** ○
MIT
330 Main St. at Carleton St. and 3 Cambridge Ctr./Cambridge

| 64-Oak Sq. (rush hours) | Shuttle bus to Cambridgeside |
| 85-Spring Hill | Galleria |

& **Charles/MGH** ○
Charles Circle, 350 Cambridge St. at 160 Charles St./Boston

& **Park St.** ○
120 Tremont St. at 1 Park St./Boston

Green Line	43-Ruggles
Orange Line via walkway to	55-Queensberry St. (Mon.-Fri.)
Downtown	

& Downtown Crossing ○
Washington
450 Washington St. at 1 Summer St./Boston

Orange Line	93-Sullivan, via Bunker Hill St.
Green Line via walkway to Park	300-Riverside (express)
St.	301-Brighton Ctr. (express)
7-City Pt., via Summer St.	304-Watertown (express)
11-City Pt., via Bayview	304A-Newton Corner (express)
49-Dudley	305-Waltham (express)
53-Roberts, via Waltham &	
Newton Corner	Special rush hour service:
54-Waverley, via Waltham &	56-Waltham Highlands or
Newton Corner	Cedarwood
92-Assembly Sq., via Main St.	58-Auburndale

& **South Station** ○
Dewey Sq., 200 Summer St. at 600 Atlantic Ave./Boston

Commuter Rail	South Sta. commuter buses*
Amtrak	6-Marine Ind. Pk.-Haymarket
Greyhound	7-City Pt., via Summer St.
Peter Pan Terminal*	

& **Broadway** ○
100 Dorchester Ave. at 1 W. Broadway/South Boston

3-Chinatown-Marine Ind. Pk.
9-City Pt.-Copley
11-City Pt.-Downtown, via
Bayview
18-Broadway

*See "Boston Terminals"
map for complete list of
carriers.

To Ashmont or Braintree

RAPID TRANSIT STATIONS	STREET ADDRESS & CONNECTING SERVICES

To Alewife via Park St.

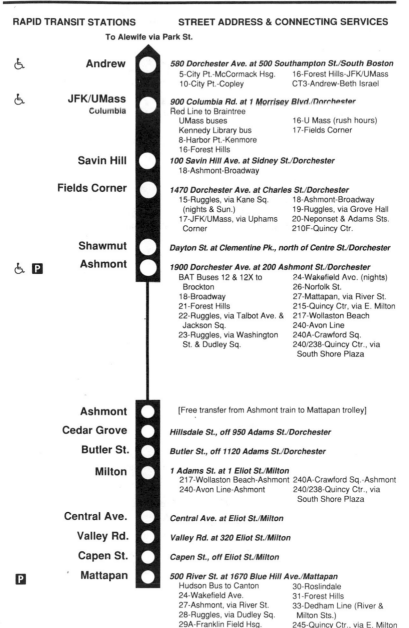

   ♿   **Andrew**

580 Dorchester Ave. at 500 Southampton St./South Boston
5-City Pt.-McCormack Hsg.   16-Forest Hills-JFK/UMass
10-City Pt.-Copley   CT3-Andrew-Beth Israel

♿   **JFK/UMass**
      Columbia

900 Columbia Rd. at 1 Morrisey Blvd./Dorchester
Red Line to Braintree
   UMass buses   16-U Mass (rush hours)
   Kennedy Library bus   17-Fields Corner
   8-Harbor Pt.-Kenmore
   16-Forest Hills

Savin Hill

100 Savin Hill Ave. at Sidney St./Dorchester
18-Ashmont-Broadway

Fields Corner

1470 Dorchester Ave. at Charles St./Dorchester
15-Ruggles, via Kane Sq.   18-Ashmont-Broadway
(nights & Sun.)   19-Ruggles, via Grove Hall
17-JFK/UMass, via Uphams   20-Neponset & Adams Sts.
Corner   210F-Quincy Ctr.

Shawmut

Dayton St. at Clementine Pk., north of Centre St./Dorchester

♿ 🅿   **Ashmont**

1900 Dorchester Ave. at 200 Ashmont St./Dorchester
BAT Buses 12 & 12X to   24-Wakefield Avc. (nights)
  Brockton   26-Norfolk St.
18-Broadway   27-Mattapan, via River St.
21-Forest Hills   215-Quincy Ctr, via E. Milton
22-Ruggles, via Talbot Ave. &   217-Wollaston Beach
  Jackson Sq.   240-Avon Line
23-Ruggles, via Washington   240A-Crawford Sq.
  St. & Dudley Sq.   240/238-Quincy Ctr., via
                South Shore Plaza

Ashmont

[Free transfer from Ashmont train to Mattapan trolley]

Cedar Grove

Hillsdale St., off 950 Adams St./Dorchester

Butler St.

Butler St., off 1120 Adams St./Dorchester

Milton

1 Adams St. at 1 Eliot St./Milton
217-Wollaston Beach-Ashmont   240A-Crawford Sq.-Ashmont
240-Avon Line-Ashmont   240/238-Quincy Ctr., via
                South Shore Plaza

Central Ave.

Central Ave. at Eliot St./Milton

Valley Rd.

Valley Rd. at 320 Eliot St./Milton

Capen St.

Capen St., off Eliot St./Milton

🅿   **Mattapan**

500 River St. at 1670 Blue Hill Ave./Mattapan
Hudson Bus to Canton   30-Roslindale
24-Wakefield Ave.   31-Forest Hills
27-Ashmont, via River St.   33-Dedham Line (River &
28-Ruggles, via Dudley Sq.   Milton Sts.)
29A-Franklin Field Hsg.   245-Quincy Ctr., via E. Milton

Red Line
Andrew – Braintree

RAPID TRANSIT STATIONS   **STREET ADDRESS & CONNECTING SERVICES**

To Alewife via Park St.

♿ **Andrew**

580 Dorchester Ave. at 500 Southampton St./South Boston
5-City Pt.-McCormack Hsg. 16-Forest Hills-JFK/UMass
10-City Pt.-Copley CT3-Andrew-Beth Israel

♿ **JFK/UMass**
Columbia

900 Columbia Rd. at 1 Morrisey Blvd./Dorchester
Red Line to Braintree 16-Forest Hills
UMass buses 16-UMass (rush hours)
Kennedy Library bus 17-Fields Corner
8-Harbor Pt.-Kenmore

P **North Quincy**

Newport Ave. at 70 W. Squantum St./Quincy
210-Quincy Ctr., via Hancock St. 211-Quincy Ctr.-Squantum
210F-Quincy Ctr.-Fields Corner 212-Quincy Ctr., via Billings Rd.

P **Wollaston**

300 Newport Ave. at 90 Beale St./Quincy
211-Quincy Ctr.-Squantum 217-Wollaston Beach-
  Ashmont

◄— FARE ZONE beyond this point:
Inbound—pay 2 tokens when boarding.
Combo pass required.
Outbound—no fare.

♿ **P** **Quincy Center**

1300 Hancock St. at Washington St./Quincy
210-N. Quincy., via Hancock St. 221-Fort Point
210F-Fields Corner 222-E. Weymouth
211-Squantum 225-Weymouth Landing
212-N. Quincy, via Billings Rd. 230-Brockton Line
214-Germantown 236-South Shore Plaza, via
215-Ashmont, via E. Milton E. Braintree
216-Hough's Neck 238-Crawford Sq.
220-Hingham 238/240-Ashmont, via
220A-Hingham Loop Randolph
  245-Mattapan, via E. Milton

◄— FARE ZONE beyond this point:
Inbound—pay 2 tokens when boarding.
Combo Plus pass required.
Outbound—pay 1 additional token when exiting.

♿ **P** **Quincy Adams**

Burgin Pkwy. and 200 Independence Ave./Quincy
238-Quincy Ctr.-Crawford Sq. 238/240-Ashmont, via
(Mon.-Sat.) Randolph (Mon.-Sat.)

♿ **P** **Braintree**

Union St. at Ivory St., west of Rt. 3/Braintree
230-Quincy Ctr.-Brockton Line Plymouth & Brockton to
236-South Shore Plaza-Quincy Marshfield, via Hanover
Ctr. Mall

RAPID TRANSIT STATIONS

STREET ADDRESS & CONNECTING SERVICES

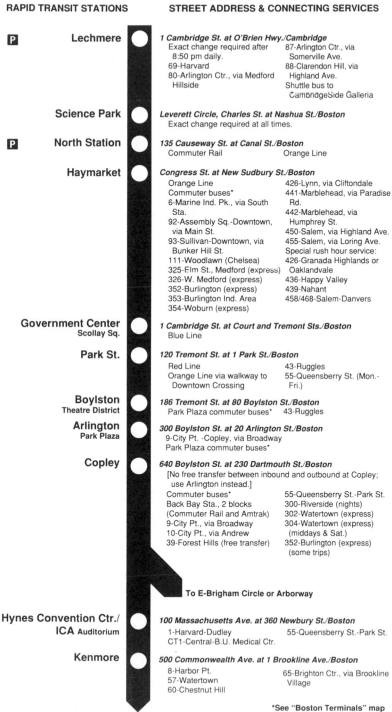

🅿 Lechmere

1 Cambridge St. at O'Brien Hwy./Cambridge
Exact change required after 8:50 pm daily.
69-Harvard
80-Arlington Ctr., via Medford Hillside

87-Arlington Ctr., via Somerville Ave.
88-Clarendon Hill, via Highland Ave.
Shuttle bus to CambridgeSide Galleria

Science Park

Leverett Circle, Charles St. at Nashua St./Boston
Exact change required at all times.

🅿 North Station

135 Causeway St. at Canal St./Boston
Commuter Rail
Orange Line

Haymarket

Congress St. at New Sudbury St./Boston
Orange Line
Commuter buses*
6-Marine Ind. Pk., via South Sta.
92-Assembly Sq.-Downtown, via Main St.
93-Sullivan-Downtown, via Bunker Hill St.
111-Woodlawn (Chelsea)
325-Elm St., Medford (express)
326-W. Medford (express)
352-Burlington (express)
353-Burlington Ind. Area
354-Woburn (express)

426-Lynn, via Cliftondale
441-Marblehead, via Paradise Rd.
442-Marblehead, via Humphrey St.
450-Salem, via Highland Ave.
455-Salem, via Loring Ave.
Special rush hour service:
426-Granada Highlands or Oaklandvale
436-Happy Valley
439-Nahant
458/468-Salem-Danvers

Government Center
Scollay Sq.

1 Cambridge St. at Court and Tremont Sts./Boston
Blue Line

Park St.

120 Tremont St. at 1 Park St./Boston
Red Line
Orange Line via walkway to Downtown Crossing

43-Ruggles
55-Queensberry St. (Mon.-Fri.)

Boylston
Theatre District

186 Tremont St. at 80 Boylston St./Boston
Park Plaza commuter buses*   43-Ruggles

Arlington
Park Plaza

300 Boylston St. at 20 Arlington St./Boston
9-City Pt. -Copley, via Broadway
Park Plaza commuter buses*

Copley

640 Boylston St. at 230 Dartmouth St./Boston
[No free transfer between inbound and outbound at Copley; use Arlington instead.]
Commuter buses*
Back Bay Sta., 2 blocks (Commuter Rail and Amtrak)
9-City Pt., via Broadway
10-City Pt., via Andrew
39-Forest Hills (free transfer)

55-Queensberry St.-Park St.
300-Riverside (nights)
302-Watertown (express)
304-Watertown (express) (middays & Sat.)
352-Burlington (express) (some trips)

To E-Brigham Circle or Arborway

Hynes Convention Ctr./
ICA Auditorium

100 Massachusetts Ave. at 360 Newbury St./Boston
1-Harvard-Dudley
CT1-Central-B.U. Medical Ctr.
55-Queensberry St.-Park St.

Kenmore

500 Commonwealth Ave. at 1 Brookline Ave./Boston
8-Harbor Pt.
57-Watertown
60-Chestnut Hill

65-Brighton Ctr., via Brookline Village

To B-Boston College, C-Cleveland Circle, D-Riverside

*See "Boston Terminals" map for complete list of carriers.

Green Line-B

Kenmore – Boston College

RAPID TRANSIT STATIONS
To Government Center via Park St.

STREET ADDRESS & CONNECTING SERVICES

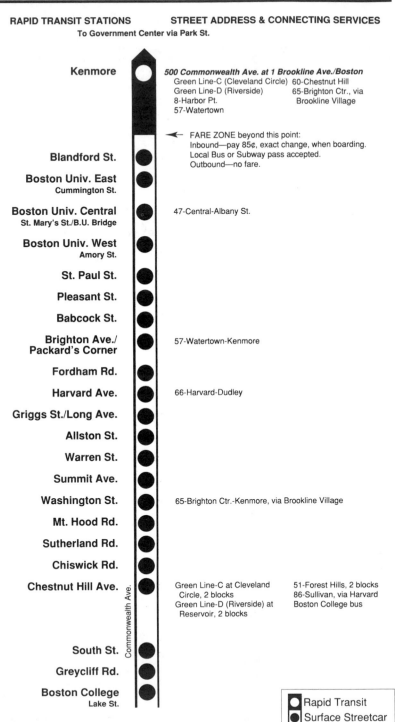

Kenmore
500 Commonwealth Ave. at 1 Brookline Ave./Boston
Green Line-C (Cleveland Circle) 60-Chestnut Hill
Green Line-D (Riverside)   65-Brighton Ctr., via
8-Harbor Pt.   Brookline Village
57-Watertown

◄— FARE ZONE beyond this point:
Inbound—pay 85¢, exact change, when boarding.
Local Bus or Subway pass accepted.
Outbound—no fare.

Blandford St.

Boston Univ. East
Cummington St.

Boston Univ. Central
St. Mary's St./B.U. Bridge
47-Central-Albany St.

Boston Univ. West
Amory St.

St. Paul St.

Pleasant St.

Babcock St.

Brighton Ave./
Packard's Corner
57-Watertown-Kenmore

Fordham Rd.

Harvard Ave.
66-Harvard-Dudley

Griggs St./Long Ave.

Allston St.

Warren St.

Summit Ave.

Washington St.
65-Brighton Ctr.-Kenmore, via Brookline Village

Mt. Hood Rd.

Sutherland Rd.

Chiswick Rd.

Chestnut Hill Ave.
Green Line-C at Cleveland   51-Forest Hills, 2 blocks
Circle, 2 blocks   86-Sullivan, via Harvard
Green Line-D (Riverside) at   Boston College bus
Reservoir, 2 blocks

Commonwealth Ave.

South St.

Greycliff Rd.

Boston College
Lake St.

○ Rapid Transit
◉ Surface Streetcar

120

Green Line-C

RAPID TRANSIT STATIONS	STREET ADDRESS & CONNECTING SERVICES

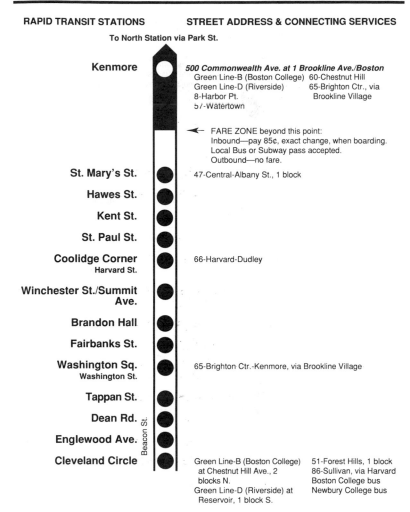

To North Station via Park St.

Kenmore

500 Commonwealth Ave. at 1 Brookline Ave./Boston
Green Line-B (Boston College)   60-Chestnut Hill
Green Line-D (Riverside)   65-Brighton Ctr., via
8-Harbor Pt.   Brookline Village
57-Watertown

◄— FARE ZONE beyond this point:
Inbound—pay 85¢, exact change, when boarding.
Local Bus or Subway pass accepted.
Outbound—no fare.

St. Mary's St.   47-Central-Albany St., 1 block

Hawes St.

Kent St.

St. Paul St.

Coolidge Corner
Harvard St.   66-Harvard-Dudley

Winchester St./Summit Ave.

Brandon Hall

Fairbanks St.

Washington Sq.
Washington St.   65-Brighton Ctr.-Kenmore, via Brookline Village

Tappan St.

Dean Rd.

Englewood Ave.

Beacon St.

Cleveland Circle   Green Line-B (Boston College)   51-Forest Hills, 1 block
at Chestnut Hill Ave., 2   86-Sullivan, via Harvard
blocks N.   Boston College bus
Green Line-D (Riverside) at   Newbury College bus
Reservoir, 1 block S.

○ Rapid Transit
● Surface Streetcar

121

Green Line-D *Kenmore – Riverside*

RAPID TRANSIT STATIONS   **STREET ADDRESS & CONNECTING SERVICES**

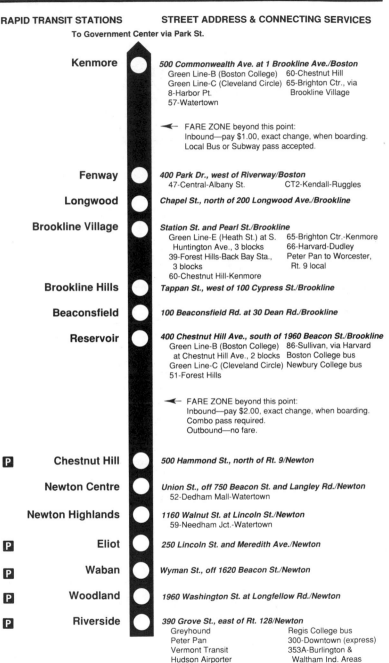

To Government Center via Park St.

Kenmore

500 Commonwealth Ave. at 1 Brookline Ave./Boston
Green Line-B (Boston College)   60-Chestnut Hill
Green Line-C (Cleveland Circle) 65-Brighton Ctr., via
8-Harbor Pt.   Brookline Village
57-Watertown

◄— FARE ZONE beyond this point:
Inbound—pay $1.00, exact change, when boarding.
Local Bus or Subway pass accepted.

Fenway

400 Park Dr., west of Riverway/Boston
47-Central-Albany St.   CT2-Kendall-Ruggles

Longwood

Chapel St., north of 200 Longwood Ave./Brookline

Brookline Village

Station St. and Pearl St./Brookline
Green Line-E (Heath St.) at S.   65-Brighton Ctr.-Kenmore
Huntington Ave., 3 blocks   66-Harvard-Dudley
39-Forest Hills-Back Bay Sta.,   Peter Pan to Worcester,
3 blocks   Rt. 9 local
60-Chestnut Hill-Kenmore

Brookline Hills

Tappan St., west of 100 Cypress St./Brookline

Beaconsfield

100 Beaconsfield Rd. at 30 Dean Rd./Brookline

Reservoir

400 Chestnut Hill Ave., south of 1960 Beacon St./Brookline
Green Line-B (Boston College)   86-Sullivan, via Harvard
at Chestnut Hill Ave., 2 blocks Boston College bus
Green Line-C (Cleveland Circle) Newbury College bus
51-Forest Hills

◄— FARE ZONE beyond this point:
Inbound—pay $2.00, exact change, when boarding.
Combo pass required.
Outbound—no fare.

P **Chestnut Hill**

500 Hammond St., north of Rt. 9/Newton

Newton Centre

Union St., off 750 Beacon St. and Langley Rd./Newton
52-Dedham Mall-Watertown

Newton Highlands

1160 Walnut St. at Lincoln St./Newton
59-Needham Jct.-Watertown

P **Eliot**

250 Lincoln St. and Meredith Ave./Newton

P **Waban**

Wyman St., off 1620 Beacon St./Newton

P **Woodland**

1960 Washington St. at Longfellow Rd./Newton

P **Riverside**

390 Grove St., east of Rt. 128/Newton
Greyhound   Regis College bus
Peter Pan   300-Downtown (express)
Vermont Transit   353A-Burlington &
Hudson Airporter   Waltham Ind. Areas
Mass. Bay Comm. College bus

RAPID TRANSIT STATIONS   **STREET ADDRESS & CONNECTING SERVICES**

To Lechmere via Park St.

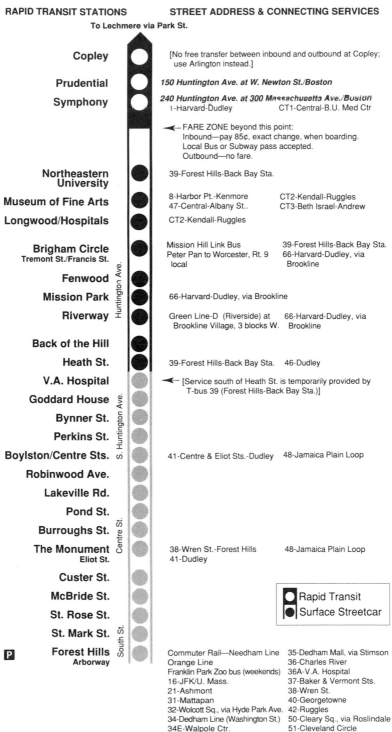

Copley — [No free transfer between inbound and outbound at Copley; use Arlington instead.]

Prudential — *150 Huntington Ave. at W. Newton St./Boston*

Symphony — *240 Huntington Ave. at 300 Massachusetts Ave./Boston*
1-Harvard-Dudley   CT1-Central-B.U. Med Ctr

◄— FARE ZONE beyond this point:
Inbound—pay 85¢, exact change, when boarding.
Local Bus or Subway pass accepted.
Outbound—no fare.

Northeastern University — 39-Forest Hills-Back Bay Sta.

Museum of Fine Arts —
8-Harbor Pt.-Kenmore   CT2-Kendall-Ruggles
47-Central-Albany St..   CT3-Beth Israel-Andrew

Longwood/Hospitals — CT2-Kendall-Ruggles

Brigham Circle
Tremont St./Francis St. —
Mission Hill Link Bus   39-Forest Hills-Back Bay Sta.
Peter Pan to Worcester, Rt. 9   66-Harvard-Dudley, via
local   Brookline

Fenwood

Mission Park — 66-Harvard-Dudley, via Brookline

Riverway —
Green Line-D (Riverside) at   66-Harvard-Dudley, via
Brookline Village, 3 blocks W. Brookline

Back of the Hill

Heath St. — 39-Forest Hills-Back Bay Sta.   46-Dudley

V.A. Hospital — ◄— [Service south of Heath St. is temporarily provided by T-bus 39 (Forest Hills-Back Bay Sta.)]

Goddard House

Bynner St.

Perkins St.

Boylston/Centre Sts. — 41-Centre & Eliot Sts.-Dudley   48-Jamaica Plain Loop

Robinwood Ave.

Lakeville Rd.

Pond St.

Burroughs St.

The Monument
Eliot St. —
38-Wren St.-Forest Hills   48-Jamaica Plain Loop
41-Dudley

Custer St.

McBride St.

St. Rose St.

St. Mark St.

Huntington Ave. / S. Huntington Ave. / Centre St. / South St.

○	Rapid Transit
◉	Surface Streetcar

Forest Hills
Arborway —
Commuter Rail—Needham Line   35-Dedham Mall, via Stimson
Orange Line   36-Charles River
Franklin Park Zoo bus (weekends)   36A-V.A. Hospital
16-JFK/U. Mass.   37-Baker & Vermont Sts.
21-Ashmont   38-Wren St.
31-Mattapan   40-Georgetowne
32-Wolcott Sq., via Hyde Park Ave. 42-Ruggles
34-Dedham Line (Washington St.)   50-Cleary Sq., via Roslindale
34E-Walpole Ctr.   51-Cleveland Circle

123

MBTA Buses

	Trip Time	Mon.–Fri. frequency (min.)			Sat. Freq.	Sun. Freq.
		Rush	Midday	Night		

1 **Harvard—Dudley**   26-38   8/7   12   16   12   18-20
via Mass. Ave.—*Cambridge:* Mass. Ave., Central Sq., MIT; Harvard Bridge; *Back Bay:* Mass. Ave., Symphony Hall; South End: Boston City Hosp.; *Roxbury:* Melnea Cass Blvd., Washington St.
➤Red Line @ Harvard, Central; Green Line-(B,C,D) @ Hynes Convention Ctr./ICA; Green Line-E @ Symphony; Orange Line @ Mass. Ave. **Free transfer** (with 85¢ fare) between Dudley Sq. and Orange Line at Mass. Ave. station.

3 **Chinatown—Marine Ind. Pk.**   17-19   20/23   —   —   —   —
Boston: Washington St., Kneeland St., Harrison Ave., Broadway; S. Boston: A St., Congress St., Fargo St., Northern Ave., Black Falcon Ave., Summer St.
➤Orange Line @ N. E. Med. Ctr., Red Line @ Broadway.

5 **City Point—McCormack Housing**   19-20   —   60   —   60   —
S. Boston: E. 4th St./E. Broadway, Perkins Sq., Dorchester St., Andrew Sq., Preble St., Old Colony Ave.
➤Red Line @ Andrew.

6 **Marine Ind. Pk.—Haymarket**   23-26   30   —   —   —   —
S. Boston: Black Falcon Ave., Summer St., Congress St.; *Boston*: South Sta., Atlantic Ave., Commercial St., Hanover St. **Add'l service Marine Ind. Pk.—South Sta. every 15 min (6am-6pm)..**
➤Red Line @ South Sta.; Blue Line @ Aquarium; Green & Orange lines @ Haymarket.

7 **City Point—Otis/Summer Sts.**   17-26   12/14   25   40   25   —
S. Boston: E. 4th St./E. Broadway, L St., Summer St., Congress St.; *Boston*: South Sta., Federal St., Franklin St., Otis St. **Nights: City Pt.—South Sta. only.**
➤Red Line @ South Sta.;

8 **Harbor Pt.—Kenmore**   29-45   20   45   45   45   45
Dorchester: UMass/Boston, Mt. Vernon St., Columbia Rd., Mass. Ave., South Bay Mall; *South End:* Boston City Hosp., Harrison Ave.; *Roxbury:* Washington St., Dudley Sq., Melnea Cass Blvd.; *Fenway:* Ruggles St., Ave. Louis Pasteur, Longwood Ave., Longwood Med. Area, Brookline Ave.
Bus 8A—*Rush hours*: add'l service Dudley-Kenmore every 13/20 min.
➤Red Line @ JFK/UMass; Orange Line @ Ruggles; Green Line-E @ Ruggles St.; Green Line-(B,C,D) @ Kenmore

9 **City Point—Copley**   16-31   8/9   15   30   15-20   30
via Broadway—*S. Boston:* E. 4th St./E. Broadway, Perkins Sq., W. Broadway; *South End:* Herald St., Berkeley/Arlington Sts.; *Back Bay:* St. James Ave./Boylston St.
➤Red Line @ Broadway; Green Line @ Copley, Arlington.

10 **City Point—Copley**   26-44   25   30   40   30   40
via Andrew—*S. Boston:* E. 4th St./E. Broadway, Perkins Sq., Dorchester St., Andrew Sq., Southampton St., South Bay Mall; *South End:* Newmarket Sq., Mass. Ave., Albany St., Boston City Hosp., E. Newton St., W. Dedham St.; *Back Bay*: Dartmouth St.
➤Red Line @ Andrew; Orange Line @ Back Bay Sta.; Green Line @ Copley.

11 **City Pt.—Downtown**   19-28   6/8   15   30   20   30
via Bayview—*S. Boston:* E. 8th St., W. 7th St., Dorchester Ave.; *Boston:* Herald St., Washington St., Chauncy St., Bedford St. **Nights: City Pt.—Kneeland & Washington Sts. only.**
➤Red Line @ Broadway; Orange Line @ N. E. Med. Ctr.; Orange Line @ Chinatown (except nights); Red & Orange lines @ Downtown Crossing(except nights).

14 **Roslindale—Dudley**   25-28   60   60   —   60   —
Roslindale: Cummins Hwy., Hyde Park Ave., Bradlees, American Legion Hwy.; *Dorchester:* Blue Hill Ave., Franklin Park, Grove Hall; *Roxbury:* Warren St.

15 **Kane Sq.—Ruggles**   21-35   7/9   13   30   16   60
Dorchester: Hancock St., Uphams Corner, Dudley St.; *Roxbury:* Dudley Sq., New Dudley St. **Nights & Sun.: Fields Corner—Ruggles**—*Dorchester:* Geneva Ave., Bowdoin St., Kane Sq., then regular route.
➤Orange Line @ Ruggles; Red Line @ Fields Corner (nights & Sun. only).

Crosstown Bus Routes

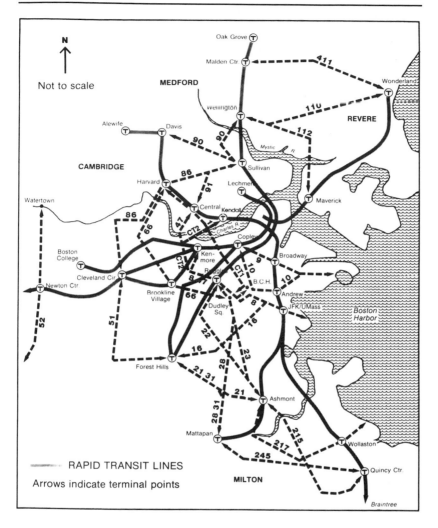

1-Harvard-Dudley
8-Harbor Pt.-Kenmore
9-City Pt.-Copley
10-City Pt.-Copley
16-Forest Hills-JFK/U.Mass.
21-Ashmont-Forest Hills
22-Ashmont-Ruggles
23-Ashmont-Ruggles
28-Mattapan-Ruggles

31-Mattapan-Forest Hills
47-Central-Albany St.
51-Cleveland Cir.-Forest Hills
52-Dedham Mall-Watertown
66-Harvard-Dudley
86-Sullivan-Cleveland Cir.
90-Davis-Wellington
91-Sullivan-Central
110-Wonderland-Wellington

112-Wellington-Maverick
215-Quincy Ctr.-Ashmont
217-Wollaston Beach-Ashmont
245-Quincy Ctr.-Mattapan
411-Revere House-Malden Ctr.

*CT1-Central-B.U. Medical Center
*CT2-Kendall-Ruggles
*CT3-Beth Israel-Andrew

* New service: see pp. 138-139 for detailed information.

MBTA Buses

		Trip Time	Mon.–Fri. frequency (min.)			Sat. Freq.	Sun. Freq.
			Rush	Midday	Night		

16 **Forest Hills—JFK/UMass**   17-23   15/18   25   40   25   40
Jamaica Plain: Morton St., J.W.V. Dr., Franklin Park; *Dorchester:* Columbia Rd., Uphams
Corner, South Bay Mall (M-Sa), Boston St., Andrew Sq., Preble St., Old Colony Ave.;
Rush hours: Forest Hills—UMass.—regular route, then Morrissey Blvd., University Rd.
➤Orange Line @ Forest Hills; Red Line @ JFK/UMass, Andrew.

17 **Fields Corner—Andrew**   13-12   12   20   40   20   —
Dorchester: Geneva Ave., Bowdoin St., Kane Sq., Hancock St., Uphams Corner, Columbia
Rd., Boston St. *Nights & Sun.:* Buses operate **Fields Corner-Ruggles** (see Bus 15).
➤Red Line @ Fields Corner, JFK/UMass.

18 **Ashmont—Andrew**   23-27   35   70   —   60   —
Dorchester: Dorchester Ave., Fields Corner.
➤Red Line @ Ashmont, Fields Corner, Savin Hill, Andrew, Broadway

19 **Fields Corner—Ruggles**   19-28   13/20   2 Trips   —   —   —
via Grove Hall—*Dorchester:* Geneva Ave., Grove Hall; *Roxbury:* Warren St., Dudley Sq.,
New Dudley St.
➤Red Line @ Fields Corner; Orange Line @ Ruggles.

20 **Fields Cor.—Neponset & Adams**   8-10   12/15   15   30   15   30-60
Dorchester: Adams St., Gallivan Blvd., Neponset Cir., Neponset Ave. (loop). Some midday
trips serve Bradlees dept. store via Victory Rd. **Middays & weekends: also serves
Hilltop St., Hallet Sq.**
➤Red Line @ Fields Corner.

21 **Ashmont—Forest Hills**   12-19   11   20   40   45   —
Dorchester: Gallivan Blvd.; Mattapan, *Jamaica Plain:* Morton St.
➤Red Line @ Ashmont; Orange Line, Green Line [Bus 39] @ Forest Hills.

22 **Ashmont—Ruggles**   20-31   10   13   20   11-16   15-25
via Jackson Sq.—*Dorchester:* Talbot Ave., Codman Sq., Blue Hill Ave., Franklin Park,
Seaver St.; *Roxbury:* Columbus Ave., Egleston Sq., Jackson Sq.
➤Red Line @ Ashmont; Orange Line @ Jackson Sq., Ruggles.

23 **Ashmont—Ruggles**   20-30   5/6   13   20   13-16   20-30
via Dudley Sq.—*Dorchester:* Talbot Ave., Codman Sq., Washington St., Grove Hall;
Roxbury: Warren St., Dudley Sq., New Dudley St.
➤Red Line @ Ashmont; Orange Line @ Ruggles.

24 **Wakefield Ave.—Mattapan**   11-22   20/25   50   60   50   60
Hyde Park: Metropolitan Ave., Highland St., Washington St., Truman Pkwy. (loop), Fairmount
Ave.*; *Mattapan:* River St. * *Nights: Through service* **Wakefield Ave.—Ashmont.**
➤Red Line @ Mattapan; Red Line @ Ashmont (nights only).

26 **Norfolk St.—Ashmont**   10-13   15   30   30   30   60
Dorchester: Washington St., Gallivan Blvd., Norfolk St. (loop); Codman Sq., Talbot Ave.
➤Red Line @ Ashmont.

27 **Mattapan—Ashmont**   11-12   30   30   30   30   60
Mattapan: River St., Mattapan Hosp.; Dorchester: Lower Mills, Dorchester Ave. **Nights:**
Through service on some trips **Wakefield Ave.—Ashmont** via Bus 24.
➤Red Line @ Mattapan, Ashmont.

28 **Mattapan—Ruggles**   23-41   8/12   13   20   15   15-20
via Dudley Sq.—*Mattapan:* Blue Hill Ave.; *Dorchester:* Franklin Park, Grove Hall;
Roxbury: Warren St., Dudley Sq., New Dudley St.
➤Red Line @ Mattapan; Orange Line @ Ruggles.

29 **Mattapan—Jackson Sq.**   17-29   16/15   30   20   —   —
Dorchester: Blue Hill Ave., Franklin Park, Seaver St.; *Roxbury:* Columbus Ave. Nighttime
service (M-Sat): Mattapan—Ruggles every 20 min, *Some midday trips serve Franklin
Field Housing Project.*
➤Orange Line @ Jackson Sq.; Red Line @ Mattapan.

MBTA Buses

	Trip Time	Mon.–Fri. frequency (min.)			Sat. Freq.	Sun. Freq.
		Rush	Midday	Night		

30   **Mattapan—Roslindale**   9-15   20   30   60   40   60
Mattapan, Roslindale: Cummins Hwy.
➤Red Line @ Mattapan.

31   **Mattapan—Forest Hills**   10-19   8   12   20   10-15   20
Mattapan: Blue Hill Ave.; *Jamaica Plain:* Morton St.
➤Red Line @ Mattapan; Orange Line @ Forest Hills

32   **Wolcott Sq.—Forest Hills**   14-22   12/8   15   30   12   30
Readville: Hyde Park Ave.; *Hyde Park:* Cleary Sq.; Roslindale, *Jamaica Plain:* Hyde Park Ave. **AM rush: add'l service Cleary Sq.—Forest Hills every 6 min.**
➤Orange Line @ Forest Hills.

33   **Dedham Line—Mattapan**   21-27   60   60   —   60   —
Readville: River St.; *Hyde Park:* Turtle Pond Pkwy., Alwin St., River St., Cleary Sq.; *Mattapan:* River St.
➤Red Line @ Mattapan.

34   **Dedham Line—Forest Hills**   13-24   9/8   15   30   15   30
W. Roxbury: Washington St.; *Roslindale:* Roslindale Sq.
➤Orange Line @ Forest Hills.

34E   **Walpole Ctr.—Forest Hills**   44-59   20   45   60   45   60
Walpole: East St., High Plain Ave., E. Walpole; *Norwood, Westwood:* Washington St.; *Dedham:* Dedham Sq., Dedham Mall; *W. Roxbury:* Washington St.; *Roslindale:* Roslindale Sq. **Nights & Sun.: E. Walpole—Forest Hills only.** Zone fares, 60¢-$1.00.
➤Orange Line @ Forest Hills.

35   **Dedham Mall—Forest Hills**   20-31   20/12   30   2 trips   30   60
via Stimson St.—*Dedham:* Washington St.; *W. Roxbury:* Stimson St., Centre St.; *Roslindale:* Belgrade Ave., Roslindale Sq., Washington St. **AM rush: Stimson St.—Forest Hills only.**
➤Orange Line @ Forest Hills.

36   **Charles River—Forest Hills**   16-21   11/12   30   30   30   30
W. Roxbury: Spring St., Centre St.; *Roslindale:* Belgrade Ave., Roslindale Sq., Washington St.
➤Orange Line @ Forest Hills.

36A   **V.A. Hospital—Forest Hills**   18-25   22/30   30   —   30   60
W. Roxbury: Spring St., Centre St.; *Roslindale:* Belgrade Ave., Roslindale Sq., Washington St.
➤Orange Line @ Forest Hills.

37   **Baker & Vermont—Forest Hills**   15-23   20/13   30   —   30   60
W. Roxbury: Vermont St., Baker St., Lasell St., LaGrange St., Centre St.; *Roslindale:* Belgrade Ave., Roslindale Sq., Washington St.
➤Orange Line @ Forest Hills.

38   **Wren St.—Forest Hills**   12-19   22   40   2 trips   40   40
W. Roxbury: Park St., Anawan Ave.; *Roslindale:* Centre St.; *Jamaica Plain:* Faulkner Hosp., Arnold Arboretum, The Monument, South St.
➤Orange Line @ Forest Hills.

39   **Forest Hills—Back Bay Sta.**   24-38   3/4   7   9   7   7
Substitutes for Green Line-E (Arborway) streetcar.
Jamaica Plain: South St., The Monument, Centre St., V. A. Hospital, S. Huntington Ave., *Mission Hill, Fenway:* Huntington Ave.; *Back Bay:* Boylston St./St. James Ave.
➤Orange Line @ Forest Hills; Green Line-E @ Heath St., Brigham Cir., Northeastern; Green Line @ Copley; Orange Line @ Back Bay Sta. **Free transfer** (with 85¢ fare) at Copley and Back Bay Sta.

40   **Georgetowne—Forest Hills**   18-25   30   50   —   60   —
Hyde Park: Alwin St., Georgetowne Dr., W. Boundary Rd.; *W. Roxbury:* Washington St.; *Roslindale:* Roslindale Sq.

MBTA Buses

	Trip Time	Mon.–Fri. frequency (min.)			Sat. Freq.	Sun. Freq.
		Rush	Midday	Night		

41

Centre & Eliot Sts.—Dudley   10-17   18/20   34   30   35   —
Jamaica Plain: Centre St., Hyde Sq.; *Roxbury:* Jackson Sq., Centre St.
➤Orange Line @ Jackson Sq.

42

Forest Hills—Ruggles   18-24   20   20   50   18   50
Jamaica Plain: Washington St.; *Roxbury:* Egleston Sq., Dudley Sq., New Dudley St.
AM Rush: add'l service Forest Hills—Dudley every 10 min.
➤Orange Line @ Forest Hills, Ruggles.

43

Ruggles—Park St.   13-21   8/10   15   20   15   20
South End: Tremont St.; *Boston:* Park Plaza, circles Boston Common.
➤Orange Line @ Ruggles, N. E. Med. Ctr.; Green Line @ Boylston; Red & Green lines @ Park St.

44

Jackson Sq.—Ruggles   17-27   10   20   30   16   45
via Humboldt Ave.—*Roxbury:* Columbus Ave., Egleston Sq.; *Dorchester:* Seaver St., Humboldt Ave.; *Roxbury:* Walnut Ave., Warren St., Dudley Sq., New Dudley St.
➤Orange Line @ Jackson Sq., Ruggles.

45

Franklin Park Zoo—Ruggles   15-25   7/8   16   30   16   45
via Grove Hall—*Dorchester:* Blue Hill Ave., Grove Hall; *Roxbury:* Dudley St., Dudley Sq., New Dudley St.
➤Orange Line @ Ruggles.

46

Heath St.—Dudley   10-13   30   30   —   30   —
Jamaica Plain: Heath St.; *Roxbury:* Jackson Sq., Centre St.
➤Green Line-E @ Heath St.; Orange Line @ Jackson Sq.

47

Central—Albany St.   24-40   20   20   30   20   35
Cambridge: Pearl/Brookline Sts.;*Fenway:* Park Dr., Brookline Ave., Longwood Med. Area, Longwood Ave., Ave. Louis Pasteur, Ruggles St.; *Roxbury:* Melnea Cass Blvd., Dudley Sq., Washington St.; *South End:* Boston City Hospital, University Hospital.
➤Red Line @ Central; Green Line-B @ B.U. Central; Green Line-C @ Mary's St. (1 block walk); Green Line-D @ Fenway; Green Line-E @ Museum Fine Arts; Orange Line @ Ruggles.

48

Jamaica Plain Loop   19   —   30   —   30   —
Jamaica Plain: Centre St., Paul Gore St., Chestnut Ave.; *Roxbury:* Jackson Sq., Egleston Sq.; *Jamaica Plain:* Washington St., Amory St., Lamartine St., Green
➤Orange Line @ Jackson Sq., Stony Brook, Green.

49

Dudley—Downtown   15-25   6/8   11   13   9-12   11-15
Roxbury, South End: Washington St.; *Boston:* Chauncy St., Bedford St.
➤Orange Line @ N. E. Med. Ctr., Chinatown; Red & Orange Lines @ Downtown Crossing. Free inbound with transfer from Orange Line at N. E. Med. Ctr. and outbound at Surface Artery.

50

Cleary Sq.—Forest Hills   15-19   20   60   —   60   —
via Roslindale—*Hyde Park:* Gordon Ave., West St.; *Roslindale:* Metropolitan Ave., Roslindale Sq., Washington St.
➤Orange Line @ Forest Hills.

51

Cleveland Cir.—Forest Hills   25-33   20   60   60   60   —
Brookline: Chestnut Hill Ave., Lee St., Newton St., Grove St., Putterham Sq., Hancock Village; *W. Roxbury:* Weld St.; *Roslindale:* Walter St., Roslindale Sq., Washington St.
➤Green Line-C @ Cleveland Circle; Green Line-D @ Reservoir; Orange Line @ Forest Hills.

52

Dedham Mall—Watertown   37   30   45   —   45   —
Dedham: V.F.W. Pkwy.;*W. Roxbury:* Charles River Loop, Spring St., Baker St.; *Newton:* Oak Hill, Wiswall Rd., Dedham St., Parker St.*, Newton Centre, Centre St., Newton Corner; *Watertown:* Galen St. *Alternate trips *Newton:* Jewish Community Ctr., Winchester St., Centre St. *instead of* Parker St. **AM rush: Charles River Loop—Watertown only.**
➤Green Line-D @ Newton Centre

MBTA Buses

	Trip Time	Mon.–Fri. frequency (min.)			Sat. Freq.	Sun. Freq.
		Rush	Midday	Night		

53 Roberts—Newton Corner 28-31 30/60 60 — 60 —
Waltham: South St., Brandeis U., Waltham Hosp., Main St., Central Sq., Moody St.;
Newton: River St., W. Newton, Austin St. (Park & Ride), Washington St., Newtonville.
Through service **Roberts—Downtown** via Bus 304.

54 Waverley—Newton Corner 35-36 30/60 60 — 60 —
Belmont: Lexington St.; *Watertown:* Belmont St.; *Waltham:* Beaver St., Bentley College,
Lyman St., Central Sq., Moody St.; *Newton:* River St., W. Newton, Washington St.,
Newtonville. *Through service* **Waverley—Downtown** via Bus 304.

55 Queensberry St.—Park St. 14-27 17/30 60 30 30 30
Fenway: Ipswich St.; *Back Bay:* Boylston St., Copley Sq.; *Boston:* circles Boston
Common. (Outbound trips: Stuart St., St. James Ave., Copley Sq., Newbury St.) Nights &
weekends: **Queensberry St.—Copley only.**
➤Green Line @ all stops from Hynes/ICA to Park St., Red & Green lines @ Park St.

56 Waltham Highnds.—Newton Cor. 27 30 60 — 60 —
Waltham: Bacon St., Dale St., Hammond St., Main St., Central Sq., Moody St., High St.;
Newton: Crafts St., Nonantum, Walnut St., Newtonville, Washington St. **Rush hours:**
alternate trips **Cedarwood—Newton Corner**—*Waltham:* Stow St., Main St., Central Sq.,
then regular route. **Rush hours:** through service **Waltham Highlands—Downtown** or
Cedarwood—Downtown via Bus 304.

57 Watertown—Kenmore 21-32 6/8 9 15 9 15-30
Watertown: Galen St.; *Newton:* Newton Corner, Tremont St.; *Brighton:* Oak Sq., Washington
St., Brighton Ctr., Cambridge St.; *Allston:* Union Sq., Brighton Ave., Commonwealth Ave.
➤Green Line-B @ Packard's Corner; Green Line-(B,C,D) @ Kenmore.

58 Auburndale—Newton Corner 27-28 30 2 trips — — —
Newton: Commonwealth Ave., Lexington St., Rumford Ave.; *Waltham:* Woerd Ave.,
Crescent St., Central Sq., River St.; *Watertown:* Pleasant St., Bemis; *Newton:* Chapel St.,
Nonantum, Adams St., Washington St. *Through service* on some trips **Auburndale—
Downtown** via Bus 304.

59 Needham Jct.—Watertown 35-40 30 45 — 45 —
Needham: Chestnut St., Needham Ctr., Highland Ave., Needham Hts., Hillside Ave., Webster
St., Central Ave.; *Newton:* Newton Upper Falls, Chestnut St., Oak St., Elliott St.*, Lincoln St.*,
Newton Highlands, Walnut St., Newtonville, Nonantum, Watertown St. * **Mon.-Fri.:** some trips
via Needham St.— *Newton:* Needham St. *instead of* Elliott & Lincoln Sts.
➤Green Line-D @ Newton Highlands.

60 Chestnut Hill—Kenmore 19-33 17/18 30 30-60 30-32 60
Brookline: Boylston St. (Rt.9), Cypress St., High St., Brookline Village; *Fenway:* Brookline
Ave., Longwood Med. Area.
➤Green Line-D @ Brookline Village; Green Line-(B,C,D) @ Kenmore.

62 Bedford V.A.—Alewife 38-42 30 60 1 trip 60 —
Bedford: V.A. Hosp., Springs Rd., Bedford Ctr., South Rd., Loomis St., Great Rd.;
Lexington: Bedford St., Lexington Ctr., Mass. Ave.; *Arlington:* Arlington Hts., Park Ave.,
Rt. 2. **Nights:** Bedford Ctr.-Alewife only. Zone fares, 60¢-$1.00.
➤Red Line @ Alewife.

64 Oak Sq.—Central 19-29 18 30 60 60 60
Brighton: Faneuil St., Hobart St., Brooks St., Birmingham Pkwy., N. Beacon St.; *Allston:*
Union Sq., Cambridge St.; *Cambridge:* Magazine St./Western Ave. **Rush hours: Oak
Sq.—Kendall**—regular route, then Cambridge: Central Sq., Main St.
➤Red Line @ Central; Red Line @ Kendall (rush hours only).

65 Brighton Ctr.—Kenmore 21-33 20/25 30 2 trips 30 —
via Brookline—*Brighton:* Washington St.; *Brookline:* Washington St., Brookline Village;
Fenway: Brookline Ave., Longwood Med. Area.
➤Green Line-B @ Washington St.; Green Line-C @ Washington Sq.; Green Line-D @
Brookline Village; Green Line-(B,C,D) @ Kenmore.

MBTA Buses	Trip Time	Mon.–Fri. frequency (min.)			Sat. Freq.	Sun. Freq.
		Rush	Midday	Night		

66 **Harvard—Dudley**   26-43   8/9   14   40   15   40
via Brookline—*Cambridge:* Kennedy St.; *Allston:* N. Harvard St., Cambridge St., Union Sq., Brighton Ave.; *Brookline:* Harvard St., Coolidge Corner, Brookline Village; *Mission Hill:* Huntington Ave., Brigham Cir., Tremont St.; *Roxbury:* Roxbury Crossing, New Dudley St.
➤Red Line @ Harvard; Green Line-B @ Harvard Ave.; Green Line-C @ Coolidge Corner; Green Line-D @ Brookline Village; Green Line-E @ S. Huntington Ave., Brigham Cir.; Orange Line @ Roxbury Crossing.

67 **Turkey Hill—Alewife**   15-20   25   45   —   —   —
Arlington: Washington St., Forest St., Summer St., Symmes Hosp., Mill St., Arlington Ctr., Pleasant St., Rt. 2.
➤Red Line @ Alewife.

69 **Harvard—Lechmere**   11-18 14/17   23   30   20   30
Cambridge: Cambridge St., Inman Sq., E. Cambridge.
➤Red Line @ Harvard; Green Line @ Lechmere.

70 **Cedarwood—Central**   32-53 14/15   30   60   40-60 30
Waltham: Stow St., Main St., Central Sq.; *Watertown:* Watertown Sq., Arsenal St.; *Brighton, Allston:* Western Ave.; *Cambridge:* River St./Western Ave. **Sat.:** *Add'l service* **Watertown Sq.—Central** every 10 min. (afternoon & early evenings only)
➤Red Line @ Central.

70A **North Waltham—Central**   31-38   60   120   —   40   —
Waltham: Trapelo Rd., Smith St., Lincoln St., Lake St., Lexington St., Central Sq., Main St., then same route as Bus 70. **Rush hours:** some trips *Waltham:* Totten Pond Rd.
➤Red Line @ Central.

71 **Watertown—Harvard***   13-16   7/9   12   30   15   50-60
Watertown, Cambridge: Mt. Auburn St., E. Watertown, Mt. Auburn Hosp.
➤Red Line @ Harvard.

72 **Huron Ave.—Harvard***   9-10   15   30   30   30   30
Cambridge: Aberdeen Ave., Huron Ave., Concord Ave.
➤Red Line @ Harvard.

73 **Waverley—Harvard***   14-22   5   12   30   12-15 50-60
Belmont: Trapelo Rd., Cushing Sq.; *Watertown:* Belmont St.; *Cambridge:* Mt. Auburn St., Mt. Auburn Hosp.
➤Red Line @ Harvard.

74 **Belmont Ctr.—Harvard**   13-22 14/15   30   40   30   40
via Concord Ave.—*Belmont:* Leonard St., Concord Ave., Bright Rd.; *Cambridge:* Blanchard Rd.*, Sancta Maria Hosp.*, Concord Ave.*, Fresh Pond*. * **some trips via Huron Towers**—*Belmont:* Leonard St., Concord Ave., Bright Rd.; *Cambridge:* Grove St., Huron Ave., Fresh Pond Pkwy., Concord Ave.
➤Red Line @ Harvard.

76 **Hanscom Field—Alewife**   36-41   30   60   60   60   —
Lexington: Wood St., Mass. Ave., Marrett Rd., Five Forks, Waltham St., Worthen Rd., Lexington Ctr., Mass. Ave., Pleasant St.; *Arlington:* Rt. 2. **Nights: Five Forks—Alewife only. Zone fares**, 60¢-$1.00.
➤Red Line @ Alewife.

77 **Arlington Hts.—Harvard**   22-35   8   11   10-12   8   15-20
Arlington: Mass. Ave., Arlington Ctr.; *Cambridge:* Mass. Ave., N. Cambridge, Porter Sq. *Rush hours:* no local stops N. Cambridge—Harvard; see Bus 77A.
➤Red Line @ Porter, Harvard.

77A **North Cambridge—Harvard*** 8-13   7/9   12   —   —   —
Cambridge: Mass. Ave., Porter Sq. **Nights & weekends:** see Bus 77.
➤Red Line @ Porter @ Harvard.

* Indicates trolley-bus route

MBTA Buses

		Trip Time	Mon.–Fri. frequency (min.)			Sat. Freq.	Sun. Freq.
			Rush	Midday	Night		
78	**Arlmont—Harvard**	15-30	14/15	30	60	30	60

Arlington: Appleton St., Wachusett Ave., Park Cir., Rt. 2; *Belmont:* Brighton St.;
Cambridge: Blanchard Rd., Sancta Maria Hosp., Concord Ave., Fresh Pond.
➤Red Line @ Harvard.

79	**Arlington Hts.—Alewife**	10-24	8/9	25	3 trips	—	—

Arlington: Mass. Ave., Arlington Ctr.; *Cambridge:* Alewife Brook Pkwy.
➤Red Line @ Alewife.

80	**Arlington Ctr.—Lechmere**	19-34	15	35	60	35	60

via Medford Hillside—*Arlington:* Medford St.; *Medford:* High St., W. Medford, Boston
Ave., Medford Hillside, Tufts U.; *Somerville:* College Ave., Powderhouse Sq., Broadway,
Ball Sq., Magoun Sq., Medford St., McGrath Hwy.
➤Green Line @ Lechmere.

83	**Rindge Ave.—Central**	16-27	10/15	30	60	25	40-60

Cambridge: Rindge Ave., Mass Ave., Porter Sq.; *Somerville:* Somerville Ave., Park St.,
Beacon St.; *Cambridge:* Inman Sq., Prospect St.
➤Red Line @ Alewife, Porter, Central.

84	**Arlmont—Alewife**	20	30	—	—	—	—

Arlington: Appleton St., Wachusett Ave., Park Ave., Rt. 2.
➤Red Line @ Alewife

85	**Spring Hill—Kendall**	10-14	30/40	40	—	—	—

Somerville: Summer St., Union Sq., Webster Ave.; *Cambridge:* Windsor/Columbia Sts.,
Hampshire St., Tech Sq.
➤Red Line @ Kendall.

86	**Sullivan—Cleveland Cir.**	24-37	20/18	35	35-60	40	70

Somerville: Washington St., Union Sq.; *Cambridge:* Kirkland St., Harvard Sq., Kennedy St.;
Allston: N. Harvard St., Western Ave.; *Brighton:* Market St., Brighton Ctr., Chestnut Hill Ave.
➤Orange Line @ Sullivan; Red Line @ Harvard; Green Line-B @ Chestnut Hill Ave.;
Green Line-C @ Cleveland Cir.; Green Line-D @ Reservoir.

87	**Arlington Ctr.—Lechmere**	22-28	16/15	25	30	24	30

via Somerville Ave.—*Arlington:* Broadway; *Somerville:* Clarendon Hill, Broadway, Teele
Sq., Holland St., Davis Sq., Elm St., Somerville Ave., Union Sq., McGrath Hwy. **Nights &
weekends: Clarendon Hill—Lechmere only.**
➤Red Line @ Davis, Porter (1 block walk); Green Line @ Lechmere.

88	**Clarendon Hill—Lechmere**	17-22	8/12	25	30	24	30

via Highland Ave.—*Somerville:* Broadway, Teele Sq., Holland St., Davis Sq., Highland
Ave., Somerville Hosp., City Hall, McGrath Hwy.
➤Red Line @ Davis; Green Line @ Lechmere.

89	**Clarendon Hill—Sullivan**	14-24	9	30	60	30	60

Somerville: Broadway, Teele Sq., Powderhouse Sq., Ball Sq., Magoun Sq., Winter Hill, E.
Somerville.
➤Orange Line @ Sullivan.

90	**Davis—Wellington**	26-28	30/35	60	60	60	—

Somerville: Highland Ave., Somerville Hosp., City Hall, Cross St., Broadway;
Charlestown: Sullivan Sq.; *Somerville:* Middlesex Ave., Assembly Sq.; *Medford:* Fellsway.
➤Red Line @ Davis; Orange Line @ Sullivan, Wellington.

91	**Sullivan—Central**	12-20	25	25	60	20	40

Somerville: Washington St., Union Sq., Newton St., Springfield St.; *Cambridge:* Inman
Sq., Prospect St.
➤Orange Line @ Sullivan; Red Line @ Central.

MBTA Buses

		Trip Time	Mon.–Fri. frequency (min.)			Sat. Freq.	Sun. Freq.
			Rush	Midday	Night		

92 **Assembly Sq.-Downtown** 18-24 10/13 30 60 30 —
via Sullivan, Main St.—*Somerville:* Middlesex Ave.; Charlestown: Sullivan Sq., Main St., Thompson Sq., City Sq.; *Boston:* N. Washington St., Haymarket, Congress St., Franklin St., Washington St. **Rush hours: Sullivan—Downtown only. Nights: Sullivan—Haymarket only.**
➤Orange Line @ Sullivan; Green & Orange lines @ Haymarket; Blue & Orange lines @ State (except nights); Red & Orange lines @ Downtown Crossing (except nights).

93 **Sullivan—Downtown** 14-24 6/7 20 30-60 20 40
via Bunker Hill St.—*Charlestown:* Bunker Hill St., Charlestown Navy Yard, Chelsea St., City Sq.; *Boston:* N. Washington St., Haymarket, Congress St., Franklin St., Washington St. Nights: **Sullivan—Haymarket** only.
➤Orange Line @ Sullivan; Green & Orange lines @ Haymarket; Blue & Orange lines @ State (except nights); Red & Orange lines @ Downtown Crossing (except nights).

94 **Medford Sq.—Davis** 13-22 22/20 40 40 22 40
via W. Medford—*Medford:* High St., W. Medford, Boston Ave., Medford Hillside, Tufts U.; *Somerville:* College Ave., Powderhouse Sq.
➤Red Line @ Davis.

95 **West Medford—Sullivan** 18-30 15 30 60 30 60
Medford: Playstead Rd., High St., Medford Sq., Mystic Ave.; *Somerville:* Assembly Sq.
➤Orange Line @ Sullivan.

96 **Medford Sq.—Harvard** 17-30 20 40 20-60 30 60
Medford: Main St., George St., Winthrop St., Medford Hillside, Boston Ave., Tufts U.; *Somerville:* College Ave., Powderhouse Sq., Davis Sq., Elm St.; *Cambridge:* Beech St., Porter Sq., Mass. Ave.
➤Red Line @ Davis, Porter, Harvard.

97 **Malden Ctr.—Wellington** 16-18 30 60 — 50 —
via Hancock St.—*Malden:* Commercial St., Medford St., Main St.; *Everett:* Belmont St., Hancock St., Everett Sq., Sweetser Cir., Broadway.
➤Orange Line @ Malden, Wellington.

99 **Upper Highland—Wellington** 22-28 20 30 60 30 60
Medford: Highland Ave.; *Malden:* Malden Hosp., Clifton St., Summer St., Malden Ctr., Malden Sq.; *Everett:* Main St. **AM rush:** add'l service **Upper Highland—Malden Ctr.**
➤Orange Line @ Malden, Wellington.

100 **Elm St.—Wellington** 10-21 20 20 60 30 60
Medford: Fellsway West, Fellsway.
➤Orange Line @ Wellington.

101 **Malden Ctr.—Sullivan** 21-38 12 30 60 30 60
via Medford Sq. & Main St.—*Malden:* Malden Sq., Pleasant St.; *Medford:* Salem St., Medford Sq., Main St.; *Somerville:* Broadway, Winter Hill, E. Somerville. **AM rush:** add'l service **Medford Sq.-Sullivan** every 6 min.
➤Orange Line @ Malden, Sullivan.

104 **Malden Ctr.—Sullivan** 17-30 12/15 30 60 30 60
via Ferry St.—*Malden:* Malden Sq., Ferry St.; *Everett:* Glendale Sq., Broadway, Everett Sq.
➤Orange Line @ Malden, Sullivan.

105 **Malden Ctr.—Sullivan** 25-31 30 60 — 65 60
via Faulkner & Main St.—*Malden:* Malden Sq., Eastern Ave., Bowdoin St., Newland St., Bryant St., Cross St.; *Everett:* Main St., Sweetser Cir., Broadway.
➤Orange Line @ Malden, Sullivan.

106 **Lebanon St.—Wellington** 21-30 20 30 60 30 60
Malden: Lebanon St., Maplewood Sq., Salem St., Malden Sq., Malden Ctr.; *Everett:* Main St., Sweetser Cir. **AM rush:** add'l service **Lebanon St.—Malden Ctr. Sun.:** via **Forest & Sylvan Sts.**
➤Orange Line @ Malden, Wellington.

MBTA Buses

		Trip Time	Mon.–Fri. frequency (min.)			Sat. Freq.	Sun. Freq.
			Rush	Midday	Night		

108   **Linden Sq.—Wellington**   23-30   25/20   30   60   30   60
Malden: Lynn St., Beach St., Salem St., Maplewood Sq., Malden Sq., Malden Ctr.,
Pleasant St., Highland Ave.; *Medford:* Middlesex Ave. **AM rush:** *add'l service* **Linden
Sq.—Malden Ctr.**
➤Orange Line @ Malden, Wellington.

109   **Linden Sq.—Sullivan**   16-27   12/15   30   60   30   60
Malden: Eastern Ave.; *Everett:* Broadway, Glendale Sq., Everett Sq., Sweetser Cir.
➤Orange Line @ Sullivan.

110   **Wonderland—Wellington**   21-30   20   30   60   30   60
Revere: Beach St., Revere Ctr., Park Ave.; *Everett:* Woodlawn, Elm St., Ferry St.,
Chelsea St., Everett Sq., Broadway. **Rush hours:** *add'l service* **Revere Ctr.—Wellington**
every 10 min. **Nights:** **Woodlawn—Wellington** *only.*
➤Blue Line @ Wonderland (except nights); Orange Line @ Wellington.

111   **Woodlawn—Haymarket**   19-31   5/6   15   15   15-25   25
Chelsea: Washington Ave., Prattville, Bellingham Sq., Chelsea Sq.; Tobin Bridge;
Charlestown: City Sq.; *Boston:* N. Washington St.
➤Green & Orange lines @ Haymarket.

112   **Wellington—Maverick**   33-42   35   35   —   35-50   50
Everett: Broadway, Everett Sq., Chelsea St.; *Chelsea:* Everett Ave., Mystic Mall, Spruce
St., Admiral's Hill, Bellingham Sq., Chelsea Sq.; *E. Boston:* Meridian St.
➤Orange Line @ Wellington; Blue Line @ Maverick.

116   **Wonderland—Maverick**   24-28   15   30   60   30   60
via Revere St.—*Revere:* Revere St., Broadway, Revere Ctr.; *Chelsea:* Bellingham Sq.,
Chelsea Sq.; *E. Boston:* Meridian St.
➤Blue Line @ Wonderland, Maverick.

117   **Wonderland—Maverick**   22-26   15   30   60   30   60
via Beach St.—*Revere:* Beach St., Revere Ctr., Broadway; *Chelsea:* Bellingham Sq.,
Chelsea Sq.; *E. Boston:* Meridian St.
➤Blue Line @ Wonderland, Revere Beach, Maverick.

119   **Northgate—Beachmont**   20-27   30   60   3 trips   60   60
Revere: Squire Rd.; *Malden:* Linden Sq.; *Revere:* Malden St., Broadway, Revere Ctr.,
Winthrop Ave., Endicott Ave. **Nights:** **Revere Ctr.—Beachmont only.**
➤Blue Line @ Beachmont.

120   **Orient Hts.—Maverick**   29-31   14/15   20   60   30   50
E. Boston: Boardman St., Waldemar Ave., Orient Ave., Orient Hts., Bennington St.,
Meridian St., Maverick Sq., Sumner St., Jeffries Pt., Maverick St.
➤Blue Line @ Orient Hts., Wood Island, Maverick.

121   **Wood Island—Maverick**   11-12   30/25   —   —   —   —
E. Boston: Chelsea St., Eagle Sq., Lexington St., Meridian St. **PM rush:** **Eagle Sq.—
Maverick only.**
➤Blue Line @ Wood Island (AM Rush only), Maverick.

130   **Lebanon St./Melrose—Malden**   14   30   60   —   60   —
Melrose: Linwood Ave., Lebanon St., Forestdale; *Malden:* Sylvan St., Forest St., Main St.,
Malden Sq.
➤Orange Line @ Malden.

130A   **Wyoming Sq.—Malden**   13   30   60   —   60   —
Melrose: Lynde Ave., Wyoming Ave., Pleasant St., Washington St.; *Malden:* Summer St.
➤Orange Line @ Oak Grove, Malden.

MBTA Buses	Trip Time	**Mon.–Fri. frequency (min.)**			Sat. Freq.	Sun. Freq.
		Rush	Midday	Night		

131 **Melrose Highlands—Malden** 27-28 30 60 — — —
Melrose: Franklin St., East Side, Porter St., Waverly Ave., Grove St., Main St.; *Malden:* Main St., Malden Sq.
➤Orange Line @ Oak Grove, (some trips) Malden.

134 **North Woburn—Wellington** 42-48 60 60 — 60 —
Woburn: Main St., Elm St., Main St., Woburn Sq.; *Winchester:* Main St., Winchester Ctr.; *Medford:* Winthrop St., High St., Medford Sq., Riverside Ave. **M-Sat**: *add'l service:* **Playstead Rd. & Winthrop St.-Wellington**. Zone fares, 60¢-$1.00.
➤Orange Line @ Wellington.

134A **Medford Sq.—Wellington** 15-22 20 30 40 30 60
Medford: Winthrop St., High St., Medford Sq., Riverside Ave. *Nights & Sun.:* **Medford Sq.—Wellington only**.
➤Orange Line @ Wellington.

136 **Reading—Malden** 32-40 30 60 — 60 —
via Lakeside—*Reading:* Reading Depot, Reading Sq., Salem St.; *Wakefield:* Main St., Wakefield Sq.; *Melrose:* Main St., Melrose Ctr.; *Malden:* Main St., Malden Sq. **Zone fares**, 60¢-$1.00
➤Orange Line @ Oak Grove, Malden.

137 **Reading—Malden** 30-38 30 60 2 trips 60 —
via North Ave.—*Reading:* Reading Depot, Reading Sq., John St.; *Wakefield:* North Ave., Main St., Wakefield Sq.; *Melrose:* Main St., Melrose Ctr.; *Malden:* Main St., Malden Sq. **Zone fares**, 60¢-$1.00.
➤Orange Line @ Oak Grove, Malden.

210 **Quincy Ctr.—N. Quincy** 12 30 60 — 30 —
via Hancock St.—*Quincy:* Hancock St.
➤Red Line @ Quincy Ctr., N. Quincy.

210F **Quincy Ctr.—Fields Corner** 22-25 30 30 — — —
Quincy: Hancock St., N. Quincy, Newport Ave.; *Dorchester:* Neponset Cir., Neponset Ave.
➤Red Line @ Quincy Ctr., N. Quincy, Fields Corner.

211 **Quincy Ctr.—Squantum** 18-24 30 60 — 60 —
Quincy: Newport Ave., Beale St., Highland Ave., Montclair, W. Squantum St., N. Quincy, E. Squantum St.
➤Red Line @ Quincy Ctr., Wollaston, N. Quincy.

212 **Quincy Ctr.—N. Quincy** 12-14 30/60 2 trips — 60 —
via Billings Rd.—*Quincy:* Hancock St., Elm Ave., Billings Rd.
➤Red Line @ Quincy Ctr., N. Quincy.

214 **Quincy Ctr.—Germantown** 12 11/20 30 — 20 —
Quincy: Coddington St., Sea St., Palmer St., Oceanview. *Nights & Sun.:* **see Bus 216.**
➤Red Line @ Quincy Ctr.

215 **Quincy Ctr.—Ashmont** 24-32 20 30 60 30 60
via Granite Ave.—*Quincy:* Hancock St., Franklin St., Water St., Copeland St., W. Quincy, Willard St., Robertson St.; *Milton:* Adams St., E. Milton Sq., Granite Ave.; *Dorchester:* Gallivan Blvd. *Sun.:* **alt. trips** *Quincy:* Whitwell St.; *Milton:* Adams St., then regular route.
➤Red Line @ Quincy Ctr., Ashmont.

216 **Quincy Ctr.—Hough's Neck** 11-17 9/20 30 60 20 40
Quincy: Coddington St., Sea St. *Nights & Sun.:* **also serves** *Quincy:* Germantown, Palmer St., Oceanview.
➤Red Line @ Quincy Ctr.

217 **Wollaston Beach—Ashmont** 23-28 30 60 — 60 —
Quincy: Beach St., Wollaston, Beale St.; *Milton:* Adams St., E. Milton Sq.; *Dorchester:* Lower Mills, Dorchester Ave.
➤Red Line @ Wollaston, Milton, Ashmont.

MBTA Buses

		Trip Time	Mon.–Fri. frequency (min.)			Sat. Freq.	Sun. Freq.
			Rush	Midday	Night		

220   **Quincy Ctr.—Hingham**   22-24   10/15   30   60   30   60
Quincy: Washington St.; *Weymouth:* Bridge St., N. Weymouth; *Hingham:* Lincoln St., Broad Cove Rd., Otis St., Station St.
➤Red Line @ Quincy Ctr.

220A   **Quincy Ctr. Hingham Loop**   22-31   10/15   60   —   60   —
Same route as Bus 220, then *Hingham:* Main St., Central St., Hingham Ctr.
➤Red Line @ Quincy Ctr.

221   **Quincy Ctr.—Fort Point**   16-18   3/1 trips   1 trip   —   —   —
Quincy: Washington St.; *Weymouth:* Bridge St., N. Weymouth, Neck St., River St.
➤Red Line @ Quincy Ctr.

222   **Quincy Ctr.—E. Weymouth**   21-23   10/15   30   60   30   60
Quincy: Washington St.; *Weymouth:* Bridge St., N. Weymouth, Sea St., North St., Commercial St., Middle St., Broad St.
➤Red Line @ Quincy Ctr.

225   **Quincy Ctr.—Weymouth Landing**   15-28   10   30   60   30   60
via Des Moines Rd.—*Quincy:* Hancock St., Quincy Ave., Scammell St., South St., Des Moines Rd., Fore River Shipyard; *Braintree:* Quincy Ave.; *Weymouth:* Front Rd., Summer St., Federal St., Washington St.
Bus 225A: *Mon.-Sat.:* **alternate trips via Quincy Ave.**—*Quincy:* Hancock St., Quincy Ave.; *Braintree:* W. Howard St., Shaw St., Hayward St., Quincy Ave., then regular route.
➤Red Line @ Quincy Ctr.

230   **Quincy Ctr.—Brockton Line**   33-43   15/20   60   60   60   60
Quincy: Hancock St., Franklin St., Independence Ave.; *Braintree:* Washington St., Braintree Sta., S. Braintree Sq., Washington St.; *Holbrook:* Franklin St., Holbrook Sq., Brookville Sq. to Brockton line. **Zone fares**, 60¢-$1.00.
➤Red Line @ Quincy Ctr., Braintree.

236   **Quincy Ctr.-South Shore Plaza**   28-32   30   60   —   60   —
via E. Braintree—*Quincy:* Hancock St., Franklin St.; *Braintree:* Commercial St., Elm St., Middle St., Union St., Braintree Sta., S. Braintree Sq., Franklin St., Five Corners, Granite St. **AM rush:** **some trips Quincy Ctr.-Braintree** *only.*
➤Red Line @ Quincy Ctr., Braintree.

238   **Quincy Ctr.—Crawford Sq.**   31-39   30   60   60   60   60
Quincy: Hancock St., Franklin St., Water St., Liberty St., Centre St., West St., Willard St.; *Braintree:* Granite St., South Shore Plaza, Five Corners, Pond St.; *Randolph:* North St. **Through service (except nights) Quincy Ctr.—Ashmont via Bus 240A.** *Sat.:* **add'l service South Shore Plaza—N. Randolph via Bus 240A, every 30 min. Zone fares**, 60¢-75¢ to Crawford Sq.; 60¢-$1.50 on Ashmont through buses.
➤Red Line @ Quincy Ctr., Quincy Adams (Mon.-Sat. only).

240   **Avon Line—Ashmont**   27-31   20   60   60   60   60
Randolph: Main St., Crawford Sq.; *Milton:* Randolph Ave., Reedsdale Rd., Milton Hosp., Central Ave.; *Dorchester:* Lower Mills, Dorchester Ave. **Zone fares**, 60¢-$1.00.
➤Red Line @ Milton, Ashmont.

240A   **Crawford Sq.—Ashmont**   23-25   10   30   60   30   60
Same route as Bus 240 except originates at Crawford Sq. **Through service** (except nights) **Quincy Ctr.—Ashmont via Bus 238. Zone fares**, 60¢-75¢ to Crawford Sq.; 60¢-$1.50 on Quincy Ctr. through buses.
➤Red Line @ Milton, Ashmont.

245   **Quincy Ctr.—Mattapan**   12-14   30   60   —   60   —
Quincy: Whitwell St., Adams St.; *Milton:* E. Milton Sq., Edge Hill Rd.*, Pleasant St.*, Reedsdale Rd.*, Milton Hosp.*, Brook Rd. * -*Rush hour:* **alternate trips via Shadowlawn**—*Quincy:* Whitwell St., Adams St.; *Milton:* E. Milton Sq., Brook Rd. *Sun.:* **see Bus 215.**
➤Red Line @ Quincy Ctr., Mattapan.

MBTA Buses

	Trip Time	Mon.–Fri. frequency (min.)			Sat. Freq.	Sun. Freq.
		Rush	Midday	Night		

300 **Riverside—Downtown**   22   5/6   —   4 trips   —   —
express—*Newton:* Riverside; Mass. Pike; *Boston:* Federal St., Franklin St., Otis St.
Nights: via **Copley Sq.** and **Newton Corner. Fare** $2.25 (10 ride = $20).
➤Green Line-D @ Riverside; Red & Orange lines @ Downtown Crossing.

301 **Brighton Ctr.—Downtown**   25   5   —   —   —   —
express—*Brighton:* Washington St., Oak Sq., Tremont St.; Mass. Pike; *Boston:* Federal St., Franklin St., Otis St. **Fare** $1.50 (10 ride = $13.50).
➤Red & Orange lines @ Downtown Crossing.

302 **Watertown—Copley**   18   10/12   —   —   —   —
express—*Watertown:* Galen St.; *Newton:* Newton Corner; Mass. Pike; *Boston:* Prudential Ctr., Boylston St. *Midday & Sat.:* **see Bus 304.** *Nights:* **see Bus 300. Fare** $1.50 (10 ride = $13.50).
➤Green Line @ Copley.

304 **Watertown—Downtown**   18-33   8/10   30   —   35   —
express—*Watertown:* Galen St.; *Newton:* Newton Corner; Mass. Pike; *Boston:* Federal St., Franklin St., Otis St. *Midday & Sat.:* *Boston:* Copley Sq. **Fare** $1.50 (10 ride = $13.50).
➤Red & Orange lines @ Downtown Crossing; Green Line @ Copley (middays & Sat. only).

304A **Newton Cor.—Downtown**   15-22   4/5   15   —   15   —
express—*Newton:* Newton Corner; Mass. Pike; *Boston:* Federal St., Franklin St., Otis St. *Through service* on most trips to Waverley, Roberts, and other Waltham points via Buses 53, 54, 56, 58. *Nights:* **see Bus 300. Fare** $1.50 (10 ride = $13.50).
➤Red & Orange lines @ Downtown Crossing.

305 **Waltham—Downtown**   30   10   1 trip   —   —   —
express—*Waltham:* Central Sq., Moody St.; *Newton:* Lexington St., Auburndale, Commonwealth Ave., Washington St., W. Newton; Mass. Pike; *Boston:* Federal St., Franklin St., Otis St. *Non-rush hours:* **see Buses 53, 54. Fare** $2.25 (10 ride = $20).
➤Red & Orange lines @ Downtown Crossing.

325 **Elm St./Medford—Haymarket**   13-20   10/12   —   —   —   —
express—*Medford:* Fellsway West, Salem St.; I-93. **Fare** $1.50 (10 ride = $13.50).
➤Green & Orange lines @ Haymarket.

326 **West Medford—Haymarket**   16-23   10/15   —   —   —   —
express—*Medford:* Playstead Rd., High St., Medford Sq.; I-93. **Fare** $1.50(10 ride = $13.50).
➤Green & Orange lines @ Haymarket.

350 **No. Burlington—Alewife**   34-54   14/20   60   60   60   50-60
Burlington: Chestnut Ave., Cambridge St., Mall Rd., Burlington Mall; *Woburn:* Cambridge Rd.; *Winchester:* Cambridge St.; *Arlington:* Mystic St., Arlington Ctr., Mass. Ave.; Alewife Brook Pkwy. **Zone fares,** 60¢-$1.00.
➤Red Line @ Alewife.

352 **Burlington—Boston**   43   10   —   —   —   —
express—*Burlington:* Chestnut Ave., Cambridge St.; Rt. 128, I-93; *Boston:* Haymarket Sq. *AM:* to Copley Sq. via Govt. Ctr., Park Plaza. *PM:* from Haymarket, except 1 trip from Park Plaza, Copley Sq. **Fare** 60¢ local, $2.25 to Boston (10 ride = $20).
➤Green & Orange lines @ Haymarket; Green Line @ Copley.

353 **Burlington Ind. Area—Haymarket**   41-46   30   —   —   —   —
express—*Bedford:* Crosby Dr.; *Burlington:* Middlesex Tpk., 2nd Ave., Mall Rd., Cambridge St.; *Woburn:* Cambridge Rd., Lexington St., Woburn Sq., Montvale Ave., Bow St., Salem St., Washington St., Cummings Ind. Pk.; I-93. *AM: from* **Boston only;** *PM: to* **Boston only. Zone fares:** 60¢ local; $2.25 to Haymarket (10 ride = $20).
➤Green & Orange lines @ Haymarket.

MBTA Buses

	Trip Time	Mon.–Fri. frequency (min.)			Sat. Freq.	Sun. Freq.
		Rush	Midday	Night		

353A **Burlington Ind. Area—Dudley**   45-60   2/1 trips   —   —   —   —
express—*Bedford:* Crosby Dr.; *Burlington:* Middlesex Tpk., 2nd Ave.; Rt. 128; *Waltham:* 2nd Ave., Bear Hill Rd.; Riverside; Mass. Pike. **AM: from Dudley only; PM: to Dudley only. Fare** $2.25 (10 ride = $13.50).
➤Green Line-D @ Riverside.

354 **Woburn—Haymarket**   28-31   10   —   —   —   —
express—*Woburn:* Cambridge Rd., Lexington St., Woburn Sq., Montvale Ave., Bow St., Salem St., Pine St.; I-93. **Fare** 60¢ local; $2.25 to Haymarket (10 ride = $20). Some buses continue to Park Sq. or Copley Sq.
➤Green & Orange lines @ Haymarket, Green line @ Copley.

400 **Lynn—Haymarket**
This bus is now combined with bus 455 (Salem-Haymarket). Some buses may still be signed "400."

411 **Revere House—Malden Ctr.**   36-47   35/50   60   —   60   —
Revere: Ocean Ave., Wonderland, Revere/Beach Sts., Malden St., Northgate Mall; *Malden:* Linden Sq., Lynn St., Granada Hlds., Kennedy Dr., Broadway, Salem St., Maplewood Sq., Malden Sq. **AM rush: Granada Hlds.—Malden Ctr. only.**
➤Blue Line @ Wonderland, Revere Beach; Orange Line @ Malden Ctr.

426 **Lynn—Haymarket**   47-60   10   60   80   60   60
via Cliftondale—*Lynn:* Lynn Common, W. Lynn, Summer St.; *Saugus:* E. Saugus, Lincoln Ave., Cliftondale; *Revere:* Salem St.; *Malden:* Lynn St., Linden Sq.; **express via Tobin Bridge.** *Rush hours:* 3/2 trips **Oaklandvale—Haymarket**—*Saugus:* Main St., Saugus Ctr., Winter St., E. Saugus, then regular route. *Rush hours:* 2 trips **Granada Hlds.—Haymarket**—*Malden:* Kennedy Dr., Lynn St., then regular route. **Zone fares**, 60¢-$2.00.
➤Green & Orange lines @ Haymarket.

429 **Lynn—North Saugus**   21-24   30   60   —   60   —
Lynn: Franklin St., Lynn Hosp., Boston St., Myrtle St., Holyoke St., O'Callaghan Way, King's Lynne, Garfield/Fairmount Aves.; *Saugus:* Walnut St.

430 **Saugus—Malden Ctr.**   30-51   35/45   60   —   60   —
Saugus: Appleton St., Summer St., Main St., Saugus Ctr., Central St., Cliftondale, Essex St., New England Shopping Ctr.; *Malden:* Broadway, Salem St., Maplewood Sq., Malden Sq.
➤Orange Line @ Malden Ctr.

433 **Lynn/Central Sq.—Pine Hill**   14   40   1 trip   —   —   —
Lynn: Lynn Common, Lynn Hosp., Mall/Park Sts., Lovers Leap Ave., Linwood St., Thistle St.

435 **Lynn—Danvers**   38-53   1 trip   60   1 trip   30-60   5 trips
Lynn: Franklin St., Lynn Hosp., Western Ave., Chestnut St., Wyoma Sq., Broadway; *Peabody:* N. Shore Shopping Ctr.; *Danvers:* Liberty Tree Mall, Sylvan St., Park St., Danvers Sq. **Sun: Lynn-Liberty Tree Mall only. Zone fares**, 60¢-$1.00.

436 **Lynn—Goodwins Cir.**   19   30   60   —   60   90
Lynn: Union St., Chestnut St., Wyoma Sq., Lynnfield St., AtlantiCare Hosp.; *Lynnfield:* Goodwins Cir. **Rush hours: 1 trip Happy Valley—Haymarket**—*Lynnfield:* Goodwins Cir.; *Lynn:* Lynnfield St., Wyoma Sq., Chestnut St., Western Ave., *through service* via Bus 450. **Fare** 60¢ local, $2.00 to Haymarket.

437 **Lynn—Lake Shore Park**   15-22   30   60   —   60   90
Lynn: Union St., Timson St., Eastern Ave., Euclid Ave., Jenness St., Saunders Rd., Broadway.

439 **Lynn—Nahant**   15-17   30   1 trip   —   —   —
Lynn: Nahant St.; *Nahant:* Nahant Rd., Castle Rd., Spring Rd., Willow Rd., Wharf St. **Rush hours: through service Nahant—Haymarket via Bus 455. Fare** 60¢ local, $2.00 to Haymarket.

440 **Lynn—Haymarket**   25-36   10   30   60   30   60*
This bus is now combined with buses 441 and 442. Some buses may still be signed "440."

MBTA Buses

	Trip Time	Mon.–Fri. frequency (min.)			Sat. Freq.	Sun. Freq.
		Rush	Midday	Night		

441 Marblehead—Haymarket   48-63   30/10   60   —   60   —
via Paradise Rd.—Marblehead: Washington St., Pleasant St., Humphrey St.;
Swampscott: Salem St., Vinnin Sq., Paradise Rd.; *Lynn:* Lewis St., Broad St., Central Sq.;
Lynnway; Gen. Edwards Bridge; *Revere:* N. Shore Rd., Wonderland, Bell Cir.; **express**
via Rt. 1A. **Mon.-Sat.:** *through service* on most trips **Marblehead—Haymarket** via 442. ***-
Sun.: Lynn—Wonderland** only. **Zone fares**, 60¢-$2.25. **Nights & Sun.:** see Bus 442.
➤Blue Line @ Wonderland; Green & Orange lines @ Haymarket.

442 Marblehead—Haymarket   47-62   15   60   60   60   60
via Humphrey St.—Marblehead: Washington St., Pleasant St., Humphrey St.;
Swampscott: Swampscott Ctr.; *Lynn:* Lewis St., Broad St., Central Sq., Lynnway; Gen.
Edwards Bridge; *Revere:* N. Shore Rd., Wonderland, Bell Cir.; **express** via Rt. 1A.
Mon.—Sat.: *through service* on most trips **Marblehead—Haymarket** via 441. ***-Sun.:
Lynn—Wonderland** *only.*, or Bus 455 (Sun.). **Zone fares**, 60¢-$2.25.
➤Blue Line @ Wonderland (Mon.-Sat.); Green & Orange lines @ Haymarket.

450 Salem—Haymarket   35-50   20   60   2 trips   60   60
via Highland Ave.—Salem: Essex St., Highland Ave.; *Lynn:* Western Ave., W. Lynn;
Saugus: Marsh Rd., (Salem Tpk.); *Revere:* American Legion Hwy., Bell Cir.; **express** via
Rt. 1A. **Rush hours:** *through service* on some trips **Danvers—Haymarket** via Bus 458.
Rush hours: add'l service Essex St.—Haymarket—Lynn: Eastern Ave., Western Ave.,
then regular route, every 10 min. **Zone fares**, 60¢-$2.25.
➤Green & Orange lines @ Haymarket.

451 North Beverly—Salem   22-27   2 trips   60   —   —   —
Beverly: Sohier Rd., Cabot St., Beverly Ctr.; *Salem:* Bridge St. **Sat.:** see Beverly
Shoppers Shuttle in Chapter 19.

455 Salem—Haymarket   60   30/15   30   60   30   60
via Loring Ave.—Salem: Lafayette St., Loring Ave.; *Swampscott:* Vinnin Sq., Essex St.;
Lynn: Union St., Central Sq., Lynn Common, Western Ave., W. Lynn; *Saugus:* Marsh Rd.
(Salem Tpk.); *Revere:* American Legion Hwy., Bell Cir.; **express** via Rt. 1A. *Through
service* on most trips **Salem—Haymarket via Bus 455, daily,** or **Marblehead—
Haymarket via Bus 442, Sun. Zone fares**, 60¢-$2.25.
➤Green & Orange lines @ Haymarket.

458/ Salem—Danvers Sq.   25-31   30/60   60   —   —   —
468 *Salem:* North St.; *Danvers:* Water St., Endicott Plaza, Liberty Tree Mall, Purchase St.,
Danvers Sq. Some trips serve Danvers State Hospital, Essex Agricultural School (see
schedule). **Rush hours:** *through service* **Danvers—Haymarket** via Bus 450. **Zone
fares**, 60¢ local; $2.50 to Haymarket.

New Crosstown Transit Service

Three new bus routes, designed primarily to improve access to the Longwood and B.U./
Boston City Hospital medical areas, were started in the Fall of 1994. The buses also make
crosstown connections among the Red, Green, and Orange rapid transit lines. All three
services are limited-stop "semi-express."

CT1 Central—B.U. Medical Center   24   15   15   —   —   —
Via the following stops *only*—University Park; M.I.T.; Hynes/I.C.A.; Symphony; Orange
Line @ Mass. Ave.
➤Red Line @ Central; Green Line @ Hynes Convention Ctr./I.C.A. (B,C,D) and Symphony
(E); Orange Line @ Mass. Ave.

CT2 Kendall—Ruggles   27   20   20   —   —   —
Via the following stops *only* —Vassar St./Mass Ave., Vassar/Memorial Dr. (inbound) or
Vassar/Amesbury Sts. (outbound), Mountfort St. (inbound) or Comm. Ave./B.U. Bridge
(outbound), Fenway Sta., Beth Israel Hosp., Children's Hospital, Huntington/Longwood
Aves., Ruggles St./Huntington Ave.
➤Red Line @ Kendall; Green Line @ Fenway (D), Longwood Med. Area (E), and Museum
of Fine Arts (E); Orange Line @ Ruggles.

MBTA Buses	Trip Time	**Mon.–Fri. frequency (min.)**			Sat. Freq.	Sun. Freq.
		Rush	Midday	Night		

CT3 **Beth Israel—Andrew**   21   20   20   —   —   —
Via the following stops *only*—Children's Hospital (outbound), Avenue Louis Pasteur (outbound), Ruggles St./Huntington Ave., Ruggles Sta., Melnea Cass Blvd./Washington St. (outbound), B.C.H. (inbound) or B. U. Med. Ctr. (outbound).
➤Green Line @ Museum of Fine Arts (E); Orange Line @ Ruggles; Red Line @ Andrew.

☞ **All T-Passes are valid on the above crosstown bus services.**

Chapter 18

MBTA Commuter Rail and Boats

The charts for commuter rail and commuter boat service show the number of trains or boats on weekdays and Saturdays and Sundays, as well as the trip time from one end of the route to the other.

The rush-hour column shows the number of trains or boats going to Boston in the morning and away from Boston in the evening (e.g., "4/4").

Numbers in parentheses—(1A), (2), etc.—indicate fare zones. A dash (—) means there is no service at the time indicated. An asterisk (*) indicates limited service (check schedule).

> Worcester-to-Boston Commuter Rail service began in September 1994. At present, there are three rush-hour trains each way (morning to Boston, evening to Worcester, Monday through Friday). All trains stop in Framingham; some trains make additional stops between Boston and Framingham. There are currently no stations between Framingham and Worcester.
>   Additional stations are planned—Ashland, Southborough, Westborough, Grafton, and Millbury are candidates; additional service is contemplated as well. Stay tuned.

MBTA Commuter Rail

	Trip Time	**Weekday Trips**			Sat. Trips	Sun. Trips
		Rush	Day	Nite		

Rockport/Ipswich Line

North Sta.—Beverly Depot   :35   8/8   8   4   12   7
Stations: Chelsea (1B), G.E. River Works* (2), Lynn (2), Swampscott (3), Salem (3), Beverly Depot (4).
➤Green & Orange lines @ North Sta.

North Sta.—Rockport   1:10   4/4   6   5   6   6
Stations: Beverly Depot (4), Montserrat (4), Prides Crossing* (5), Beverly Farms (5), Manchester-by-the Sea (6), W. Gloucester (7), Gloucester (7), Rockport (8).
➤Green & Orange lines @ North Sta.

North Sta.—Ipswich   :55   4/4   4   2   5   —
Stations: Beverly Depot (4), N. Beverly (5), Hamilton/Wenham (5), Ipswich (6).
➤Green & Orange lines @ North Sta.

Reading/Haverhill Line

North Sta.—Reading   :30   7/7   6   5   6   6
Stations: Malden Ctr. (1B), Wyoming Hill (1), Melrose/Cedar Park (1), Melrose Hlds. (1), Greenwood (2), Wakefield (2), Reading (2).
➤Green & Orange lines @ North Sta.; Orange Line @ Malden Ctr.

MBTA Commuter Rail	Trip	**Weekday Trips**			Sat.	Sun.
	Time	Rush	Day	Nite	Trips	Trips

North Sta.—Haverhill   1:05   6/3   2   6   6   5
Stations: Reading (2), N. Wilmington (3), Ballardvale (4), Andover (5), Lawrence (6), Bradford (7), Haverhill (7).
➤Green & Orange lines @ North Sta.; Orange Line @ Malden Ctr.

Lowell Line

North Sta.—Lowell   :45   6/6   7   5   8   8
Stations: W. Medford* (1B), Wedgemere (1), Winchester Ctr. (1), Lechmere Sales office* (2), Mishawum (2), Wilmington (3), N. Billerica (5), Lowell (6).
➤Green & Orange lines @ North Sta.

Fitchburg Line

North Sta.—S. Acton   :50   5/5   5   4   8   7
Stations: Porter (1B), Belmont Ctr.* (1), Waverley* (1), Waltham (2), Brandeis/Roberts (2), Kendal Green (3), Hastings* (3), Silver Hill* (3), Lincoln (4), Concord (5), W. Concord (5), S. Acton (6).
➤Green & Orange lines @ North Sta.; Red Line @ Porter.

North Sta.—Fitchburg   1:30   4/4   4   2   5   4
Stations: S. Acton (6), Littleton/495 (7), Ayer (8), Shirley (8), N. Leominster (9), Fitchburg (9).
➤Green & Orange lines @ North Sta.; Red Line @ Porter.

Framingham Line

South Sta.—Framingham   :45   5/5   4   3   9   7
Stations: Back Bay Sta. (1A), Newtonville* (1), W. Newton* (2), Auburndale* (2), Wellesley Farms (3), Wellesley Hills (3), Wellesley Sq. (3), Natick (4), W. Natick (4), Framingham (5).
➤Red Line @ South Sta.; Orange Line @ Back Bay Sta.

Needham Line

South Sta.—Needham Jct.   :30   5   4   4   9   —
Stations: Back Bay Sta. (1A), Ruggles* (1A), Forest Hills* (1B), Roslindale (1), Bellevue (1), Highland (1), W. Roxbury (1), Hersey (Bird's Hill) (2), Needham Jct. (2). *Connects w/T-Bus 59 to Needham Ctr. and Needham Hts.*
➤Red Line @ South Sta.; Orange Line @ Back Bay Sta., Ruggles, Forest Hills.
South Sta.—Needham Hts.   :40   3/5   4   4   9   —
Stations: Needham Jct. (2), Needham Ctr. (2), Needham Hts. (2).
➤Red Line @ South Sta.; Orange Line @ Back Bay Sta., Ruggles, Forest Hills.

Franklin Line

South Sta.—Forge Park/495   1:00   6/4   4   4   9   7
Stations: Back Bay Sta. (1A), Ruggles* (1A), Readville (2), Endicott (2), Dedham Corp. Ctr. (2), Islington (3), Norwood Depot (3), Norwood Central (3), Windsor Gardens (4), Plimptonville* (4), Walpole (4), Norfolk (5), Franklin (6), Forge Park/495 (7).
➤Red Line @ South Sta.; Orange Line @ Back Bay Sta.; Ruggles.

Attleboro/Stoughton Line

South Sta.—Attleboro   :50   6/5   4   3   9   7
Stations: Back Bay Sta. (1A), Ruggles* (1A), Hyde Park (1), Rt. 128 Sta. (2), Canton Jct. (3), Sharon (4), Mansfield (6), Attleboro (7).
➤Red Line @ South Sta.; Orange Line @ Back Bay Sta., Ruggles.

South Sta.—Providence, RI   1:05   4/4   —   —   —   —
Stations: Attleboro (7), S. Attleboro (7), Providence, RI (9).
➤Red Line @ South Sta.; Orange Line @ Back Bay Sta., Ruggles.

South Sta.—Stoughton   :40   4/4   4   3   —   —
Stations: Back Bay Sta. (1A), Ruggles* (1A), Hyde Park (1), Rt. 128 Sta. (2), Canton Jct. (3), Canton Ctr. (3), Stoughton (4).

MBTA Commuter Rail

	Trip	Weekday Trips			Sat.	Sun.
	Time	Rush	Day	Nite	Trips	Trips

➤Red Line @ South Sta.; Orange Line @ Back Bay Sta., Ruggles.

Fairmount Line

South Sta.—Readville	:19	7/6	7	3	—	—

Stations: Uphams Corner (1A), Morton St. (1B), Fairmount (1), Readville (2).
➤Red Line @ South Sta.

MBTA Commuter Boats

	Trip	Weekday Trips			Sat.	Sun.
	Time	Rush	Day	Nite	Trips	Trips

Long Wharf—Charlestown

	:10	10/12	15	1	17	17

Navy Yard Water Shuttle to Pier 4, Charlestown Navy Yard. *Operated for the MBTA by Boston Harbor Cruises.* **Fare** $1.00. Rush hour service operates every 15 min.; off-peak and weekends, every 30 min. Free connecting shuttle bus service to points within the Navy Yard. Bikes free.
➤Blue Line @ Aquarium.

Rowes Wharf—Hingham

	35	9/7	4	1	—	—

Operated by Boston Harbor Commuter Service and by Massachusetts Bay Lines. **Fare** $4.00. Bikes free.
➤Blue Line @ Aquarium; Red Line @ South Sta.

Airport Water Shuttle—see Chapter 6 ("Logan Airport")
For other non-MBTA ferry services, see Chapter 19.

Commuter Rail Station Locations

DOWNTOWN BOSTON

Back Bay Station—145 Dartmouth St., S of Stuart St., at BACK BAY STATION (Orange Line)
Ruggles—800 Columbus Ave. at Melnea Cass Blvd., at RUGGLES (Orange Line)
North Station—126 Causeway St., at NORTH STATION (Green and Orange lines)
South Station—200 Summer St. & 600 Atlantic Ave., at SOUTH STATION (Red Line)

SUBURBS

ROCKPORT/IPSWICH LINE (from North Station)

Beverly Depot—Park St. across from Post Office
Beverly Farms—West St. (Rt. 127) at Oak St.
Chelsea—Arlington & Sixth sts.
Gloucester—Washington St. at Railroad Ave.
Hamilton/Wenham—Bay Rd. at Walnut St.
Ipswich—S of Topsfield Rd., downtown
Lynn—Market & Munroe sts.
Manchester-by-the-Sea—Beach St., S of Summer St.
Montserrat—Between Spring & Essex sts., Beverly
North Beverly—Enon St. at Dodge St.

Prides Crossing—Hale St. (Rt. 127), Beverly
Rockport—Railroad Ave., off Rt. 127
Salem—Bridge & North sts.
Swampscott—Burrill St. at Railroad Ave.
West Gloucester—Essex Ave. (Rt. 133), S of Magnolia Ave.

HAVERHILL/READING LINE (from North Station)

Andover—17 Railroad Ave., between Main & Essex sts.
Ballardville—Andover St., near River St., Andover
Bradford—Railroad & Laurel aves., Haverhill
Greenwood—907 Main St., behind bank, Wakefield
Haverhill—Washington St. at Railroad Sq.
Lawrence—Merrimack & Parker, at I-495/Sutton St. exit
Melrose/Cedar Park—W. Emerson & Tremont sts.
Melrose Highlands—Franklin St. & Chipman Ave.
North Wilmington—Middlesex Ave., W of I-93/Rt. 63 Jct.
Malden Center—Commercial & Pleasant sts.
Reading—High & Lincoln sts.
Wakefield—Tuttle St. & North Ave.

Wyoming Hill—W. Wyoming Ave. & Pleasant St., Melrose

LOWELL LINE (from North Station)

Lowell—Thorndike St., N of Lowell Connector
Mishawum—Mishawum Rd., off Washington St. exit Rt. 128, Woburn
North Billerica—Ruggles St., off Mt. Pleasant St.
Wedgemere—Mystic Valley Pkwy. at Bacon St., Winchester
West Medford—High St. & Playstead Rd.
Wilmington—N of intersection of Rt. 62 & Rts. 129/38
Winchester—Between Common & Church sts.

FITCHBURG LINE (from North Station)

Ayer—Depot Sq., on S side of Main St.
Belmont—Common St. & Concord Ave., behind Lions Club
Brandeis/Roberts—South & Sawyer sts., Waltham
Concord—Thoreau St., between Sudbury Rd. & Belknap St.
Fitchburg—Rt. 2A, E of Jct. with Rt. 12
Hastings—Viles St., 1 block S of Rt. 117, Weston
Kendal Green—Church St., block S of Rt. 117, Weston
Lincoln—Lincoln Rd., 2 blocks N of Rt. 117
Littleton/495—Foster St., off Taylor St.
North Leominster—568 Main St. (Rt. 13), behind Victory Shopping Center
Porter Sq.—1900 Mass. Ave. at PORTER (Red Line), Cambridge
Shirley—Main & Phoenix sts.
Silver Hill—Silver Hill Rd., off Merriam St., Weston
South Acton—Central St. near Main St. (Rt. 27)
Waltham—Center St., between Elm & Moody sts.
Waverly—Trapelo Rd. & Lexington St., E of Rt. 60, Belmont
West Concord—Commonwealth Ave. & Main St.

FRAMINGHAM/WORCESTER LINE (from South, and Back Bay stations)

Auburndale—Lexington St., at Mass. Turnpike, Newton
Framingham—Rts. 126 & 135
Natick—Walnut St. & Rt. 27
Newtonville—Between Harvard & Walnut sts.
Wellesley Farms—90 Glen Rd.
Wellesley Hills—339 Washington St., W of Cliff Rd.
Wellesley Square—Washington St. & Crest Rd.
West Natick—Rt. 135 & Boden Ln.
Worcester—45 Shrewsbury St. (Amtrak Station)

NEEDHAM LINE (from South, Back Bay and Ruggles stations)

Bellevue—Colbert & Centre sts., W. Roxbury
Forest Hills—Washington St. at FOREST HILLS (Orange Line)

NEEDHAM LINE, cont.

Hersey—Great Plain Ave., Needham
Highland—Corey & Hastings sts.
Needham Center—Great Plain Ave. at Eaton Sq.
Needham Heights—West St., W of Highland Ave.
Needham Junction—Junction St., off Chestnut St.
Roslindale Village—Belgrade & South sts.
West Roxbury—LaGrange St., N of Centre St.

FRANKLIN LINE (from South, Back Bay and Ruggles stations)

Dedham Corporate Ctr.—East St. off Rt. 128 to Allied Dr.
Endicott—Washington Ave., off East St., Dedham
Forge Park/495—Rt. 140 off Rt. I-495, Franklin
Franklin—Depot St., off E. Central & Main sts.
Hyde Park—Hyde Park Ave. at Cleary Sq., Boston
Islington—Carol St., off East St., Westwood
Norfolk—Rt. 115 at Norfolk Ctr.
Norwood Central—Broadway St., E of Washington St.
Norwood Depot—Railroad Ave. & Hill St.
Plimptonville—Plimpton St., E of Rt. 1A, Walpole
Readville—Hyde Park Ave., Readville, (Boston)
Walpole—West St., 3 blocks W of Walpole Ctr.
Windsor Gardens—Windsor Gardens apts., Rt. 1A, Norwood

ATTLEBORO/STOUGHTON LINE (from South, Back Bay and Ruggles stations)

Attleboro—So. Main St. & Wall St.
Canton Center—Washington St., near BayBank
Canton Junction—Sherman & Beaumont sts.
Hyde Park—Hyde Park Ave. at Cleary Sq., Boston
Mansfield—Crocker St., off Rt. 106 (Chauncy St.)
Providence, RI—100 Gaspee St. (Amtrak Station)
Route 128 Station—University Ave., off Rt. 128, Westwood
Sharon—Rt. 27, near Sharon Ctr.
South Attleboro—Newport Ave. (Rt. 1A), off Rt. I-95
Stoughton—Wyman St. at RR crossing

FAIRMOUNT SHUTTLE (from South Station)

Fairmount—Fairmount Ave. & Truman Hwy., Hyde Park (Boston)
Morton Street—Morton St., near Star Market, Mattapan (Boston)
Readville—Hyde Park Ave., Readville (Boston)
Uphams Corner—Dudley St., Dorchester (Boston)

Commuter Rail System

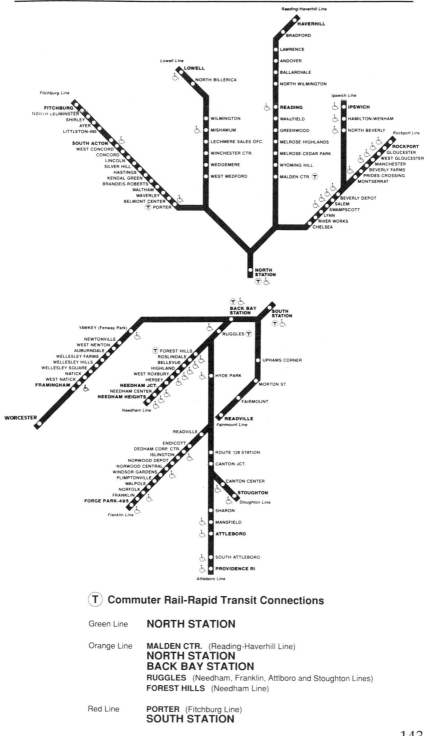

(T) **Commuter Rail-Rapid Transit Connections**

Green Line   **NORTH STATION**

Orange Line   **MALDEN CTR.** (Reading-Haverhill Line)
NORTH STATION
BACK BAY STATION
RUGGLES (Needham, Franklin, Attlboro and Stoughton Lines)
FOREST HILLS (Needham Line)

Red Line   **PORTER** (Fitchburg Line)
SOUTH STATION

Chapter 19
Other Trains, Ferries, Buses

The Americans With Disabilities Act (ADA), requires all public carriers to provide services for persons with disabilities. Call the individual carriers for the latest information on these services.

There are possible service changes on Amtrak; call them for latest information. The Boston Terminals map is found on page 16.

Trains

Amtrak
800-USA-RAIL or 482 3660
Boston terminals:
South Station; Back Bay Station
Suburban terminals:
Route 128 Sta. (Dedham/Westwood); Framingham (downtown). Bikes $5, box provided, checked baggage trips only.
Northeast Corridor (Shore Line)
Boston-New York, NY
Via Rt. 128 Sta., Providence RI; New London, New Haven, CT; through trains to Philadelphia, PA, and Washington, DC.
  Daily: 13 trips
  Trip time: 4 3/4–5 hours
Inland Route
Boston-New York, NY
Via Framingham, Worcester, Springfield; Hartford, New Haven, CT; through trains to Philadelphia, PA, and Washington, DC.

Daily: 2 trips from Boston;
plus 7 trips Springfield-New York
Trip time: 6 1/4 hours
Lake Shore Limited
Boston-Chicago
Via Framingham, Worcester, Springfield, Pittsfield; Albany, Buffalo, NY; Cleveland, OH; connecting train to Michigan points.
  Daily: 1 trip
  Trip time: Boston-Albany, 5 1/2 hours; Boston-Chicago, 21 1/2 hours
Cape Codder
New York, NY-Hyannis, MA
Via New Haven, New London, CT; Providence, RI; Taunton, Wareham, Buzzards Bay, Sandwich, W. Barnstable. *Does not stop in Boston.*
  July-Labor Day only:
  Fri, Sat, & Sun, 1 trip
  Trip time: 6 1/4–7 hours. No bikes.

Ferries

A.C. Cruise Line
800-422-8419 or 261-6633
Boston terminal: 290 Northern Ave.
Boston-Gloucester (Rocky Neck)
Late June-Labor Day: 1 trip Tue-Sun & Holidays
Mem'l Day-mid June : weekends only
Trip time: 2 1/2 hours. Bikes $2.

Airport Water Shuttle
800-23-LOGAN or 330-8680
Boston terminal: Rowes Wharf
Downtown Boston-Logan Airport
Connecting shuttle bus to all airline terminals.
  M-F: every 15 min., 6:00 am-8:00 pm.

Fri eves every 30 min. until 11 pm.
Sat every 30 min. 10 am-11 pm.
Sun every 30 min. 10 am-8 pm
Trip time: 7 min. Bikes free.

Bay State Cruise Co.
723-7800. Boston terminals:
Long Wharf; Commonwealth Pier
Unless noted otherwise, all Bay State boats operate daily, mid June-Labor Day; and weekends only, early May-early June & mid Sept.-late Oct.
Boston-Georges Island
From Long Wharf.
  May-Mid June, Sept-mid Oct

M-F: 3 trips
Sat-Sun-Hol: 4 trips
Mid June-Labor Day
M-F 6 Trips
Weekends, Hourly 10 am-5 pm
Trip time: 45 min. No bikes.
Boston-Pemberton (Hull)
From Long Wharf
M-F rush hours: 1 trip (year-round)
Trip time: 50 min. Bikes free.
Boston-Provincetown
*From Commonwealth Pier; shuttle
boat available from Long Wharf.*
Mid June-Labor Day: 1 trip daily
*Memorial Day-mid June &
Labor Day-mid Sept.:* weekends only
Trip time: 3 hours. Bikes $5.
Hingham-Georges Island
3 trips daily
Trip time: 40 min. No bikes.

Boston Harbor Commuter Service
740-1253
Boston terminal: Rowes Wharf
Boston-Hingham
See *"MBTA Commuter Boat"* in
Ch. 18.

Boston Harbor Cruises
227-4321
Boston terminal: Long Wharf
Navy Yard Water Shuttle
Boston-Charlestown Navy Yard
See "MBTA Commuter Boat" in Ch. 18.
Boston-JFK Library
M-F: 4 trips
Trip time: 45 min. Bikes free.

Cape Island Express Lines
508-997-1688
**New Bedford-Martha's Vineyard
(Vineyard Haven)**
Mid June-Labor Day: 3-4 trips daily
*Mid May-early June & Labor Day-
Columbus Day:* 1-3 trips daily
Trip time: 1 1/2 hours. Bikes $2.50.

City Water Taxi
775-7301 Serving: World Trade
Center, Downtown, Charlestown,
Chelsea, North End and Logan Airport.
M-F: 6 trips
Trip time: 1 hour. Bikes free
*Also daily on-demand service,
5:30 am-11 pm.)*

Cuttyhunk Boat Lines
508-922-1432
New Bedford-Cuttyhunk Island
Connects w/American Eagle buses at

New Bedford on Mon-Fri only.
Mid June-mid Sept.: 1-2 trips daily
*Memorial Day-early June & late Sept.-
Columbus Day:* Tue, Fri, Sat, Sun,
& Hol, 1 trip
Rest of year: Tues & Fri only
Trip time: 1 3/4 hours. Bikes $1.

Harbor Islands Water Taxi
723-7800 Operated by Bay State Cruise
Co. Service operates 10 am-5:30 pm.
Boats dock at Hingham (4 times),
Grape I. (3 times), Georges I. (5 times),
Bumpkin I. (2 times), Gallops I.
(3 times), and Lovells I. (3 times). Daily
June-Aug. Weekends only May, Sept.-
Oct. No bikes.

Hy-Line
508-778-2600
**Hyannis-Martha's Vineyard
(Oak Bluffs)**
*Connects w/Plymouth & Brockton buses
from Boston at Hyannis.*
Mid June-mid Sept.: 4 trips day
Late May-early June 3 trips daily
Early May, lateSept.-Oct.: 1 trip daily
Trip time: 1 3/4 hours. Bikes $4.50
Hyannis-Nantucket
*Connects w/Plymouth & Brockton buses
from Boston at Hyannis.*
Mid June-early Sept. 6 trips daily
*Early May-early June & mid- Sept.-late
Oct.:* 1-4 trips daily
Trip time: 2 1/4 hours. Bikes $4.50
**Martha's Vineyard (Oak Bluffs)-
Nantucket**
Mid June-mid Sept.: 3 trips daily
Trip time: 2 1/4 hours. Bikes $4.50.

Island Queen
508-548-4800
**Falmouth-Martha's Vineyard
(Oak Bluffs)**
Mid June-early Sept.: 7-8 trips daily
*Late May-early June & mid
Sept.-Columbus Day:* 2-5 trips daily
Trip time: 30 min. Bikes $6.

Massachusetts Bay Lines
542-8000
Boston terminal: Rowes Wharf
Boston-Hingham
See "MBTA Commuter Boat" in Chapter
18.

Steamship Authority
508-477-8600
Hyannis-Nantucket
Connects w/Plymouth & Brockton buses

from Boston at Hyannis.
  Late May-early Sept. 6 trips daily
  Rest of year: 3 trips daily
  Trip time: 2 1/4 hours. Bikes $5.
**Woods Hole-Martha's Vineyard
(Oak Bluffs)**
*Connects w/Bonanza Bus from Boston
at Woods Hole.*
  Late May-late Sept. only: 4 trips daily

Trip time: 45 min. Bikes $5.
**Woods Hole-Martha's Vineyard
(Vineyard Haven)**
*Connects w/Bonanza Bus from Boston
at Woods Hole.*
  Mid March-late Oct.: 9-14 trips daily
  Rest of year: 6-7 trips daily
  Trip time 45 min. Bikes $5.

Buses

Buses operated by Regional Transit Authorities are listed in Chapter 20.

Alewife Shuttle
890-0093
Alewife-Lexington & Waltham
*Connects w/Red Line at Alewife.
Limited to employees of participating
companies.*

American Eagle Motor Coach
508-993-5040
Boston terminal: Peter Pan
Boston-New Bedford-Fairhaven
Some trips stop at Taunton (Silver City
Galleria Mall)
  M-F: every 2 hours until 11:30 pm
  Rush hours: every 15 min.
  Sat: every 2 hours until 9:00 pm
  Sun: every 3 hours until 8:00 pm
  Trip time: 1 1/2 hours. Bikes $3.

Barrett's Tours
508-228-0174
Barrett's Tours operates summer-only
local buses on Nantucket.
  June 15-Sept. 1.

Brockton Area Transit (BAT)
508-580-1170
12 Ashmont–Brockton
Dorchester: Dorchester Ave., Lower
Mills;*Milton:* Randolph Ave.; *Randolph:*
Main St., Crawford Sq.; *Avon:* Avon
Sq., W. Main St. (some trips via E.
Main St.); *Brockton:* N. Main St. (No
local stops between Ashmont and
Randolph/Avon line.) *Connects w/Red
Line at Ashmont.*
  M-Sat: every 40 min.
  Rush hours: every 20 min.
  Nights: every hour until 11:40 pm M-F
  (until 10:50 pm Sat)
  Trip time: 40 min.

12X Ashmont-Brockton *(express)*
Via Rt. 24; *Brockton:* Pleasant St.
Connects w/Red Line at Ashmont.
  M-F rush hours only: every 20 min.

Trip time: 32 min.
See Chapter 20 for BAT local buses in
Brockton and Stoughton.

Beverly Shoppers Shuttle
508-921-0040
Shoppers Shuttle Commuter Bus
Beverly: loop via Beverly Depot, Cabot
St., Balch St., N. Beverly (Sat. only),
Herrick Rd., Beverly Hosp., Brimball
Rd., Essex St., Montserrat, Colon St.,
Elliott St., Bridge St. *Connects w/T-
Commuter Rail at Beverly Depot
(Rockport/Ipswich Lines) and
Montserrat (Rockport Line).*
  M-Sat: every hour.

Bloom Bus Lines
508-822-1991
Boston terminal: Peter Pan
Boston-Taunton
Via Raynham; some off-peak trips stop
at Westgate Mall, Brockton. Stops at
Silver City Galleria Mall in Taunton.
  Daily: every 2-2 1/2 hours
  Rush hours: every 30 min.
  Trip time: 1 hour. Bikes $2.
Taunton-Fall River
  M-F: 2 Trips
  Trip time: 25 Min. Bikes $2.

Bonanza Bus Lines
800-556-3815
Boston terminal: Back Bay Station
Bikes free except where noted.
Boston-Bangor, ME
Via Portland, ME, some trips via
Searsport, Belfast, Lincolnville,
Camden/Rockport, Rockland,
Waldoboro, Damariscotta,Wiscasset,
Bath, Bowdin College, Brunswick,
UMaine Orono. Most trips serve Logan
Airport.
  Daily: 5 trips
  Trip time: 5-7 Hours.

Boston-Newport, RI
Via Fall River. *Also serves Logan Airport.*
Daily: every 2 hours until 8: 00 pm
(until 10:00 pm Sun)
Trip time: 1 1/2 hours.

Boston-New York, NY
Via Providence, RI (change buses),
Hartford, Danbury, CT.
Daily: 5 trips
Trip time: 5 hours.

Boston-Providence, RI *(express)*
Via Pawtucket, RI.
Daily: every hour until 12:15 am
Trip time: 1 1/4 hours.

Logan Airport-Providence, RI
Via Foxboro, MA, and Pawtucket, RI.
Does not stop in downtown Boston.
Daily: every hour until 12:15 am
Trip time: 1 1/4 hours.

Boston-Wareham
Express; rush hour 1 trip also serves
Buzzards Bay.
M-F: 3 trips
Sat-Sun: 7 trips
Trip time: 1 1/4 hours.

Boston-Woods Hole
Via Bourne, Otis AFB, Falmouth. *Also
serves Logan Airport.*
Daily: every 2 hours until 10:00 pm
Rush hours: every hour
Summer: daily, every hour
Trip time: 1 3/4 hours, Bikes $3.

New York, NY-Hyannis
Via Providence, RI, Fall River, New
Bedford, Bourne; connecting buses to
Falmouth and Woods Hole. *Does not
stop in Boston.*
Daily: every 2-3 hours.
Trip time: 6 1/2 hours.

Brush Hill Transportation
986-6100
Boston terminals: Park Plaza;
South Station

Boston-Milford
Via Rt. 109, Westwood, Medfield, Millis,
W. Medway.
M-F rush hours only: 2 trips
Trip time: 1 1/4 hours. Bikes free.

Burlington Bus (The B Line)
270-1965
Local buses serving the town of
Burlington. All buses depart from the
Common at Cambridge & Bedford Sts.,
where they connect w/T- Buses 350
and 352. Some buses connect w/ T-
bus 350 at the Burlington Mall. Service
operates Mon-Fri 8:00 am-6:00 pm.

C & J Trailways
800-258-7111
Boston terminal: Peter Pan

Boston-Durham, NH
Via Logan Airport, Newburyport,
Portsmouth, and 5 trips to Dover, NH.
Daily: every 1-1 1/2 hours (15 trips)
until 10:00 pm (11:20 pm Fri & Sun)
Trip time: 2 hours. Bikes free.

Carey's Bus Lines
447-5555

Boston-Whitman
From South Sta. and Govt. Ctr.: via E.
Braintree, Weymouth Landing, S.
Weymouth; 1 trip serves Rockland; 2
trips serve N. Abington, Abington Ctr.; 3
trips serve Whitman Ctr., E. Whitman.
M-F rush hours only: 5 trips
Trip time: 1-1 1/2 hours. Bikes free.

Cavalier Coach
391-3331

Boston-Northborough
From Government Center, South
Station and Park Plaza, Via: Weston,
Wayland, Sudbury and Marlboro.
M-F 1 rush hour trip.
Trip time: 1 1/4 hours.

City Transportation
236-1888
Logan Airport-Downtown Boston
Serves most Boston hotels.
Daily, every 30 min. until 9:15 pm
on the quarter hour.

The Coach Company
603-382-4699
Departs from St. James Ave. and
Haymarket. Bikes free.

Boston-Portsmouth, NH
Via Newburyport, Hampton, NH
Inbound trips serve Logan Airport.
M-F rush hours only:
every 10-30 min.
Trip time: 2 hours

Boston-Plaistow, NH
Via Lynnfield, Danvers, Boxford,
Georgetown, Groveland, Haverhill.
M-F rush hours only: 2 trips
Trip time: 1 1/2 hours.

Concord Trailways
800-639-3317
Boston terminal: Peter Pan

Boston-Berlin, NH
via: Londonderry, Manchester,
Concord, Tilton, Laconia, Meredith,

Conway, Pinkham Notch. *Serves*
Logan Airport.
   1 Trip Daily to Berlin.
   2 Trips Daily to Conway.
   6 Trips Daily to Laconia.
   Trip time: 5 1/2 hours. Bikes free.
Boston-Concord, NH
Via Londonderry, Manchester, NH.
Also serves Logan Airport.
   M-F: every 1-1 1/2 hours (12 trips)
   Rush hours: every 30 min.
   Trip time: 1 1/2 hours. Bikes free.
Boston-Littleton,NH
Via Manchester, Concord, Plymouth,
Lincoln, Franconia, NH.
   Daily: 2 Trips.
   Trip time: 4 1/2 hours. Bikes free .
Boston-Nashua, NH
   M-F: 4 Trips.
   3 Trips serve Logan Airport.
   Sat-Sun: 3 Trips.
   Trip Time: 2 3/4 hours. Bikes free .
Boston-Portland, ME
Express. *Also serves Logan Airport.*
   Daily: 6 trips.
   Trip time: 2 hours. Bikes free .
Boston-Bangor, ME
Via Portland, ME. *Also serves Logan*
Airport.
   Daily: 3 trips.
   Trip time: 4 1/2 hours. Bikes free.

Concord Free Bus
371-3660
Local bus service in Concord, connecting
to shopping areas in neighboring towns.
Buses operate Mon., Wed., and Fri.
mornings, except holidays.

Dedham Local Bus
461-5987
Spring St.-Readville Manor
Dedham: Riverdale, Bridge St., Ames
St., Dedham Sq., High St., Dedham
Mall, E. Dedham Sq., Oakdale Sq.,
Cedar St., Endicott Cir., Sprague St.,
Trenton Rd. *Connects w/T-Bus 36 at*
Spring St. (W. Roxbury) and w/T-Bus
34E at Dedham Sq.
   M-F: 9 trips
   Trip time: 30 min.

Flight Line
800-245-2525
Logan Airport-Andover, Chelmsford,
Haverhill, Lawrence, Lowell, Methuen
and Tewksbury. Daily scheduled, on
demand and door-to-door service. Call
for details. Bikes $6-$10.

H. T. Drummond, Inc.
293-6264
Commuter van service to downtown
Boston from Duxbury, Hanover,
Kingston, Marshfield, Pembroke,
Plymouth, Rockland and Whitman.
Monthly tickets only.

Green Harbor Transportation
837-1234
Logan Airport-Plymouth
Van Service Via Braintree, Rockland,
Pembroke, Kingston, Plymouth Ctr.
   Daily: every hour (15 trips)

Greyhound Lines
800-231-2222
Boston terminal: South Sta.
Suburban terminal:
Riverside *(Green Line-D)*
Bikes $10, box required.
Boston-Albany, NY
Via Riverside, Worcester; some trips
also serve Springfield, Lee, Lenox,
Pittsfield.
   Daily: 4 trips
   Trip time: 3 3/4–4 3/4 hours
Boston-New York, NY *(express)*
Via Riverside, Hartford, CT.
   Daily: every hour (19 trips)
   Trip time: 4 3/4 hours
Boston-New York, NY *(local)*
Via Riverside, Worcester, Hartford,
Providence, RI, New Haven and other
Connecticut points; White Plains, NY.
   Daily: 4 trips
   Trip time: 6 1/2 hours
Boston-Portland, ME
Via Newburyport, Portsmouth, NH; 2
trips stop at Biddeford/Saco ME;
through buses to Bangor, ME; summer
service to Bar Harbor, ME, Moncton, NB.
   Daily: 6 trips
   Trip time: 2 1/2 hours.

Gulbankian's Bus Lines
508-460-0225
Boston-Hudson
From Park Plaza and Copley Sq.; via
Mass. Pike, Southborough, Marlborough.
   M-F: 3 trips
   Trip time: 1 1/4 hours. Bikes free.
Framingham-Hudson
From Shoppers World, via
Southborough, Marlborough.
   Sat only: 1 trip
   Trip time: 35 min. Bikes free.

Hudson Bus Lines
722-3200 (MBTA info line)
Fulton St.-Meadow Glen Mall
Medford:Highland Ave., Fulton St.,
Medford Sq., Riverside Ave.
> Mon-Sat: every 30 min. rush hours.
> Hourly off peak.
> Trip timo: 15 min.

Mattapan-Canton
This run is currently operated by
People Care-iers (361-1515).
Milton: Blue Hill Ave.;
Canton:Washington St., Canton Ctr.,
Cobbs Corner. *Connects w/Red Line at
Mattapan.; connects w/BAT 14 at
Cobbs Corner.*
> M-Sat: hourly until 5:30 pm (except no
> service M-F 10:00 am-2:00 pm).
> Trip time: 30 min.

Interstate Coach
800-BUS-UNDA
Boston-Middleborough
From Park Plaza and Lincoln St.: via
Bridgewater, W. Bridgewater, Easton
and Stoughton.
> M-F: rush hours, every 30 min.;
> 1 midday trip; 1 "reverse commute"
> trip Sat-Sun: 3 trips
> Trip time: 1 1/4 hours. Bikes free.

Island Transport
508-693-0058
Operates seasonal local buses on
Martha's Vineyard. No bikes.
**Vineyard Haven-Oak Bluffs-
Edgartown via Beach Road**
*Connects w/ferries at Vineyard Haven
and Oak Bluffs.*
> *Late June-Labor Day:*
> Daily: every 15-30 min.
> Nights: every hour until 11:30 pm
> Trip time: 45 min.

**Vineyard Haven-Oak Bluffs-
Edgartown via Beach Road and
Edgartown Road**
Connects w/ferries at Vineyard Haven.
> Late June-Labor Day
> Daily: every hour
> Trip time: 45 min.

Vineyard Haven-Gay Head
Via Oak Bluffs, W. Tisbury, Chilmark; 1
trip via Edgartown. *Connects w/ferries
at Vineyard Haven and Oak Bluffs.*
> Late June-Labor Day
> Daily: every 2 hours (4 trips)
> Trip time: 1 1/4 hour

Lexpress
861-1210
Lexpress operates local buses in
Lexington; one route also serves
Burlington Mall. All buses depart from
Depot Sq. in Lexington Center, where
they connect w/T-Buses 62 and 76.
Service operates Mon.-Fri. 7:00 am-
6:00 pm and Sat. 10:00 am-5:30 pm;
there is no Sat. service in July or Aug.

LIFT
508-620-4823
Local Intra-Framingham Transit
LIFT operates local buses in
Framingham, Ashland, Hopkinton, and
part of Natick. Service operates Mon-
Sat. All routes operate hourly. All LIFT
routes depart from Concord & Howard
Sts. in downtown Framingham, where
they connect w/T-Commuter Rail.
Routes 2,3,4 & 6 also connect w/Peter
Pan buses to Boston, w/Logan Express,
and w/the Natick Neighborhood Bus at
Shoppers World.
1 Industrial Park Express
Via Union Ave., Framingham Ctr., Rt. 9.
> M-F rush hours only: 6 trips
> Trip time: 1 hour

2 Malls via Nobscot
3 Nobscot via Malls
Via Union St., Framingham Ctr., Edgell
Rd., Nobscot, Water St., Pinefield,
Saxonville, Shoppers World, Natick
Mall, Sherwood Plaza, Concord St.
*Route 2 operates in a clockwise loop;
Route 3 operates counter-clockwise.*
> M-F: 6:30 am-5:30 pm
> Sat: 9:00 am-4:00 pm
> Trip time: 1 hour

4 Framingham Station
To Downtown, via Route 135, Route 9,
Cloverleaf Mall, McCall West Office
Center, Route 30, Shoppers World.
> M-F: 6 trips, rush hours only
> Trip time: 1 hour

5 Framingham-Hopkinton
Via Rt. 135. *Framingham*:Waverly St.;
Ashland: Union St.; *Hopkinton*: Main St.
> M-F: 6:45 am-5:45 pm, hourly
> Trip time: 45 min.

6 Milford-Framingham
Via Holliston (Route 16), Ashland
(Route 126), Framingham Commutrer
Rail, Downtown Framingham,
> M-F: 6 trips
> Sat.: 5 trips, every 2 hours
> Trip time: 1 hour

Logan Express
800-23-LOGAN
Logan Airport-Braintree
Express to Braintree T. Operated by
Plymouth & Brockton.
  M-F: every 30 min.
  Nights: every hour until 11:00 pm
  Sat: every hour
  Sun: every 30-60 min.
Logan Airport-Framingham
Via Mass. Pike, to Shoppers World.
  M-F: every 30 min. until 11:45 pm
  Sat: every hour until 11:00 pm
  Sun: every 30-60 min. until 11:45 pm
Logan Airport-Woburn
To the Marriott Hotel on Mishawum Road.
  M-F: every 30 min. until 8:00 pm
  Sat: every hour until 10:00 pm
  Sun: every 30-60 min. until 10:00 pm

LMA Shuttle
632-2800
**Cambridge-Longwood Medical and
Academic Area**
*Limited to students, faculty, and staff of
Harvard, MIT, and other Medical and
Academic Area institutions.*

Lower Cape Bus
508-487-3353
Lower Cape Bus operates summer-only
local buses in Provincetown.
Town Loop
Via Sandcastle Condominiums,
Howland St., MacMillan Pier, Shank
Painter Rd.
  Daily: every hour until 12:00 mid
Beach Loop
Via Sandcastle Condominiums,
MacMillan Pier, Provincetown Inn,
Herring Cove Beach
  Daily: every hour until 6:30 pm

Lynn East/West Loop Bus
508-535-2963
East Lynn Loop
Lynn: Central Sq., Broad St., Lewis St.,
Eastern Ave., Timson St., Union St.,
Rockaway St., High Rock St., Washing-
ton St., Lynn Hosp., Boston St.,
Broadway, Wyoma Sq., return to
Central Sq.
  M-Sat: 6 trips
  Trip time: 35 min.
West Lynn Loop
Lynn: Central Sq., Franklin St., Lynn
Hosp., Boston St., Cottage St., Barry
Park, Summer St., Neptune Towers,

return to Central Sq.
  M-Sat: 6 trips
  Trip time: 25 min.

M & L Transportation
665-7791
Logan Airport-Merrimack, NH
Via Boston (Quincy Market), Woburn,
Burlington, Bedford, Lowell,
Chelmsford, Nashua NH.
  M-F: every 30 min. until 11:00 pm
  Sat-Sun: every 30-60 min.
  Trip time: 1 1/2 hours. Bikes $7

Mass Limousine Co.
800-342-5894
Logan Airport-S. Attleboro
Via Middleborough, Taunton,
Foxborough, Mansfield.
  M-F only: 5 trips and by request
  Trip time: 1 1/4 hours

Michaud Bus Lines
800-MICHAUD
**Salem, Peabody, Northshore
Shopping Ctr. & Lakeshore Park**
Peabody: Lakeshore Park, Lynn St.,
Main St., Washington St., Peabody
Sq.,Central St., Andover St.
Salem: Riley Plaza, Broad St. Jackson
St., Shaughnessy Hospital, Jefferson
Ave., Canal St., Derby St., Washington
St., Bridge St., Boston St.
  M-Sat: every 1-2 hours (6 trips)
  Trip time: 1 3/4 hours

Mission Hill Link Bus
Serves the Mission Hill neighborhood of
Boston. All buses depart from Osco
Drug on Tremont St. near Brigham
Circle, where they connect w/Green
Line-E trains and T-Buses 39 and 66.
Service operates Mon-Sat 5:30 am-
9:00 pm.
Green Route
Via Tremont St., St. Alphonsus St.,
Calumet St., Parker St., Fisher Ave.,
Wait St.
  M-Sat 2:00-6:40 pm: every 20 min.
Blue Route
A variation of the Green Route which also
serves Roxbury Crossing*(Orange Line),*
Parker St., Hillside St.
  M-Sat 7:00-9:30 am: every 30 min.
  and 7:30-9:00 pm: every 30 min.
Red Route
A variation of the Green Route which
also serves Ward St., Annunciation
Rd., Parker St., Hillside St.
  M-Sat 10:30 am-1:30 pm: every 30 min.

Natick Neighborhood Bus
508-651-7262
Natick Common-Shoppers World
Most Natick neighborhoods are served by either fixed-route or on-request service. *Connects w/Peter Pan buses to Boston, Logan Express, and LIFT (Framingham local buses) at Shoppers World (Framingham); connects w/T-Commuter Rail (Framingham Line) at Natick and W, Natick stations.*
M-F: every hour, 7:15 am-5:45 pm
Sat: every hour, 10:00 am-4:00 pm

Paul Revere Bus
539-1993
Paul Revere operates local buses in Winthrop. Service operates 5:00 am-12:30 am Mon-Sat and 7:25 am-11:00 pm Sun.
Orient Heights-Winthrop Beach *via Centre*
East Boston: Saratoga St.; Winthrop Main St., Hermon St., Pauline St., Pleasant St., Washington St. *Connects w/blue line at ORIENT HEIGHTS*
Rush hours: every 7-15 min.
Nights: every 40 min.
Sun: every 80 min.
Trip time: 15 min.
Orient Heights-Winthrop Beach *via Highlands*
East Boston: Saratoga St.; *Winthrop:* Main St., Revere St., Crest Ave., Veterans Rd. *Connects w/Blue Line at Orient Hts.*
M-Sat: every 30-35 min.
Rush hours: every 12-18 min.
Nights: every 40 min.
Sun: every 80 min.
Trip time: 15 min.
Winthrop Beach-Pt. Shirley
Winthrop: Shirley St., Tafts Ave. *Through service from Orient Hts.*
M-Sat: every 30 min.
Nights & Sun: every 40 min.
Trip time: 20 min.

People Care-iers
361-1515
Canton-Mattapan (see Page 149)
Hingham Depot-Pt. Pemberton, Hull
Hingham: Summer St., Rockland St. *Hull:* Nantasket Ave., Spring St., Main St., to Pemberton. *Connects w/T-Bus 220 at Hingham Depot; connects w/Bay State ferry at Pt. Pemberton.*
M-Sat: every 45-60 min. until 7:30 pm (5:30 pm Sat)
Trip Time: 25 min.

Peter Pan Bus Lines
800-343-9999
Boston terminal: Peter Pan
Suburban terminal:
Riverside *(Green Line-D)*
Bikes free as checked baggage.
Boston-Albany, NY
Via Springfield, Lee, Lenox, Pittsfield; 2 trips via Riverside.
Daily: 3 trips
Trip time: 4-4 1/2 hours
Boston-Amherst/UMass *(express)*
Via Northampton, Holyoke.
M-F: 3 trips; 4 trips Fri & Sun during the school year
Trip time: 2-2 1/2 hours
Boston-Amherst
Via Springfield, Holyoke, Northampton; some trips stop at S. Hadley, Palmer, Sturbridge, Worcester, Framingham Center, Shoppers World, Riverside.
Daily: every hour (16 trips)
Trip time: 3-3 1/2 hours
Boston-Bennington, VT
Via Riverside, Springfield, Lee, Pittsfield, Adams, North Adams, Williamstown. M-F: 1 trip.
Trip time: 4 1/4 hours.
Boston-Framingham *(express)*
From Peter Pan terminal, Park Plaza, Copley Sq.; some rush hour trips from State House; via Mass. Pike to Shoppers World.
M-F only: every 2 hours until 9:15 pm
Rush hours: every 15 min.
Trip time: 35 min.
Boston-Greenfield
Via Deerfield, Amherst, Northampton, Holyoke, Springfield. Some trips serve Riverside, Worcester, Palmer.
Daily: 3 trips
Trip time: 3 1/2 hours
Boston-Hartford, CT
via Springfield, Northampton, Amherst. Serves Logan Airport.
Daily: 5 trips
Trip Time: 3 3/4 hours
Boston-New York, NY (Express)
Via Riverside.
Daily: 8 trips
Trip time: 4 1/2 hours
Boston-New York, NY (Local)
Via Riverside, Hartford, CT. Some trips serve Framingham, Worcester, Middletown CT, Meriden CT, New Haven CT, Bridgeport CT, Norwalk CT, White Plains NY, New Rochelle NY.
Daily: 11 Trips
Trip Time: 4 3/4-5 3/4 hours
(2 hours to Hartford)

Boston-Springfield
Via Mass. Pike; some trips serve
Riverside, Framingham, Worcester,
Palmer. *Connecting service from Logan
Airport.*
  Daily: 15 trips
  Trip time: 2 hours
Boston-Sturbridge
Via Worcester, Old Sturbridge Village.
  Daily: 2 trips
  Trip time: 1 3/4 hours
Boston-Westfield
Via Riverside, Springfield.
  Sun during school year only, 1 trip
  Trip time: 2 1/2 hours
Boston-Worcester*(express)*
Via Mass. Pike, Millbury. *Connecting
service from Logan Airport.*
  Daily: every hour (21 trips)
  Rush hours: every 30 min.; also stops
  at Park Plaza, Copley Sq.,
  Framingham and Auburn.
  Trip time: 1 hour
Boston-Worcester *(Rt. 9 Local)*
From Peter Pan terminal, Park Plaza,
Copley Sq.; via Brigham Circle,
Brookline Village, Newton Highlands,
Wellesley, Natick, Shoppers World,
Framingham Ctr., Southborough,
Westborough, Northborough,
Shrewsbury.
  M-F: every 2 hours (7 trips)
  Trip time from Boston:
  Shoppers World, 1 hour;
  Worcester, 1 3/4 hours
Logan Airport-Downtown Boston
Connects w/Peter Pan Treminal.
  Daily: 4 trips
  Trip time: 20 min.
Logan Airport-Worcester
Via Downtown Boston.
  Daily: 4 trips
  Trip time: 1 1/2 hours
Springfield-Bradley Airport
*Connects w/buses from Boston at
Springfield.*
  Daily: every 2 hours
  Trip time: 30 min.

Plymouth & Brockton Street Railway Co.
508-746-0378
Boston terminals: Park Plaza (Broad-
way St.); South Station; Peter Pan.
Some buses serve Logan Airport (as
noted). Bikes $5-10.
Boston-Brockton
Direct service from Park Plaza and

South Station to downtown Brockton.
  M-F: 6 trips.
  Trip time: 1 hour
Boston-Hyannis
*From Logan Airport (most trips), Park
Plaza and/or Peter Pan;* via Rockland,
Plymouth, Sagamore, Barnstable.
Most trips serve Logan Airport.
  M-F: hourly (27 trips)
  Rush hours: every 10-15 min.
  Sat-Sun: 12 trips
  Trip time: 1 1/2 hours
Boston-Logan Airport
From Park Plaza and South Station;.
  M-F hourly service
  Trip time: 20 min.
Boston-Plymouth Ctr. (Rt 53 Local)
From Park Plaza & South Sta.; Various
local and express routes via Rockland,
Norwell, Hanover, Pembroke, Duxbury,
Kingston.
  M-F: every 2 hours
  Rush hours: every 15 min.
  Trip time: 1 1/4 hours
Boston-Provincetown
*From Logan Airport, Peter Pan
Terminal, Park Plaza.* Via Plymouth,
Barnstable, Hyannis, Yarmouth,
Dennis, Brewster, Orleans, Eastham,
Wellfleet, Truro.
  Daily: 2 trips
  Trip time: 4 1/2 hours
Boston-Rockland
*Express from Peter Pan, Park Plaza
and South Station (Logan Airport on
Weekends).*
  M-F: Every 2 hours.
  Rush hours: Every 10-15 min,
  Sat-Sun: 7 trips.
  Trip time: 20-30 min.
Boston-Scituate (Rt. 228 Local)
*From Park Plaza, Peter Pan & South
Sta.;* via Rockland (Rt. 228), Hingham,
Cohasset, N. Scituate, Egypt,
Greenbush; 1 trip via Norwell.
  M-F rush hours: every 30 min., plus
  1 late-morning and 1 afternoon trip
  Trip time: 1 1/4 hours
Boston-Marshfield
From Park Plaza & South Sta.; via
Rockland, Brant Rock, Green Harbor,
Duxbury.
  M-F rush hours only: 2 trips
  Trip time: 1 hour

Trombly Commuter Lines
508-937-3626
Boston-Lawrence
From Government Ctr, Park Plaza and

Essex St.; via I-93, Andover, Lawrence. 1 trip serves Salem, NH.
M-F: 5 inbound trips every 20 min. beginning at 6:20 am. 5 outbound trips every 20 min. beginning at 4:15 pm
Trip time: 1 hour. Bikes free.

Vermont Transit Lines
800-451-3292
Boston terminal: South Station
Bikes free.
Boston-Rutland, VT
Via Riverside, Fitchburg Jct., Gardner, Winchendon; Fitzwilliam and Keene, NH; Bellows Falls, VT, Springfield, VT, Ludlow, VT:connecting buses to Springfield, MA, Hartford, CT and Brattleboro, VT. *1 trip serves Logan Airport.*
Daily: 2 trips
Trip time: 4 1/2 hours

Boston-Burlington, VT
Via Manchester, NH, White River Junction and Montpelier, VT. Some trips serve Lowell, MA, Nashua, Concord and New London, NH, Barre and Waterbury, VT; connecting buses to Montreal. *Also serves Logan Airport.*
Daily: 4 trips
Trip time: 5 1/4 hours

Yankee Line
1-800-942-8890
Boston-Littleton
From Essex St., Park Plaza, Copley Sq.; via Concord, Acton, Rt. 119.
M-F rush hours only: 1 trip
Trip time: 1 1/4 hour. Bikes free.

Chapter 20

Regional Transit Authorities

Regional Transit Authorities are responsible for transit in Massachusetts communities outside the Boston area. There are 14 RTAs serving 90 cities and towns across the Commonwealth. This chapter also includes services of the Rhode Island Public Transportation Authority (RIPTA).

All RTAs have reduced fares for elderly and handicapped riders. Many RTAs offer discounted monthly passes or multiple-ride tickets.

Besides the regular buses described here, every RTA offers special services for the elderly and handicapped. RTA services are wheelchair accessible.

BAT
☎ **508-580-1170**

Brockton Area Transit local buses operate Mon.-Fri. 6:00 am-8:40 pm, Sat. 7:20 am-6:00 pm; there is no Sunday service. Most routes operate every 40 minutes, or every 20 minutes in rush hours and late afternoons. The local fare is 60¢. Transfers are free.

Brockton—12 local routes depart from the Transfer Centre at Crescent and Main Sts. in downtown Brockton.

Stoughton—BAT Bus 14 departs from Westgate Mall, where it connects with BAT Buses 4 and 4A from Brockton and the Mini-Maller (MM).

Brockton-Ashmont, via Milton, Randolph, and Avon—BAT Buses 12 and 12X operate Mon.-Fri. 5:00 am-11:25 pm, Sat. 5:20 am-10:45 pm. Fare, $1.20.

Connecting services: BAT Buses 12 and 12X (Ashmont) connect with the MBTA Red Line at Ashmont. BAT Bus 10 (Lisa & Howard) connects with T-Bus 230 (Quincy Ctr.-Holbrook) at S. Franklin and Howard Sts. BAT Bus 14 (Stoughton) connects with Hudson Bus (Mattapan-Canton) at Cobbs Corner. Plymouth & Brockton buses from Boston stop at the BAT Transfer Centre.

BRTA   ☎ 800-292-BRTA; 413-499-BRTA

Berkshire Regional Transit Authority, or "The B," serves Pittsfield, North Adams, and other Berkshire County towns. BRTA buses operate Mon.-Sat. Most routes operate hourly. The fare is 60¢ per community traveled. Transfers are free.

Pittsfield—10 local routes in Pittsfield, Dalton, Hinsdale, and Lanesboro. Buses depart from Park Square in Pittsfield. *Connecting services:* Greyhound and Peter Pan stop at 57 S. Church St. (413-442-4451), 4 blocks southwest of Park Square. Amtrak stops at Depot St., off North and Center Sts., 2 blocks north of Park Square.

North Adams—4 local routes in North Adams and Williamstown. Buses depart from Main St. in North Adams. *Connecting services:* Peter Pan stops at Angelina's Subs (413-664-0315); one Bonanza trip serves North Adams.

Pittsfield-Great Barrington, via Lenox, Lee, Housatonic, and Stockbridge—hourly, Mon.-Sat. *Also:* Bonanza has 3 daily trips via Lenox, Lee, and Stockbridge. *Connecting services:* Greyhound and Peter Pan stop opposite the police station in Lenox and at 43 Main St. in Lee.

Pittsfield-North Adams, via Lanesboro (Berkshire Village), Cheshire, and Adams—hourly, Mon.-Sat. *Connecting services:* See "Pittsfield" and "North Adams." *Additional connecting services:* Peter Pan stops at the Williams Inn (413-458-2665) in Williamstown. Bonanza has 2 daily trips from Pittsfield to Williamstown via New Ashford (one trip serves North Adams).

Visitor information: 413-443-9186.

CATA   ☎ 508-283-7916

Cape Ann Transportation Authority buses operate Mon.-Sat. Most routes operate every 2 hours with additional rush hour service. The fare is 60¢, or 75¢ for two-zone trips. Trips in the "downtown zones," between the railroad station and downtown in both Gloucester and Rockport, cost only 25¢.

Gloucester—4 local routes depart from Dunkin Donuts at the corner of Rogers St. and Manuel Lewis Dr. in downtown Gloucester. *Connecting services:* The T-Commuter Rail station is on Railroad Ave., off Washington St., 1/2 mile north of downtown. (See map on page 90.) Two of CATA's routes stop at the train station. CATA's Green Line (Business Express) offers shuttle service from the train station to downtown, every 30 min. Mon.-Fri. The Sat. Business Express schedule is irregular but there is service to downtown from arriving trains. Rush hour trains are met by specially-scheduled trips on 3 CATA routes. The AC Cruise boat from Boston lands at Rocky Neck, across the harbor from downtown Gloucester. CATA's Red Line (East Gloucester) bus stops at Rocky Neck.

Gloucester-Rockport—hourly service via 3 different routes. In Rockport, buses depart from the Richdale store on Broadway. *Connecting service:* The T-Commuter Rail station is behind Whistlestop Mall, off Railroad Ave., 1/2 mile from Dock Sq. and Bearskin Neck. CATA's Blue Line bus (Rockport-Gloucester via Lanesville) stops on Railroad Ave. and makes this connection. (See map on page 92.)

Visitor information: 508-283-1601.

CCRTA
☎ 800-352-7155; 508-385-8326

Cape Cod Regional Transit Authority
Barnstable Village-Woods Hole, via Cape Cod Community College, Cape Cod Mall, Plymouth & Brockton Bus Terminal, Hyannis, Cape Cod Hospital, Centerville, Osterville, Cotuit, Mashpee, Waquoit, East Falmouth, Teaticket, Falmouth—6 trips Mon.-Fri., 3 trips Sat., no Sun. service. Fares on the 25-mile trip range from 75¢ to $4.00. *Connecting services:* CCRTA stops at bus stations in Hyannis, Falmouth, and Woods Hole, and at Steamship Authority ferry terminals in Hyannis and Woods Hole. (See Hyannis and Falmouth maps on pages 90 and 88.)

Hyannis-Provincetown—see the "Plymouth & Brockton" listing in Chapter 19.

Yarmouth Easy Shuttle, Plymouth & Brockton Bus Terminal, Hyannis to Yarmouth, via Thunder Falls, Christmas Tree Plaza, Zooquarium Visitors Center, Pirates Cove, Bass River Beach, Red Jacket. Free, hourly, daily service late June to early September.

CCRTA also operates door-to-door service by advance reservation, Mon.-Sat., throughout Cape Cod. This service is open to the general public.
Visitor information: 508-362-3225.

FRTA
☎ 413-774-2262

Franklin Regional Transit Authority operates 3 routes in Greenfield, Bernardston, Charlemont, Deerfield, Northfield, and Shelburne Falls. Service on all routes is limited, 3 or fewer trips per day, with most service operating during the school year only. Buses leave from Court Sq. in Greenfield. The fare is: zone 1, $1.25, zone 2, $1.75, zone 3, $2.00. *Connecting services:* See the GMTA listing.

GATRA
☎ 508-222-6106

Most **Greater Attleboro-Taunton Regional Transit Authority** routes operate hourly, Mon.-Sat. The local fare is 60¢.

Attleboro—4 local routes in Attleboro, N. Attleboro, Plainville, and part of Seekonk. Buses depart from the bus shelter on Union St. *Connecting services:* The T-Commuter Rail station is 1/2 block from the bus shelter. GATRA Bus 12 (S. Attleboro) connects with RIPTA Bus 77 for service to Providence, RI. GATRA Bus 16 (Seekonk) connects with RIPTA Buses 76 and 77.

Taunton—6 local routes depart from the Bloom bus complex bus at 10 Oak St. *Connecting service:* Bloom buses depart from the Oak St. complex.

Attleboro-Taunton, via Norton—Hourly Mon.-Fri., except there is no midmorning service. Fare, $1.40.

Taunton-Providence, RI, via Rehoboth and Seekonk—Every 90 minutes Mon.-Sat. (every 45 min. in rush hour). Fare, $2.25.

GMTA
☎ 413-773-9478

Most **Greenfield-Montague Transportation Area** buses depart from Court Sq. in downtown Greenfield. The fare is 75¢, plus 35¢ per zone, to a maximum of $1.80.

Greenfield—5 local routes in Greenfield. Routes operate Mon.-Sat. *Connecting services:* Peter Pan stops near Court Square. GMTA's "GCC" bus stops at Colrain Rd. and Rt. 2, near Rich's Mall, Mon.-Fri.

Greenfield-Montague, via Millers Falls—4 trips Mon.-Fri.; 2 trips Sat.

Greenfield-Amherst, via Turners Falls, Montague, Millers Falls—2 trips Mon.-Fri.

Greenfield-Turners Falls, Every 30-60 min. Mon-Fri, 2 trips serve Montague, 2 trips serve Amherst. 5 trips on Saturday.

LRTA   ☎ 508-452-6161

Lowell Regional Transit Authority operates 17 routes in Lowell, Billerica, Chelmsford, Dracut, Tewksbury, and Tyngsboro. Buses operate Mon.- Sat. All LRTA buses depart from the Transit Center between Merrimack and Paige Sts. in downtown Lowell. Most routes operate hourly. The fare is 60¢ in Lowell, increasing to a maximum of $1.00 outside the city limits; transfers are 20¢.

Connecting services: T-Commuter Rail and intercity buses stop at Gallagher Terminal (508-459-7101), 145 Thorndike St., 1 mile south of downtown. LRTA's 30¢ downtown shuttle bus stops at the Terminal every 15 min. Mon.-Fri. 6:00am-6:00 pm (every 30 min. in summer); every 30 min. Sat. 10:00 am-4:00 pm. (See map on page 92.)

Lowell-Lawrence—This MVRTA bus stops at the LRTA Transit Center.

MART   ☎ 800-922-5636; 508-345-7711

Montachusett Area Regional Transit serves Fitchburg, Leominster, and Gardner in north central Massachusetts. Buses operate Mon.Sat. Most routes operate hourly. The local fare is 50¢.

Leominster-Fitchburg—9 local routes depart from Monument Square, Leominster, and the MART Intermodal Center (508-343-3064). *Connecting services:* T-Commuter Rail stops at the Intermodal Center; this is also the stop for Peter Pan buses. The T-Commuter Rail also stops 1 mile North of Monument Square (North Leominster stop). Vermont Transit stops at Bickford's restaurant (508-537-6669) at Rts. 2 and 12.

Fitchburg— is also served by 2 additional routes departing from Intermodal Center.

Gardner—2 local routes operate in a loop, Mon.- Sat. The Mount Wachusett Community College Express connects Gardner to Fitchburg and Leominster.

Leominster-Fort Devens—2 trips Mon.-Fri. 5 trips during the school year; $1.00.

MVRTA   ☎ 800-231-RIDE

Merrimack Valley Regional Transit Authority serves Haverhill, Lawrence, Methuen, Merrimac, Salisbury, Amesbury, Lowell, Andover, North Andover and Newburyport. Buses operate Mon.-Sat. Most routes operate hourly on weekdays, and every 80 min. on Saturday. Most local fares are 75¢; transfers are free.

Haverhill—8 local routes in Haverhill. Buses depart from the Transit Station in Washington Square. The T-Commuter Rail station is at Railroad Sq., 3 blocks west of the MVRTA Transit Station. Buses to New York, NY, and Portland, ME, stop at the MVRTA Transit Station (508-372-3900).

Lawrence—14 local routes in Lawrence, Andover, N. Andover, and Methuen. Buses depart from the Intown Mall on Essex St. (westbound) and Common St. (eastbound). A 35¢ downtown shuttle bus operates every 15-30 min., Mon.-Fri. The T-Commuter Rail station is across the river from downtown Lawrence, a 1/2-mile walk across the Parker St. bridge. Trombly buses from Boston stop at Common St. (508-686-9577) in the Intown Mall, as do buses to New York, NY, Concord, NH, and Portland, ME.

Newburyport—Buses from Boston stop at the Park and Ride off I-95, 2 1/2 miles west of downtown. (Some The Coach Co. rush hour trips stop in downtown Newburyport.) MVRTA buses connect the Park and Ride to downtown Newburyport and to Amesbury.

Andover—Two free local buses operate every half hour, Mon.-Fri.; plus MVRTA Bus 32 from Lawrence, Mon.-Sat. MVRTA local buses serve T-Commuter Rail stations at Andover and Ballardvale. Trombly buses stop on Main St., served by all MVRTA routes.

Methuen—A local route connects with MVRTA buses from Lawrence at Methuen Sq. and at Methuen Mall.

Newburyport-Haverhill, via Amesbury—every 60-90 min., Mon-Sat.; $1.00

Haverhill-Lawrence, via Methuen Mall—Every 45 min., Mon.-Sat.; $1.00

Lawrence-Lowell, via Merrimack Plaza (Methuen)—Every 45 min., Mon.-Fri.; every 80 min., Sat.; $1.00

Lawrence-Salisbury Beach, via Methuen Mall, Haverhill, Merrimac, and Amesbury—2 trips Mon.-Sat. in July and Aug.; $2.00.

PVTA ☎ 413-781-PVTA

Pioneer Valley Transit Authority serves 20 cities and towns in the Connecticut River valley, including Springfield, Holyoke, Northampton, and Amherst.

Springfield—20 local routes in Springfield, Agawam, Chicopee, E. Longmeadow, part of Holyoke, Longmeadow, Ludlow, Westfield, W. Springfield, Wilbraham, and Enfield, CT. Most buses operate Mon.-Sat. 5:00 am-9:00 pm, with no Sunday service. Buses depart from Baystate West at Main St. and Boland Way in downtown Springfield. The fare is 65¢, plus 15¢ per zone to a maximum of 95¢; transfers are free within one zone. *Connecting services:* Peter Pan and Greyhound stop at 1776 Main St. (413-781-3320), 4 blocks north of Baystate West. PVTA Buses 101, 102, 103, 105, 107, 109, 217, 221, 401, 402, 403, 404, and 406 stop on Main St. near the bus station (see map on page 102.)

Holyoke —9 local routes in Holyoke, Chicopee, Granby, S. Hadley, and Westfield. Buses operate Mon.-Sat. Buses depart from Maple St. The fare is 65¢, or 80¢ for 2-zone trips; transfers are free. *Connecting services::* PVTA Bus 204 stops at Northampton and Dwight Sts., 1 block from the bus station, every 80 min. PVTA Buses 217 and 221 offer frequent service to downtown Holyoke from the Springfield bus station.

Northampton —3 local routes in Northampton, Easthampton, Williamsburg, and part of Holyoke. Routes operate Mon.-Sat. During fall and winter semesters, service is free; at other times, the fare is 65¢. *Connecting services:* Peter Pan stops at 1 Roundhouse Plaza (413-586-1030), off Old South St., 1 block from the PVTA bus stop and 3 blocks from Smith College.

Amherst—13 local routes in Amherst, Belchertown, Hadley, S. Deerfield, S. Hadley, and Sunderland. During the college year, buses daily; during school vacations, there is no Sat. or Sun. service. Buses depart from N. Pleasant St. adjacent to the University of Massachusetts. The Amherst buses are free.

Five Colleges —Frequent shuttle buses during the school year, connecting Amherst College, Hampshire College, Mount Holyoke College, Smith College, and UMass/Amherst. Service operates daily. This service is free and open to the public. *Connecting services:* Peter Pan stops in Amherst Ctr. at 79 S. Pleasant St. (413-256-0431), at the UMass Hotel (413-256-0431), and at the Hampshire College Bookstore (413-549-4600). There are daily trips from Springfield, via Holyoke, Northampton, and Hadley. The Amherst-Greenfield GMTA bus stops at UMass.

Springfield-Holyoke—3 routes: via Chicopee, via W. Springfield, or express in rush hour. Fare, 90¢.

Northampton-Amherst, via Hadley and Williamsburg—Same schedule as Five College buses during the school year; reduced service in summer.

Visitor information: 413-787-1548.

RIPTA   ☎ 401-781-9400

The **Rhode Island Public Transit Authority** operates all public transit service in Rhode Island, both local and intercity. The system serves 36 of the state's 39 cities and towns. The fare is 85¢ for one zone (25¢ for a "short zone" in Providence), increasing to a maximum of $2.50 for 4 zones; transfers are 15¢.

Providence—28 local routes in Providence, Centredale, Cranston, E. Providence, Johnston, and N. Providence. Service operates Daily. All buses depart from Kennedy Plaza in downtown Providence. *Connecting services:* Amtrak and T-Commuter Rail trains stop at 100 Gaspee St., 1/4 mile north of Kennedy Plaza; RIPTA Buses 56 and 57 stop on Gaspee St. in front of the train station. The Bonanza bus terminal is at 1 Bonanza Way (401-751-8800), 2 miles north of downtown Providence. Bonanza buses to Boston stop at both the Bonanza terminal and Kennedy Plaza. Buses to other destinations, including Logan Airport, stop only at the Bonanza terminal, but passengers may use the hourly Boston bus for connections from Kennedy Plaza. RIPTA Buses 98 and 99 (Providence-Pawtucket) stop at the Bonanza terminal. (See map on page 106.)

Pawtucket—9 local routes in Pawtucket, Central Falls, Cumberland, and Lincoln. Service operates daily. Buses depart from Main & Roosevelt Sts., where they connect with RIPTA Buses 98 and 99 from Providence.

Newport—3 local routes operate daily. Buses depart from Gateway Center at 23 America's Cup Ave. *Connecting service:* Bonanza buses from Boston stop at Gateway Center.

Woonsocket, Wakefield, and *Galilee*—local buses operate Mon.-Sat.

Providence-Pawtucket—Service operates daily.

Providence-Newport, via Bristol, Warren, Middletown, and Portsmouth—daily service.

Providence-Woonsocket—Service operates daily.

Providence-Kingston, via S. Kingstown—4-6 trips daily.

Other Providence services—Mon.-Sat. to E. Greenwich, Galilee, Jamestown, Narragansett, N. Kingstown, Wakefield, Warwick; Mon.-Fri. to most other points in the state.

Newport-Kingston, via Jamestown, Narragansett, Wakefield—every hour Mon.-Fri.; every 90 minutes Sat. This bus serves the Amtrak station, which is 2 miles west of downtown Kingston.

Visitor information: 401-274-1636.

SRTA ☎ 508-999-5211

Southeastern Regional Transit Authority serves New Bedford and Fall River in southeastern Massachusetts. The fare on all SRTA buses is 75¢ per zone.

New Bedford—14 local routes in New Bedford, Acushnet, Dartmouth, Fairhaven, and Mattapoisett. Buses operate Mon.-Sat. with limited service Sun. Buses depart from the Transportation Center at Elm and Pleasant Sts. *Connecting service:* American Eagle stops at the SRTA terminal (508-999-5211x34).

Fall River—13 local routes in Fall River, Somerset, and Swansea. Buses operate Mon.-Sat. Buses leave from the SRTA terminal at 221 Second St.*Connecting service:* Bonanza stops at the SRTA terminal (508-679-2335).

New Bedford-Fall River, via Dartmouth and Westport—Daily, every hour until 6:00 pm.

Visitor information: New Bedford, 508-991-6200; Fall River, 508-679-0922.

VTA ☎ 508-627-9663

Martha's Vineyard Transit Authority operates 4 summer-only routes, 2 in Vinyard Haven and 2 in Edgartown.

Vinyard Haven, Downtown loop—Flag stop service every 2 hours, daily, 10:00 am-10:00 pm. Fare; $1.00.

Park and Ride Shuttle— Every 15 min, daily, 5:30 am-10:30 pm. Fare 25¢. *Connecting service:s::* see "Steamship Authority" and "Cape Island Express" ferries and "Island Transport" bus (see Chapter 19).

Edgartown, Downtown loop—Every 10 minutes, daily, 7:30 am-11:30 pm, July and August. 7:30 am-7:00 pm, mid May-June, early Sept. Fare; 25¢.

Katama Beach shuttle—Every 15 min., 9:00 am-5:30 pm, daily, mid June-early Sept.; $1.50. *Connecting services:* See "Island Transport" in Chapter 19. All buses stop on Church St. in Edgartown, next to the police station.

Visitor information: 508-693-0085.

WRTA ☎ 508-791-WTRA

Worcester Regional Transit Authority operates routes in Worcester, Auburn, Boylston, Brookfield, Clinton, E. Brookfield, Holden, Leicester, Grafton, Webster, Oxford, Millbury, Shrewsbury, Spencer, and W. Boylston. Most buses operate daily. Most routes operate every half hour on weekdays, hourly at night and on Sat., and every two hours on Sun. Buses depart from Worcester City Hall. The fare is 75¢, plus 25¢ per zone outside Worcester to a maximum of $1.50; transfers are 25¢. *Connecting services:* Peter Pan and Greyhound stop at 75 Madison St. (508-754-3247), 4 blocks south of City Hall. WRTA buses 6S, 19S, 26S, 30S, and 33 stop at Main and Madison Sts., 2 blocks west of the bus station. The 10 and 25 buses stop 1 block away at the registry. The Amtrak station is at 45 Shrewsbury St., 1/2 mile east of City Hall. (See map on page 106.)

Visitor information: 508-753-2920.

Transit in New England and Beyond

You don't need a car to travel around New England. Buses and trains serve major cities and small towns throughout the region. The map in this chapter shows some of the places where you can go.

Connecticut

Connecticut is served by two different Amtrak routes from Boston, as well as Peter Pan (617-426-7838), Greyhound (617-423-5810), and Bonanza (617-720-4110) buses.

Amtrak's scenic "Shore Line" has nine trains daily, via Mystic, New London, and Old Saybrook. At Mystic, the Mystic Seaport museum village is just a few blocks from the train station. A second Amtrak route, with two trains daily, operates via Hartford. Both routes converge at New Haven, the home of Yale University, before continuing to Bridgeport and Stamford.

New Haven, Bridgeport, and Stamford are transfer points from Amtrak to Metro-North Commuter Railroad (800-638-7646) for local trains to Westport, Norwalk, New Canaan, Greenwich, and other towns. Shore Line East commuter trains (800-ALL-RIDE or 203-777-RIDE outside Connecticut) serve points east of New Haven.

Hartford, the state capital and the site of Mark Twain's house, has frequent bus service from Boston via Peter Pan, Greyhound and Bonanza. Greyhound and Peter Pan also serve New Haven.

Other towns and cities you can reach from Boston by public transportation include Canaan, Danbury, Danielson, Fairfield, Kent, Meriden, Middletown, Milford, New Britain, Southbury, Storrs, Stratford, Wallingford, Willimantic, and Waterbury.

There are ferries across Long Island Sound from New London and Bridgeport. The ferry docks are adjacent to the Amtrak station:

New London—Block Island, RI (summer only): 203-442-7891
New London—Fishers Island, NY (year-round): 203-443-6851
New London—Orient Point, NY (year-round): 203-443-5281
New London—Montauk, NY (May-October): 800-MONTAUK
Bridgeport—Port Jefferson, NY (year-round): 203-367-3043

The following Connecticut cities have local bus service:

Bridgeport 203-333-3031	New Haven 203-624-0151
Danbury 203-748-203	Hartford 203-525-9181
New London 203-886-2631	Norwalk 203-852-0000
Meriden 203-235-6851	Stamford 203-327-RIDE
Middletown 203-346-0212	Wallingford 203-294-2160
Milford 203-783-3258	Waterbury 203-753-2538
New Britain 203-828-0511	Westport 203-226-7171

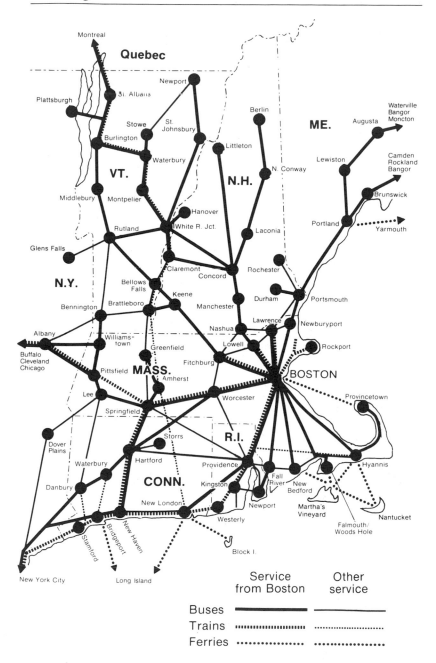

Maine

Portland, Maine's largest city, is served by Bonanza (800-556-3815),Greyhound (800-231-2222),Concord Trailways (800-639-3317) and Vermont Transit (800-451-3292) buses from Boston.

Bonanza and Vermont Transit buses then continue north from Portland, following either the inland route via Lewiston, Augusta, and Waterville, or the coastal route via Brunswick, Rockland, and Camden. Both routes meet at Bangor, where you can connect to buses for northern Maine and "down East" points, including Bar Harbor, the gateway to Acadia National Park. Concord Trailways buses continue nonstop to Bangor.

Vinalhaven, North Haven, and Matinicus islands are reached by ferry from Rockland. Call 207-596-2202.

Other towns and cities you can reach from Boston by public transportation include Bar Harbor, Bath, Belfast, Berwick, Biddeford, Calais, Caribou, Ellsworth, Freeport, Houlton, Machias, Orono, Presque Isle, Saco, Waterville, and Wiscasset.

The following Maine cities have local bus service:

> Augusta 207-622-4761   Lewiston/Auburn 207-783-2033
> Bangor 207-947-0536   Portland 207-774-0351
> Berwick 603-862-2328   S. Portland 207-767-5556
> Biddeford/Saco 207-282-5408

For Maine tourist information, call 800-533-9595 or 207-289-2423. For Portland, call 207-772-5800.

New Hampshire

Central New Hampshire is served by Concord Trailways (603-238-3300) and Vermont Transit (617-292-4700) buses from Boston. Both companies have several trips daily to Manchester and to Concord, the state capital.

Concord Trailways buses then continue north into the Lake Winnipesaukee and White Mountains regions. Hiking trails are accessible at many of the stops along the route. Several ski areas are also near bus stops such as Lincoln (North Woodstock), Conway, and Jackson.

One of Concord Trailways' stops is at the Appalachian Mountain Club camp in Pinkham Notch. In summer, the AMC has a "hiker's shuttle service" which connects the camp with several nearby trailheads. Call 603-466-2727 for details and reservations.

Vermont Transit goes to Lebanon and Hanover (site of Dartmouth College), with one bus daily to Newport, Claremont, and Mt. Sunapee. Another Vermont Transit route stops at Keene.

Portsmouth, on the seacoast, is served by C & J Trailways (617-426-7838). C & J Trailways also serves the University of New Hampshire, at Durham.

C & J Trailways, Concord Trailways, The Coach Co. (800-225-4846), and Vermont Transit operate commuter schedules to Boston from several southern New Hampshire cities.

All C & J Trailways, Concord Trailways, and Vermont Transit buses from Boston also serve Logan Airport. For additional airport service, see Chapter 19 listings for M & L Transportation (1-800-225-4846).

The following New Hampshire cities have local bus service:

Dover/Durham 603-862-2328   Nashua 603-880-0100
Hampton Beach 603-926-8717   Portsmouth 603-862-2328
Hanover/Lebanon 603-448-2815   Rochester 603-862-2328
Manchester 603-623-8801

For New Hampshire tourist information, call 603-271-2666. For Portsmouth, call 603-436-1118.

Rhode Island

Rhode Island is served by Bonanza buses (617-720-4110) and Amtrak (617-482-3660) trains from Boston. Bonanza has frequent service to Providence, Pawtucket, and Newport from both downtown Boston and Logan Airport; and Amtrak stops at Providence, Kingston, and Westerly. In addition, MBTA Commuter Rail (617-227-5070) serves Providence, the state capital.

Block Island can be reached by ferry from Providence and Newport, and from New London, CT (Amtrak).

All bus service within Rhode Island is operated by Rhode Island Public Transit Authority (RIPTA); see Chapter 20, "Regional Transit Authorities," for details.

For Rhode Island tourist information, call 800-556-2484.

Vermont

Most intercity buses in Vermont are operated by Vermont Transit, a private company. Virtually all points in the state can be reached directly from Boston or by connections at White River Jct. or Rutland.

Bennington, in the southwestern part of the state, is served by Peter Pan buses (800-343-9999) from Boston.

Peter Pan has winter service to the Mount Snow ski area.

The following Vermont cities have local bus service:

Barre/Montpelier 802-479-1071   Rutland 802-773-3244
Burlington 802-864-0211   White River Jct. 603-448-2815

For Vermont tourist information, call 802-828-3236.

Beyond New England

New York

Amtrak (617-482-3660), Peter Pan (800-343-9999), Greyhound (800-231-2222), and Bonanza (800-556-3815) all have frequent daily service from Boston to New York City. Many Amtrak trains also stop at New Rochelle, and connecting Metro-North commuter trains are available from Stamford, CT, to Rye, Mt. Vernon, and other towns.

Long Island Railroad trains depart from Amtrak's Pennsylvania Station in New York City; ferries to Long Island are described above, in the Connecticut listing.

Fishers Island can be reached by two ferries from New London, CT.

For information on bus, train, limousine, and ferry service from LaGuardia, Kennedy, and Newark airports, call 800-AIR-RIDE.

Albany, the state capital, is served by Peter Pan and Greyhound buses from Boston and Amtrak's daily "Lake Shore Limited." All have through or connecting service across New York state to Utica, Syracuse, Rochester, and Buffalo. Connections may also be made at the Albany bus terminal for other New York state points.

Here are transit information numbers for major New York cities:

Albany 518-482-8822	New Rochelle 914-682-2020
Buffalo 716-855-7211	New York City 718-330-1234
Long I. (Nassau) 516-222-1000	Rochester 716-288-1700
Long I. (Suffolk) 516-360-5700	Syracuse 315-442-3400

Three different commuter railroads serve New York City:

Long Island Railroad 718-217-LIRR
Metro-North Commuter Railroad 800-638-7646
New Jersey Transit 201-460-8444
For New York state tourist information, call 800-I-LOVE-NY.

Canada

Bus service is available from Boston to several Canadian cities. Vermont Transit has a daily bus to Montreal, with connections to Quebec city. Buses to Toronto leave from Buffalo, NY, and Montreal.

Amtrak's overnight "Montrealer" goes from Washington, DC, to Montreal; connections from Boston can be made at New Haven or New London, CT. [Note: may be discontinued.]

In summer, Prince of Fundy Cruises operates an overnight ferry from Portland, ME, to Yarmouth, Nova Scotia, with connecting bus service to Halifax. Call 800-341-7540 for reservations. Concord Trailways has seven buses to Amherst, Truro, Halifax, Antigonish, and Sydney, Nova Scotia.

For Canadian tourist information, call 536-1730 in Boston; for passenger train information, call VIA Rail Canada at 800-561-3949.

Index

For transit information on cities, towns, and neighborhoods, see the alphabetical list in Chapter 16; other text mentions of these localities are covered in the index.

A

Access, 15. *See also* Disabilities, persons with
Adams National Historic Site, 42
Airport Handicapped Van, 15
Airport, Logan. *See* Logan Airport
Airport Water Shuttle, 30-32
American Antiquarian Society, 43
Americans with Disabilities Act (ADA), 15
Amtrak, 11
   schedule, 144
Arnold Arboretum, 47
Assn. for Public Transportation (APT), *vi*
Attleboro, 155
Auditoriums, cinemas, and theaters. *See* alphabetical list in Ch. 10

B

Back Bay, 36
Back Bay Fens, 46
Back Bay Station, 19, 27, 141
Battle Green, 40
Battleship Cove, 40
Beaches, 44-54
Beacon Hill, 36
Bearskin Neck, 40
Beaver Brook, 54
Berkshire Regional Transit Authority (BRTA), 155
Bicycles, 13-14
   bikepaths, 13-14
   on the T, 14
   rentals, 45
Billiards, 65
Black Heritage Trail, 36
Blue Hills, 52
Blue Line
   fares, 3-4, 8
   first and last trains, 110
   map, 113
   schedule, 111
   tips for subway riders, 2
   transfer points, 3
Bonanza terminal, 28
Boott Cotton Mills Museum, 41
Boston African American National Historic Site, 36
Boston Common, 44
Boston Garden, 27

Boston Harbor Islands, 46
Boston maps
   Back Bay, 20-21
   downtown, 22-23
   terminals, 16
Boston Marathon, 69
Boston National Historical Park, 38
Boston Passport, 10
Boston terminals, 16
Brighton, 47
Brockton Area Transit (BAT), 146
Brookline, 47
   Brookline Village map, 24
Bumpkin Island, 46
Bunker Hill, 37
Buses
   commuter bus stops, 27-28
   crosstown (map), 125
   MBTA. *See* Buses, MBTA
   non-T lines, 11, 146-153 (schedules)
   subscription, 13
   terminals, 30. *See also* Individual terminals, e.g., Bonanza
Buses, MBTA, 4-5
   crosstown (map), 125
   fares, 5, 8
   schedules, 124-139

C

Cambridge, 19, 39, 48
Camping, 45
Canada, 164
Canoeing, 45
Cape Ann
   maps, 90, 92
Cape Ann Transportation Authority (CATA), 154
Cape Cod, 48-49
Cape Cod Regional Transit Authority (CCRTA), 155
Car rentals, 13
Carpools, 13
Carson Beach, 47
Castle Island, 47
Central Sq. (Cambridge) map, 24
Charles River, 44, 46, 53
Charlestown, 37
Charters, 12
"Cheers" (Bull & Finch Pub), 36
Chestnut Hill Reservoir, 47
Children's fares, MBTA, 8
Chinatown, 37
Christian Herter Park, 48
Cinemas, theaters, and auditoriums. *See* alphabetical list in Ch. 10
Cleveland Circle (map), 25
Colleges. *See* alphabetical

list in Ch. 14
Comedy Clubs, 65-66
Commonwealth Pier, 29
Community Boating, 46
Commuter boats, MBTA, 6
   schedules, 141
Commuter info. phone, 13
Commuter Rail, MBTA, 5-0
   fares, 6, 8
   schedules, 145-146
   station locations, 141-142
   transfer points, 5
   zones, 139-141
Concord, 39
Copley Sq. (commuter bus stop), 27
Connecticut, 160
Constitution (ship), 37
Constitution Beach, 46
Crane Beach, 50

D

Davis Sq. (map), 25
DeCordova Museum, 50
Devereux Beach, 51
Disabilities, services for persons with, 15
   accessible stations (maps), 113-118
   accessible taxis, 15
   Airport Handicapped Van, 15
   Americans with Disabilities Act (ADA), 15
   MBTA services, 15
   Ride, the, 15
   Transportation Access Pass, 8
Dog racing, 68-69
Downtown Boston, 46
Drumlin Farm, 50
Duckling statues, 36

E

Echo Bridge, 53
Educational institutions. *See* alphabetical list in Ch. 14
Emerald Necklace, 44-47
Essex Institute, 43

F

Fall River, 39-40
Falmouth (map), 66
Faneuil Hall, 38
Fares, MBTA. *See* Buses, MBTA, fares; Commuter boats, MBTA, fares; Commuter Rail, MBTA, fares; Rapid Transit, MBTA, fares; Special Fares
Fens and Fenway, 46
Fenway (map), 19
Fenway Park, 68
Ferries, 144-146. *See also* Commuter Boats, schedules

Ferry Docks, 29
First Night, 7
Fitchburg, 156
FleetCenter, 27
Fowl Meadow, 52
Foxboro Stadium, 69
Framingham (map), 88
Franklin Park, 46
Franklin Regional Transit
    Authority (FRTA), 155
Freedom Trail, 38
Fresh Pond, 48
G
Gallops Island, 46
Gardner, 156
Georges Island, 46
Gloucester, 45
    map, 90
Golf, 45
Good Harbor Beach, 50
Government Center, 2, 3
Grape Island, 46
Great Esker Park, 54
Great Meadows, 49
Greater Attleboro-Taunton
    Regional Transit
    Authority (GATRA), 155
Green Line
    fares, 4, 8
    first and last trains, 110
    maps, 119-123
    schedules, 112
    tips for subway riders, 2
    transfer points, 2, 3
Greenfield, 155-156
Greenfield-Montague
    Transportation Area
    (GMTA), 155-156
Greyhound terminal, 28
H
Half Moon Beach, 49
Halibut Point, 53
Hammond Pond, 53
Harbor cruises, 35, 36
Harbor islands, 46
Harvard Sq., 39
    map, 26
Haverhill, 156
Haymarket (commuter bus
    stop), 28
Head of the Charles
    Regatta, 69
Hemlock Gorge, 53
Higgins Armory Museum, 43
Hingham, 50
Holyoke, 157
Horseback riding, 60
Hospitals. *See alphabetical
    list in Chapter 15*
Houghton's Pond, 52
House of Seven Gables, 43
Hyannis, 49
    map, 90
I

Ice skating, 45
ID cards, senior citizen, 8
Inbound and Outbound
    defined, 2
Information
    MBTA, 2, 6
    visitor, 34
Ipswich, 50
J
Jamaica Pond, 47
K
Kalmus Beach, 49
King's Beach, 50
L
Lawrence, 156-157
Leominster, 156
Lexington, 40
Limousines, airport, 32
Lincoln, 50
Logan Airport
    Airport Handicapped Van,
        15
    Airport Water Shuttle, 30
    buses to, 30, 32
    Rapid Transit to, 30
    taxis to, 32
    telephone numbers, 32
    terminal map, 31
Long Wharf, 29
Longwood area (map), 19
Longwood Cricket Club, 69
Lost and Found (MBTA),
    168
Lovells Island, 46
Lowell, 41
    map, 92
Lowell Regional Transit
    Authority (LRTA), 156
Lynn Beach, 50
Lynn Woods, 50
M
M St. Beach, 47
Maine, 162
Make Way for Ducklings
    (statues), 36
Malibu Beach, 46
Manchester-by-the-Sea, 51
Marblehead, 41, 51
Martha's Vineyard, 51
Martha's Vineyard Transit
    Authority (VTA), 156
Mass. Inst. of Technology,
    39
Mass. State House, 36
MBTA
    accessible stations
        (maps), 113-118
    Advisory Board, 10
    buses. *See* Buses, MBTA
    commuter boats. *See*
        Commuter boats, MBTA
    commendations and
        complaints, 10
    fares. *See individual*

services, e.g., Buses,
    MBTA, fares
first and last rapid transit
    trains, 110
holiday services, 7
hours of operation, 6-7
information, 2, 6
Lost & Found, 168
passes. *See* Passes,
    MBTA
schedules, 6
services for persons with
    disabilities. *See*
    Disabilities, services for
    persons with
special fares, 8
suggestions, 10
Merrimack Valley Regional
    Transit Authority
    (MVRTA), 156-157
Metro-North Railroad, 164
Metro Parks, 44
Middlesex Falls, 51
Milton, 52
Montachusett Area Regional
    Transit (MART), 156
Monthly passes, 7-10
Museums. *See alphabetical
    list in Ch. 9*
Mt. Auburn Cemetery, 48
Music Clubs, 66-68
Mystic Lakes, 65
Mystic River, 51
N
Nahant Beach, 50
Nantasket, 52
Nantucket, 52
Neponset Marshes, 53
New Bedford, 41
    map, 92
Newburyport, 157
New England map, 161
New England Science
    Center, 43
New Hampshire, 162
Newport, RI, 41
New York, 164
Newton, 53
Newton Corner map, 96
Nightlife, 65-68. *See also
    individual categories,
    e.g., Comedy Clubs,
    Music Clubs*
North Adams, 154
North End, 38
North Station, 27
O
Old North Bridge, 39
Old North Church, 38
Old Sturbridge Village, 42
Olmsted Park, 47
Orange Line
    accessible stations, 114-
        115

fares, 4, 8
first and last trains, 110
maps, 114-115
schedule, 111
tips for subway riders, 2
transfer points, 3
Outbound and Inbound
defined, 2

P

Park-and-ride facilities, 82-107
Park Plaza, 28
Park Sq. *See* Park Plaza
Passes, MBTA, 7-10
Paul Revere House, 38
Pavillion Beach, 49
Peabody Museum (Salem), 43
Peter Pan terminal, 28
Pine Banks Park, 51
Pioneer Valley Transit
Authority (PVTA), 157-158
Plymouth, 42
Ponkapoag Pond, 52
Porter Sq. station, 28
Portland, ME, 162
Portsmouth, NH, 162
Providence, RI, 42
map, 106
Provincetown, 49
Public Garden, 44

Q

Quincy, 42, 43
Quincy Market, 38

R

Railroad stations, 27-28.
*See also individual
station, e.g.,* North
Station
Railroads, 11-12. *See also*
Commuter Rail
Rapid Transit
accessible stations, 113-118
fares, 3-4, 8
tips for subway riders, 2
transfer points, 2, 3
Raynham Park, 68
Red Line
accessible stations, 113-118
fares 4, 8
first and last trains, 110
maps, 116-118
schedule, 111
tips for subway riders, 2
transfer points, 2, 3
Regional Transit Authorities
(RTAs), 12, 153-159.
*See also individual
transit authorities, e.g.,*
Cape Ann Transit
Authority (CATA)

Rental cars, 13
Revere Beach, 53
Rhode Island, 163
Rhode Island Public Transit
Authority (RIPTA), 158
Ride, The, 15
Ridesharing, 13
Riverbend Park, 40
Riverway, 47
Rockport, 53
map, 92
Rockport Beach, 53
Roger Williams Park, 42
Rowes Wharf, 29

S

Sailing, 45
Salem, 43
map, 102
Savin Hill Beach, 46
Schedules, MBTA, 6
bus, 124-139
commuter boat, 141
commuter rail, 139-141
rapid transit, 111-112
Senior citizen fares, 8
Shopping centers. *See
alphabetical list in Ch. 13*
Sightseeing. *See* Tours
Singing Beach, 51
Skiing, 45
Slater Mill, 42
Somerville, 53
South Boston, 47
South Bridge Boat House, 49
South Station, 27, 28
Southeastern Regional
Transit Authority
(SRTA), 159
Southwest Corridor Park, 47
Special fares, 8
Sports, spectator, 68-70 *See
also individual sport
(e.g., Golf), team (e.g.,
Boston Bruins), or event
(e.g., Boston Marathon)*
Springfield (map), 102
St. James Ave. (commuter
bus stop), 28
Stage Fort Park, 49
State House, 36
Stony Brook Reservation, 47
Sturbridge, 42
Subscription buses, 13
Subway. *See* Rapid Transit
Suffolk Downs, 70

T

T. *See* MBTA
Taunton, 155
Taxicabs, 13
accessible, 15
Telephone numbers, 168-169
Logan Airport, 32
Theaters, cinemas, and
auditoriums. *See*

alphabetical list in Ch. 10
Tips for subway riders, 2
Tourist attractions and
museums. *See
alphabetical list in Ch. 9*
Tours, 12, 35-36
Trailside Museum (Milton), 52
Transportation Access Pass,
8
Transfer points, 2, 3, 5
Travelers Aid, 34

V

Vanpools, 13
Vermont, 163
Visitor information, 34
Visitor pass, 10

W

Walden Pond, 49
Walk to the sea "tour," 39
Waterfront, 38-39. *See also*
Ferries, Harbor cruises
Watertown Sq. map, 28
Waverly Oaks, 54
Weston Ski Track, 54
Weymouth, 54
Whaling Museum, 41
Winthrop Beach, 54
Wollaston Beach, 53
Women's Heritage Trail, 38
Wompatuck State Park, 50
Woods Hole, 48
map, 88
Worcester, 43
commuter rail service, 139
map, 106
Worcester Regional Transit
Authority (WRTA), 159
World's End, 50

Transit Telephone Numbers

All telephone numbers in this book are in area code 617 unless noted otherwise. A "1" means the number is a toll call from Boston, but still in the 617 area. Toll-free "800" numbers are valid from eastern Massachusetts unless noted. "TDD" numbers are for the hearing impaired.

MBTA

Travel Information Line 722-3200; 800-392-6100
    TDD 722-5146
Commuter Rail 800-392-6099
    Commuter Rail Group Travel 722-3663
MBTA General Offices 722-5000
Monthly Pass Program 722-5218
Customer Relations, Commendations and Complaints 722-5215
Senior Citizen ID cards/Transportation Access Pass 722-5438
    TDD 722-5854
Transportation Access/The Ride 722-5123
    TDD 722-5415
Lift-Bus Info & Reservations 800-LIFT-BUS
Elevator Service Update 451-0027
MBTA Police Emergency 722-5151
MBTA Police Business Office 722-5747
Bikes on the T Program 722-5438
Lost & Found:

Blue Line 722-5533		Buses
Green Line 722-5635		Cambridge, Arlington, Belmont,
Orange Line 722-5404		Watertown 722-5560
Red Line 722-5317		Charlestown, Everett, Malden,
Red Line—Mattapan 722-5213		Medford, Revere 722-5607
Park Street Station 722-5644		Dorchester, Kenmore, Harvard-
Trackless Trolleys		Dudley, Mass. Pike 722-5203
Cambridge, Belmont, Watertown.		Lynn & North Shore 722-5263
.... 722-5562		Quincy & South Shore .. 722-5367
Commuter Rail		West Roxbury, Jamaica Plain,
North Station 722-3600		Newton 722-5819
South Station 345-7456		

COMMUTER INFORMATION

Caravan for Commuters, Inc. .... CAR-POOL; 800-248-5009

LOGAN AIRPORT INFORMATION

Ground Transportation Information 800-23-LOGAN
Public Information Office 561-1800
Airport Handicap Van 561-1769
Airlines .... See Chapter 6

VISITOR ASSISTANCE

Boston Visitor Information .... See page 34
Travelers Aid Society 542-7286
U.S.O. 720-4949

RAILROADS

Amtrak 482-3660; 800-USA-RAIL
    TDD 800-523-6590

FERRIES

A. C. Cruises 261-6633; 800-422-8419	Harbor I. Water Taxi 723-7800
Airport Water Shuttle 330-8680	Hy-Line 508-778-2600
Bay State Cruise Co. 723-7800	Island Queen 508-548-4800
Boston Harbor Commuter 740-1253	Massachusetts Bay Lines 542-8000
Boston Harbor Cruises 227-4321	Steamship Authority........508-477-8600
Cape Island Express 508-997-1600	Hyannis 508-771-4000
City Water Taxi...................... 755-1301	Woods Hole 508-548-3788
Cuttyhunk Boat 508-992-1432	TDD 508-540-1394

BUSES

Alewife Shuttle.......................890-0093	LMA Shuttle.........................632-2800
American Eagle . 426-7838; 508-993-5040	Logan Express 800-23-LOGAN
Barrett's Tours 508-228-0174	Lower Cape Bus 508-487-3353
BAT (Brockton) 508-580-1170	LRTA (Lowell) 508-452-6161
Beverly Shoppers Shuttle ... 508-921-0040	Lynn East/West 508-535-2963
Bloom Bus 426-7838; 508-822-1991	M & L Transp. 665-7791
Bonanza 720-4110; 800-556-3815	from NH 800-225-4846
BRTA 800-292-BRTA	MART 800-922-5636
Pittsfield 413-499-BRTA	Fitchburg 508-345-7711
Brush Hill 986-6100	Gardner 508-632-7373
Burlington Bus.......................270-1965	Mass Limousine ....
C & J Trailways...................................	.... 508-285-5536; 800-342-5894
.................800-258-7111; 426-6030	Michaud ... 508-745-1000; 800-MICHAUD
from NH 603-742-5111	Mission Hill Link .... (No phone)
Carey's 471-4098; 1-447-5555	MVRTA 800-231-RIDE
Cavalier..................................391-3331	Haverhill 508-372-3900
CATA (Gloucester) 508-283-7916	Mybus 356-5170
CCRTA 800-352-7155	Natick Neighborhood Bus .. 508-651-7262
Coach Co.,The 800-874-3377	Paul Revere 539-1993
from NH........................603-382-4699	Peter Pan 426-7838; 800-343-9999
Concord Trailways 426-7838	Riverside 965-7040
from NH 800-639-3317	People Care-iers 361-1515
Concord Free Bus..........508-371-6330	Plymouth & Brockton Street Railway ....
Crystal Transport 787-1544	.... 508-746-0378; 800-433-7800
Dedham Local Bus 461-5987	PVTA
Flight Line........................800-245-2525	Springfield 413-781-PVTA
H. T. Drummond Inc. 1-293-6264	Northampton 413-586-5806
FRTA (Greenfield) 413-774-2262	RIPTA
GATRA	Providence 401-781-9400
Attleboro 508-222-6106	Newport 800-221-3797
Taunton 508-823-8828	from RI 800-244-0444
GMTA (Greenfield) 413-773-9478	SRTA
Green Harbor Transp. 1-837-1234	Fall River 508-672-6071
Greyhound 800-231-2222	New Bedford 508-999-5211
Riverside 969-8660	Trombly 508-937-3626
Gulbankian's 508-460-0225	Vermont Transit 800-451-3292
Hudson...............................(No phone)	Burlington, VT 802-864-6811
Interstate 800-BUS-UNDA	Riverside 969-8660
Island Transport 508-693-0058	VTA 508-627-7448
Lexpress 861-1210	WRTA (Worcester) 508-791-WRTA
LIFT (Framingham) 508-620-4823	Yankee Line 800-942-8890

Freshness Guaranteed

The Car-Free
Absolutely Free
Update Program

As long as this edition of *Car-Free in Boston* is on sale in bookstores and at newsstands, we will publish update reports of changes in transit services. Our goal is to give our readers access to the latest information throughout the shelf-life of this guide.

We promise a *minimum* of two updates, scheduled for Spring 1996 and Spring 1997. Additional updates will be issued if circumstances (including "Big Dig" construction-related changes) dictate.

All you have to do to get on our Update Mailing List is to send us your **name**, **address,** and **zip code**. You can do this by either:

- Sending a postcard to Car-Free/APT, P. O. Box 1029, Boston MA 02205 or

- Calling our answering machine, 24 hours a day, at (617) 482-0282. Please indicate that you wish to be on the Update mailing list

Car-Free Updates are not sold in stores. Call or write today!